MULTIMODAL COMPOSITION

Resources for Teachers

NEW DIMENSIONS IN COMPUTERS AND COMPOSITION
Gail E. Hawisher and Cynthia L. Selfe, editors

Digital Youth: Emerging Literacies on the World Wide Web
Jonathan Alexander

Role Play: Distance Learning and the Teaching of Writing
Jonathan Alexander and Marcia Dickson (eds.)

Aging Literacies: Training and Development Challenges for Faculty
Angela Crow

Writing Community Change: Designing Technologies for Citizen Action
Jeffrey T. Grabill

Literacies, Experiences and Technologies: Reflective Practices of an Alien Researcher
Sibylle Gruber

Datacloud: Toward a New Theory of Online Work
Johndan Johnson-Eilola

Digital Writing Research: Technologies, Methodologies and Ethical Issues
Heidi A. McKee and Danielle DeVoss (eds.)

At Play in the Fields of Writing: A Serio-Ludic Rhetoric
Albert Rouzie

Integrating Hypertextual Subjects: Computers, Composition, Critical Literacy
and Academic Labor
Robert Samuels

Multimodal Composition Resources for Teachers
Cynthia L. Selfe (ed.)

Sustainable Computer Environments: Cultures of Support in English Studies
and Language Arts
Richard Selfe

Doing Literacy Online: Teaching, Learning, and Playing in an Electronic World
Ilana Snyder and Catherine Beavis (eds.)

Labor, Writing Technologies and the Shaping of Composition in the Academy
Pamela Takayoshi and Patricia Sullivan (eds.)

forthcoming

Webbing Cyberfeminine Practice: Communities, Pedagogy and Social Action
Kristine Blair, Radhika Gajjala, and Christine Tully (eds.)

Going Wireless: A Critical Exploration of Wireless and Mobile Technologies
for Composition Teachers and Scholars
Amy C. Kimme Hea

MULTIMODAL COMPOSITION

Resources for Teachers

editor

Cynthia L. Selfe
The Ohio State University

HAMPTON PRESS, INC.
CRESSKILL, NEW JERSEY

Printed in the United States of America

Library of Congress Cataloging-in-Publication Data

Multimodal composition: resources for teachers / editor: Cynthia L. Selfe.
    p. cm. -- (New dimensions in computers and composition)
  Includes bibliographical references and index.
  ISBN 1-57273-702-6 (pbk.)
  1. English language--Composition and exercises--Study and teaching. 2. English language--Rhetoric--Study and teaching. 3. English language--Computer-assisted instruction. 4. Report writing--Study and teaching. I. Selfe, Cynthia L., 1951-
  PE1404.M85 2007
  808'.042071--dc22
               2006102859

Hampton Press, Inc.
23 Broadway
Cresskill, NJ 07626

CONTENTS

Foreword   xx
    Bronwyn Williams

1   Thinking about Multimodality   1
    Pamela Takayoshi & Cynthia L. Selfe
2   Words, Audio, and Video: Composing and the Processes of Production   13
    Cynthia L. Selfe, Stephanie Owen Fleischer, & Susan Wright
3   Composing Multimodal Assignments   29
    Mickey Hess
4   Collaborating on Multimodal Projects   39
    Anne-Marie Pedersen & Carolyn Skinner
5   Thinking Rhetorically   49
    Daniel Keller
6   Saving, Sharing, Citing, and Publishing Multimodal Texts   65
    Iswari Pandey
7   Experimenting with Multimodality   83
    John Branscum & Aaron Toscano
8   Responding and Assessing   99
    Sonya C. Borton & Brian Huot
9   More about Reading, Responding, and Revising: The Three Rs   113
    of Peer Review and Revision
    Kara Poe Alexander
10   When Things Go Wrong   131
    Sylvia Church & Elizabeth Powell
11   Making Connections with Writing Centers   153
    Jo Ann Griffin
12   Sustaining Multimodal Composition   167
    Richard J. Selfe
13   Learning and Teaching Digital Literacies   181
    Marilyn M. Cooper

Afterword   187
    Debra Journet
Glossary: Technical Terms   193
Collected Resources   203

APPENDICES

Appendix 1   Sample Assignment #1   211
    Audio Autobiography: Sound and Literacy
Appendix 2   Sample Assignment #2   214
    Video Biography: Literacy Practices and Values
Appendix 3   Sample Assignment #3   217
    Documentary as creative Non Fiction

Appendix 4   Sample Timeline   218
Appendix 5   Interviewing   220
Appendix 6   Interview Release Consent Form   221
Appendix 7   Homemade Documentation   222
Appendix 8   Technology Survey   224
Appendix 9   Student Expertise Grid   225
Appendix 10   Collaborative Project Log   226
Appendix 11   Heuristic for Audio Essays   227
Appendix 12   Planning Audio Essays   228
Appendix 13   Planning Video Essays   229
Appendix 14   Self Evaluation—Audio Essays   230
Appendix 15   Group Evaluation—Video Essays   231
Appendix 16   Collaboration Checklist   232
Appendix 17   Bridging Alphabetic and Multimodal Composition   233
Appendix 18   Rhetorically Powerful Images   234
Appendix 19   Rhetorically Powerful Sounds   235
Appendix 20   Rhetorically Powerful Camera Work   237
Appendix 21   Discovering about Audio   239
Appendix 22   Discovering about Video   240
Appendix 23   Equipment Checkout Sheets   242
Appendix 24   Class Equipment Schedule   245
Appendix 25   Check-In and Check-Out Procedures   246
Appendix 26   Sources of Documentation on the Web   247
Appendix 27   Web Sites for Audio and Video Genre Examples   249
Appendix 28   Teacher's Progress-Assessment Journal   252
Appendix 29   Student's Progress Journal   253
Appendix 30   Media, Modalities, and Genres of Composing   254
Appendix 31   Affordances of Modalities   255
Appendix 32   Audio Checklist   256
Appendix 33   Video Checklist   257
Appendix 34   Audio-Editing Log   258
Appendix 35   Video-Editing Log   259
Appendix 36   Connecting Sound and Writing   260
Index   263

CONTENTS FOR DVD

Glossary: Technical Terms

Collected Resources

Appendices

Appendix 1   Sample Assignment #1
     Audio Autobiography: Sound and Literacy
Appendix 2   Sample Assignment #2
     Video Biography: Literacy Practices and Values
Appendix 3   Sample Assignment #3
     Documentary as creative Non Fiction
Appendix 4   Sample Timeline
Appendix 5   Interviewing
Appendix 6   Interview Release Consent Form
Appendix 7   Homemade Documentation
Appendix 8   Technology Survey
Appendix 9   Student Expertise Grid
Appendix 10   Collaborative Project Log
Appendix 11   Heuristic for Audio Essays
Appendix 12   Planning Audio Essays
Appendix 13   Planning Video Essays
Appendix 14   Self Evaluation—Audio Essays
Appendix 15   Group Evaluation—Video Essays
Appendix 16   Collaboration Checklist
Appendix 17   Bridging Alphabetic and Multimodal Composition
Appendix 18   Rhetorically Powerful Images
Appendix 19   Rhetorically Powerful Sounds
Appendix 20   Rhetorically Powerful Camera Work
Appendix 21   Discovering about Audio
Appendix 22   Discovering about Video
Appendix 23   Equipment Checkout Sheets
Appendix 24   Class Equipment Schedule
Appendix 25   Check-In and Check-Out Procedures
Appendix 26   Sources of Documentation on the Web
Appendix 27   Web Sites for Audio and Video Genre Examples
Appendix 28   Teacher's Progress-Assessment Journal
Appendix 29   Student's Progress Journal
Appendix 30   Media, Modalities, and Genres of Composing
Appendix 31   Affordances of Modalities
Appendix 32   Audio Checklist
Appendix 33   Video Checklist
Appendix 34   Audio-Editing Log
Appendix 35   Video-Editing Log
Appendix 36   Connecting Sound and Writing

SAMPLE MULTIMODAL COMPOSITIONS

Audio Essays

"Legacy of Music" (audio essay, 5:30), *Sonya C. Borton*
     Bibliography, Legacy of Music"

"Lord of the Machines: Reading the Human Computer Relationship" (audio essay, 12:40), *Daniel Keller*

Bibliography, "Lord of the Machines"

"Lost in Translation" (audio essay, 8:13), *Iswari Pandey*
Bibliography, "Lost in Translation"

"Interview with Taylor Mali: Performance Poet" (audio essay, 7:12), *Mickey Hess*
Bibliography, "Interview with Taylor Mali"

"Yelling Boy" (audio essay, 3:05), *Wendy Wolters Hinshaw*

"What's at Stake" (audio essay, 2:45), *Michael Harker*

"Re-learning How to Argue" (audio essay, 4:00), *Aaron McKain*

"Sheets and Hollers" (audio essay, 2:46), *Julia Applegate*

"A Thread of Literacy" (audio essay, 2:51), *Envera Dukaj*

"The Next Chapter Book Club (audio essay, 2:48), *Hallisy Bruchs*

Video Essays

"Literacy and Public Transportation: A Case Study" (video essay, 5:31), *Elizabeth Powell*
Bibliography, "Literacy and Public Transportation"

"Literacy Practices and Literacy Events of a 21st Century American Child" (video essay, 13:40),
Kara Poe Alexander
Bibliography, "Literacy Practices and Literacy Events"

"Skate 18" (video essay, 6:17), Michael Fardal

"What is Style?" (video essay, 6:16), *Nick Sullivan* & *Jason Gamm*

"Made Actual Through Pain" (video essay, 5:17),
Michael Harker, Aaron McKain, & *Cormac Slevin*

"Nina West and the Performative Affordances of Drag" (video essay, 10:51),
Shawn Casey & *Envera Dukaj*

"The Changing Nature of Literacy: A Case Study" (video essay, 6:07),
Cynthia L. Selfe

FOREWORD

Bronwyn Williams

As students and teachers of English, and more particularly of rhetoric and composition, our colleagues and we have begun to consider how new media and new technologies are expanding and revising our understanding of literacy. Yet even as many are beginning to compose in multiple modes and media and encouraging their students to do so as well, there is still sometimes a gap between theories of multimodal communication and effective classroom practices.

This book is a result of efforts to address such gaps. In the spring of 2004, Cindy Selfe was the Thomas R. Watson Visiting Distinguished Professor of Rhetoric and Composition at the University of Louisville. As Watson Professor, Cindy offered a graduate seminar entitled "Literacy, Technology, and Education" and gave several presentations to students and faculty. Much of this book is the result of the fruitful conversations that were stimulated and enriched by Cindy's visit. The book also draws on the theoretical grounding presented by many theorists of literacy (Barton & Hamilton, 2000; Gee, 2004; Kress, 2003) and digital literacy (Lankshear & Knoble, 2003; Wysocki, Johnson-Eilola, Selfe, & Sirc, 2004; Snyder & Beavis, 2004) The book's authors outline some of the achievements and complications inherent in integrating multimodal literacies into writing classes. As practitioners (and lovers) of narrative, we preface their work with a set of stories that we hope will locate the challenges that students, teachers, and writing program administrators face as they move toward multimodal literacies. This book captures the energy and creativity that inspired these innovative projects and practices so that others can both learn from them and explore new ways of writing and communication.

WRITING OFF THE PAGE: THE NECESSITY OF EXPLORING MULTILITERACIES

Recently a graduate student teacher approached me and asked if it would be permissible for the students in her composition course, which was going to focus on the rhetoric of the upcoming political campaign, to do a multimedia project on a political issue as one of their assignments for the course. I was delighted to say yes, and told her that, given my interests in popular culture and multiliteracies, I could hardly say "no." But what I found particularly intriguing about her request was that not only did she feel she needed my permission to create such an assignment, but that she also needed to ask if there were "minefields" she would be walking into—specifically if this would get her or the program into trouble with the department or other departments on campus.

As we talked about how to explain and work through such assignments with students who would not be expecting to encounter them in a first-year composition class, including issues of revision and assessment, I was struck by the sense that we both assumed that students and other faculty would regard the Composition Program as a bastion of print, essayistic literacy. What's more, as director of the program I somehow seemed to stand atop the battlements guarding linear, rational print arguments from the forces of change. We both sensed that encouraging students to create multimodal projects would be seen by others on campus as being either unrigorous or downright subversive.

The interaction gave me a sense of the simultaneous excitement and uncertainty this moment of changing technological possibilities has created. Although some scholars, such as Tom Romano, have long advocated multigenre essays in writing classes, the rapid evolution of digital technology has pushed the possibilities of composition well beyond print to visual, audio, and video texts. It is an exciting time when the electronic communicative tools that used to be available only to groups of people with lots of money are increasingly accessible to individuals with time and creativity. We are quickly moving toward the moment that Mitchell Stephens predicted only a few years ago when producing video texts will:

> Become an art form kids learn at about the age they learn how to draw a face, play the guitar or navigate the Internet. Video should no longer be the private tool of professionals in the employ of advertising agencies and media conglomerates or of well-funded artists. Teenagers should be playing with it; friends should be staying in touch on it; radicals may challenge the status quo through it; academics should eventually be warned to produce it or perish. Video will be shot by amateurs and freelancers; it will be edited in basements, in garrets. (p. 168)

For Stephens we are in a moment akin to when print literacy moved from the province of priests and scribes to the individual seeking to express thoughts on a page.

Yet if we want to bring such exciting possibilities to first-year composition classes we have to face the reality that many, if not most, people who got into literacy and teaching writing did so because they were in love with print literacy, whether poetry, fiction, or the essay. Certainly that was the case for me. I wanted to be a novelist from sixth grade on (though I never had the talent for it). I embraced teaching writing because I loved the craft of it, the joy I could see students find in writing well, the precision, the improvisation, all the things that make us love print literacy. And, like many of my colleagues I felt it was somehow a higher calling than teaching some of the other subjects students had to take in college.

So now as the technology changes what is possible to teach, I find myself, like many teachers, to be off balance. Though I may still believe that there is a place for extended essayistic print texts, I've no desire to throw my lot in with those such as Sven Birkerts or Neil Postman, who Barry Brummet so accurately describes as "discursive nostalgics" who "long for a lost, golden age of discourse (and) perceive a degraded state of public communication today" (p. 56) traceable to the rise of electronic texts and multimodal genres. Moments of uncertainty always produce those with either utopian or dystopian visions, whose loud voices often overwhelm more considered ideas like those found in the chapters of this book.

KEEPING UP WITH STUDENTS

In fact, my earlier narrative of my love of print literacy is not all the story. I did love reading and did dream of being a novelist, a writer. Yet I was also a devoted and intense fan of movies and of television. And if on Mondays, Wednesdays, and Fridays I wanted to be novelist; on Tuesdays and Thursdays I dreamed of being a film director. I loved the way images were juxtaposed on film and blended with speech and music. Years later as a journalist I worked for a public radio station and found great pleasure and challenge in exploring the ways sound and narrative could be combined to tell stories. Still, though I often used film, television, music, and audio when I taught writing, it was always in the service of print literacy. I could say I didn't teach multimodal communication because I lacked the technological capabilities to do so, but it would be closer to the truth to say that I didn't know how to teach it or what the point would be for my students.

It has been my students, more than most theorists, who have demonstrated for me the point of composing multimodal texts. Unconcerned about whether I feel comfortable, I have seen students during the past decade go from downloading images into their essays to creating webpages to accompany assignments to creating short films for those websites, often without being asked to do so in the assignment. And, when I talk with them, I find that what I see in class is only a glimmer on the surface of their explorations of new forms of electronic texts. The energy and creativity I see in students' multimodal texts convince me that they are the ones who are pushing us to engage in a more complex understanding of writing and reading in the academy, the workplace, and our daily lives.

Sometimes I find this energy and creativity unnerving, in part because I do not always think I know how to teach the use of images or video or sound to create an argument or explore an issue. Even if I know how to teach it, I'm not convinced I know how to respond to a "draft" in such forms the way I do with a print literacy, let alone know how I would grade it or explain the grading process to a student. For other teachers the concern is that images will somehow not be as rigorous in the production of intellectual work in the academy as words can be. Yet these concerns are either ill-considered shadows, as in the case of the latter, or addressable through the thoughtful application of theory and practice, as is laid out so productively in this book.

As teachers then, what we are faced with now is how best to connect our classroom practices with the thoughtful voices that have begun to theorize how all of these ways of communicating fit together. As scholars such as David Barton and Mary Hamilton have argued, literacy is not a set of standalone skills, but is better comprehended as meaning-making practices that must be in understood in context. If we accept that there are "different literacies associated with different domains of life" (p. 11) and that the boundaries between such domains are flexible and often permeable, then we have to confront how students' reading and interpretation of electronic texts outside the classroom connect or conflict with their work in our classes. If we accept that "literacy practices change and new ones are frequently acquired through processes of informal learning and sense making as well as formal education and training" (p. 14), then we have to re-imagine both the ways in which our students are learning to compose and communicate as well as the goals and outcomes we create for our writing courses. Many scholars has pointed out that print on the page is no longer the only option for individuals wanting to communicate across space and time, and it is certainly no longer the dominant communicative technology in the culture at large. Gunther Kress maintains that we have shifted from a world where the image was fitted in around the demands and logic of the print text on a page to one where "writing appears on the screen subject to the logic of the image" (p. 8).

The use of multimodal assignments (assignments that draw on multiple modalities, including words, still images, animation, video, and sound) is not, then, part of an argument about whether there will or won't be writing. Such an argument is as reductive and useless as those who argue about whether the book is always better than the movie. In doing so they miss the point that the book is always different from the movie and each offers strengths and weaknesses. Even as the movie communicates powerfully through layers, speed, juxtaposition, and the blending of sound and image, the book offers an ease of recursiveness, reflection, interiority, and the ability to be dropped in the bathtub and still be useful. We should instead regard the ability to use multiple modalities of communication as a call to examine how new ways of conceiving of literacy and composing produce new possibilities for different rhetorical situations. The multiple purposes and audiences for which we write demand multiple approaches for communicating our message. It is also important to remember that such multiple approaches to literacy are not limited to what can be produced with electronic technology but include other combinations of image and print that may be less expensive and more available to more people in a given culture (Lankshear & Knobel, p. 17).

YES, MULTIMODAL TEXTS BELONG IN WRITING AND COMPOSITION COURSES

Of course, there are potential pitfalls in engaging in the teaching and composing of multimodal texts. As a colleague from Australia related to me she had recently attended a conference where the word "multiliteracies" was on everyone's' lips, but nothing much had changed in the pedagogy, presentations, or research. It would be quite easy to see concepts such as multiliteracies or multimodality become easy buzzwords that are addressed only superficially in classrooms in which the pedagogical foundations of the class remain unchanged. In short order the term "multimodal" could become as general and useless as "multicultural" has become. Another potential problem is the introduction of multimodal assignments by teachers who have not studied how to teach or assess still image and audio and video texts and production. Even worse this could be forced on unwilling teachers without their support and engagement, as has happened with such movements as critical pedagogy and service learning. Finally there is the almost certain backlash of conservative, back-to-basics colleagues, administrators, parents, and politicians, who will regard the use of new technologies and literacies as evidence of a lack of seriousness in the classroom and argue that each multimodal assignment must inevitably result in the loss of the poetry, drama, and philosophy of our greatest books.

Because of these and similar objections there are those writing teachers who would argue that the field of Composition and Rhetoric, embedded as it is so many places in the United States in Departments of English, is no place for the study of multimodal forms of communication. It is worth remembering that there is nothing new in having a chorus of skepticism and resistance greet changes in communication technologies and genres, from writing to the printing press to the novel to photography to film (Stephens, 1998, pp. 30-33). But more to point is that we must recognize that English Departments no longer sustain culture behind impenetrable walls of print. Culture, the product of our human relations, now produces texts in multiple, often overlapping forms. If it has become acceptable to recognize the work of scholars in English Departments who use cultural studies approaches to texts in everything from film to clothing to museum exhibits, it should be part of an English Department's mission to regard its students as capable of composing intellectual work in forms other than traditional print essays. And we should also recognize that other disciplines across campus are increasingly moving to multimodal texts in their courses and that our students need to know how to write to learn and write to inform and persuade in these forms as well as they do in print. We need to teach the forms of literacy that are producing the culture on our campuses and in our communities. The most severe potential consequences for English Departments if they choose to turn their backs on multimodal texts are perhaps summed up by David Marc:

> By ignoring and stereotyping the vital new vessels of language and imagination, the humanities have placed themselves at the margins of contemporary thinking. Valued more by the university as an antiquarian ornament than a dynamic epistemology—sort of like a charmingly nostalgic, if somewhat dysfunctional old building that the campus just wouldn't be the same without. (p. 38)

The purpose of this book, however, is not to sound dire warnings of what might go wrong with teaching literacy and writing if we ignore all but conventional academic print literacy. If we are to move from teaching the dominance of print literacy to teaching the use of multiliteracies and the creation of multimodal texts for different purposes, we need to connect our theory and our practice in productive ways. Such a large project requires "much debate, and an uncommon generosity of view. . . . It will require from us a different kind of reflection on what writing is, what forms of imagination it fosters" (Kress, p. 8). If any pedagogical change is to be meaningful and long lasting, such debate and reflection must take place in the classroom, with our students, as much as it does in the pages of scholarly books. This book, by joining theory and pedagogy, will help us engage in our best reflective teaching practices as we all explore new ways to analyze, imagine, and communicate our thoughts and experiences to one another.

WORKS CITED

Barton, D., & Hamilton, M. (2000). Literacy practices. In D. Barton, M. Hamilton, & R. Ivanic (Eds.), *Situated literacies: Reading and writing in context* (pp. 7-15). London: Routledge.

Brummett, B. (1991). *Rhetorical dimensions of popular culture.* Tuscaloosa: University of Alabama Press.

Gee, J. (2004). *What video games have to teach us about learning and literacy.* New York: Palgrave Macmillan.

Kress, G. (2003). *Literacy in the new media age.* London: Routledge.

Lankshear, C., & Knobel, M. (2003). *New literacies: Changing knowledge and classroom learning.* London: Open University Press.

Marc, D. (1995). *Bonfire of the humanities: Television, subliteracy, and long-term memory loss.* Syracuse, NY: Syracuse University Press.

Snyder, I., & Beavis, C. (Eds.). (2004). *Doing literacy online: Teaching, learning and playing in an electronic world.* Cresskill, NJ: Hampton Press.

Stephens, M. (1998). *The rise of the image, the fall of the word.* Oxford: Oxford University Press.

Wysocki, A.F., Johnson-Eilola, J., Selfe, C.L., & Sirc, G. (Eds.). (2004). *Writing new media: Theory and applications for expanding the teaching of composition.* Logan: Utah State University Press.

CHAPTER 1
Thinking about Multimodality

Pamela Takayoshi
Cynthia L. Selfe

WHY MULTIMODAL COMPOSITION?

It is fast becoming a commonplace that digital composing environments are challenging writing, writing instruction, and basic understandings of the different components of the rhetorical situation (writers, readers, texts) to change. Such changes are both significant and far reaching—and they promise to be disruptive for many teachers of English composition. For many such teachers at both the secondary and collegiate levels, the texts that students have produced in response to composition assignments have remained essentially the same for the past 150 years. They consist primarily of words on a page, arranged into paragraphs. This flow of words is only occasionally interrupted by titles, headings, diagrams, or footnotes.

These texts resemble—in many ways—other texts that students have been producing elsewhere in the academy (or in other formal educational settings) in response to more conventional assignments like essay tests, lab reports, and research papers. The information within these is conveyed primarily by two modalities—words and visual elements (e.g., layout, font, font size, white space)—and is often distributed in the medium of print. Importantly, however, these texts do not resemble many of the documents we now see in digital environments that use multiple modalities to convey meaning—moving and still images, sounds, music, color, words, and animations—and that are distributed primarily, albeit not exclusively, via digital media (e.g., computers, computer networks, CDs, DVDs). Although composition theories have evolved to acknowledge and study these new ***multimodal*** texts (texts that exceed the alphabetic and may include still and moving images, animations, color, words, music and sound), the formal assignments that many English composition teachers give to students remain alphabetic and primarily produced via some form of print media. And the papers that students submit in response to these conventional assignments have remained essentially the same: 8.5 by 11 inch pages, double-spaced, 1-inch-margins, 12 or 10 inch fonts. Thus, while time marches on *outside* of U.S. secondary and college classrooms, while people on the Internet are exchanging texts composed of still and moving images, animations, sounds, graphics, words, and colors, *inside* many of these classrooms, students are producing essays that look much the same as those produced by their parents and grandparents.

Why the astonishing lack of change in both classroom assignments and student-authored writing? It's been many years since Patricia Sullivan (2001) pointed out that, with computer technologies, writers have more control over the page than they've ever enjoyed. Her claims today suggest that authors could expand that notion of control *beyond* the page, that they could think in increasingly broad ways about texts—not only about pages, words, layout, and design, but also about still and moving visual imagery (photos, photo-editing programs, movie-authoring programs, animation programs) and aural components of communication (music, audio recordings, sounds). Why should composition teachers, researchers, and scholars be interested in taking more advantage of these opportunities?

Agreeing that literacy pedagogy must account for the multiplicity of texts allowed and encouraged by digital technologies, many teacher/scholars and others in fields outside writing studies have articulated compelling arguments for why people concerned with writing and literacy should turn their attention to the cultural shifts in meanings of writing, composing, and texts:

> Cindy Selfe (2004) has elsewhere written: " . . . if our profession continues to focus solely on teaching only alphabetic composition—either online or in print—we run the risk of making composition studies increasingly irrelevant to students engaging in contemporary practices of communicating" (p. 72).

> Arguing that "new communications media are reshaping the way we use language," the New London Group (1996) contends that "effective citizenship and productive work now require that we interact effectively using multiple languages, multiple Englishes, and communication patterns that more frequently cross cultural, community, and national boundaries" (p. 64).

> "To be responsible teachers," Anne Wysocki (2003) maintains, "we need to help our students (as well as ourselves) learn how different choices in visual arrangement in all texts (on screen and off) encourage different kinds of meaning making and encourage us to take up (overtly or not) various values" (p. 186).

> James Gee (2003), writing about video games and literacy, asserts the importance this way: "People need to be literate in new semiotic domains [by which he means any set of practices which relies on multiple modalities to communicate meanings] throughout their lives. If our modern, global, high-tech and science-driven world does anything, it certainly gives rise to new semiotic domains and transforms old ones at an ever faster rate" (p. 19).

In a world where communication between individuals and groups is both increasingly cross-cultural and digital, teachers of composition are beginning to sense the inadequacy of texts—and composition instruction—that employs only one primary semiotic channel (the alphabetic) to convey meaning. In internationally networked digital environments, texts must be able to carry meaning across geo-political, linguistic, and cultural borders, and so texts must take advantage of multiple semiotic channels. At the same time, however, many composition teachers—raised and educated in the age and the landscapes of print—feel hesitant about the task of designing, implementing, and evaluating assignments that call for multimodal texts—texts that incorporate words, images, video, and sound. These teachers understand both the possibilities and the challenges posed by a curriculum that accommodates multimodal literacy practices and students who compose texts from video, sound, still images, and animations, as well as from words. It is a difficult situation, and composition instruction is poised on the precipice of the change.

This collection is designed to provide a beginning point for composition teachers who want to make this theoretical shift in their understanding of literacy and develop effective and sound pedagogical approaches in response. This book provides a basic set of resources for teachers who want to experiment with multimodal composition assignments—particularly those that incorporate video and audio production—in their classrooms.

As we've indicated above, the authors represented in this volume argue for the importance of paying attention to multimodal composing. Our reasoning can be summarized in the following list of claims:

1 **In an increasingly technological world, students need to be experienced and skilled not only in reading (consuming) texts employing multiple modalities, but also in *composing* in multiple modalities, if they hope to communicate successfully within the digital communication networks that characterize workplaces, schools, civic life, and span traditional cultural, national, and geopolitical borders.**

Whatever profession students hope to enter in the 21st century—game design (Gee, 2003), archeology (Boxer, 2005), science and engineering (Tufte, 1990, 1993, 2001, 2003), the military (D.C. Comics, 2005), the entertainment industry (Daly, 2003), and medicine (Hull, Mikulecky, St. Clair, & Kerka, 2003)—they can expect to read and be asked to help compose multimodal texts of various kinds, texts designed to communicate on multiple semiotic channels, using all available means of creating and conveying meaning. Instructors of composition need to teach students not only how to read and interpret such texts from active and critical perspectives, they also need to teach students how to go *beyond the consumption* of such texts—learning how to *compose* them for a variety of purposes and audiences.

In peer-review workshops or studio sessions (where compositions are viewed or heard and responded to), students are simultaneously put in the familiar position of audience member and the perhaps unfamiliar position of critical responder. Many people have argued for a pedagogical commitment to critical and active response, especially to technologies. Grounded in the knowledge that comes from authoring multimodal compositions themselves, students can constructively respond to audio and visual compositions, developing critical perspectives that will serve them well as citizens who respond to any texts.

2 **If composition instruction is to remain relevant, the definition of "composition" and "texts" needs to grow and change to reflect peoples' literacy practices in new digital communication environments.**

Although it may sound like technological determinism to some (i.e., that our professional work and values should take into account changes and developments in communication technologies), the authors of this book believe that it is important to remain in step with the ways in which students, workers, and citizens are communicating, the changing nature of the texts these people produce, and the ways in which such texts are now being used around the world.

The more channels students (and writers generally) have to select from when composing and exchanging meaning, the more resources they have at their disposal for being successful communicators. Aural and video compositions sometimes reveal and articulate meanings students struggle to articulate with words; audio and visual compositions carry different kinds of meanings that words are not good at capturing. It is the thinking, decision making, and creative problem solving involved in creating meaning through any modality that provide the long-lasting and useful lessons students can carry into multiple communicative situations. In this way, the new composing processes, and problem-solving approaches that students learn when composing with modalities other than words can later serve to illuminate the more familiar composing processes associated with words and vice versa.

Effective technologies often function invisibly in our lives. Think of how visible technologies become when they break down; it's when they are not running invisibly in the background of our work that we become most conscious of them and their roles in our lives. When computers were first introduced to writing instruction, many teachers marveled at how the new writing technologies revealed the processes of writing that over time had become largely invisible to students and teachers of composition. With the new technologies now mediating composition—the web, digital video, digital photography, digital sound—different aspects of composing meaning, of communicating, have been foregrounded in ways that have encouraged many teachers to take note.

3   **The authoring of compositions that include still images, animations, video, and audio—although intellectually demanding and time consuming—is also *engaging*.** It is certainly true that one of the challenges of teaching multimodal composition is the learning curve involved for both teachers and students new to thinking about different modalities. This learning curve varies, however, depending on whether or not multimodal composing involves computers (many such projects do not, and we provide sample assignments in Chapters 3 and 9 that are nondigital), the size of the project (a 5-minute original video project or an 8-minute montage of still images set to an audio track), the complexity of the compositional elements (still images, audio, or video downloaded from a web source; still images, video or audio recorded by students, downloaded onto a computer, and edited by students; or a combination of these elements), and the time frame (several smaller projects in one semester or one culminating project worked on throughout the semester). In addition, increasing numbers of students coming into composition classes have experience in multimodal composing that teachers can tap.

The collective experiences of the authors represented in this book also indicate that audio and visual compositions are *engaging for students*. Like the majority of Americans, many students are already active consumers of multimodal compositions by virtue of their involvement in playing and even creating digital music, watching television, shooting home videos, and communicating within web spaces. As a result, students often bring to the classroom a great deal of implicit, perhaps previously unarticulated, knowledge about what is involved in composing multimodal texts, and they commonly respond to multimodal assignments with excitement.

For students, such instruction is often refreshing (because it's different from the many other composing instruction experiences they've had), meaningful (because the production of multimodal texts in class resemble many of the real-life texts students encounter in digital spaces), and relevant (students often sense that multimodal approaches to composing will *matter* in their lives outside the classroom). Indeed, the teachers writing for this collection have watched students become so engaged in their compositions that they push themselves beyond the boundaries of the assignments and demonstrate learning that goes well beyond teachers' expectations as they begin to understand how multimodal texts look, act, and function. As James Gee (2003) has speculated about the intense engagement some computer gamers experience, "Wouldn't it be great if kids were willing to put in this much time on task on such challenging material in school and enjoy it so much?" Yes, it would be, and this kind of engagement is marvelous to witness.

Additionally, students engage—sometimes very personally and emotionally—with multimodal compositions as readers/listeners/viewers for their peers' compositions. When was the last time you or anyone in your class was moved to tears by a student composition? Multimodal composition may bring the often neglected third appeal—pathos—back into composition classes (which often emphasize logos and ethos while devaluing pathos as an ethical or intellectual strategy for appealing to an audience). Students authoring multimodal compositions often demonstrate a strong awareness and understanding of how music and images are used as appeals in arguments and, further, how effective these modalities can be in creating and establishing meaning. Maybe classes that draw on such understandings can produce the *driveway effect*, a state of engagement so strong that radio listeners remain in their cars after they've arrived at their destinations to listen to the end of a program. Wouldn't it be

> "There was what they call the *'driveway effect*,' Mozetich says. People stayed in their cars in their driveways long after they'd arrived home in order not to miss the ending."
>
> —Hugh Fraser (2001)

great to re-articulate Gee's question, if students experienced that kind of engagement and connectedness in the peer-response workshops that characterize composition classrooms?

4   **Audio and visual composing requires attention to rhetorical principles of communication.** Conventional rhetorical principles such as audience awareness, exigence, organization, correctness, arrangement, and rhetorical appeals are necessary considerations for authors of successful audio and visual compositions. In some ways, many classical rhetorical principles of communication—in which the study of composition is grounded—may be more difficult to ignore in audio and visual compositions. These rhetorical principles of communication—which composition teachers have applied primarily to *literate* communication—also apply, just as appropriately, to multimodal compositions. Teachers less than willing to make such a leap might be encouraged to remember that the rhetorical principles currently used to teach written composition are, themselves, principles translated from the study of oral communication. To include additional oral and visual elements in composition might be seen as a return to rhetoric's historical concerns.

Further, the authors of this book agree with many contemporary scholars and teachers (Cope & Kalantzis, 2000; Gee, 2003; Hocks, 2003; Kalantzis, Varnava-Skoura, & Cope, 2002; Lankshear & Knobel, 2003; Wysocki, Johnson-Eilola, Selfe, & Sirc, 2004) that the study of literacy and composing using a full range of visual and aural modalities can teach students new strategies and approaches which can be productively applied to their efforts at composing more traditional written compositions. Thus, the time spent on multimodal composition, far from being a distraction, will enrich the teaching of composition in general. The following chapters provide suggestions for teachers who want to experiment with multimodal compositions and test this hypothesis for themselves—in both small or more extensive ways.

5   **Teaching multimodality is one pathway to accomplishing long-valued pedagogical goals.** In *Experience and Education*, first published in 1938, John Dewey outlined a vision for "progressive education," as opposed to education in which "the kind of external imposition which is so common in the traditional school limited rather than promoted the intellectual and moral development of the young" (p. 22). In contrast, Dewey envisioned education as an enterprise involving teachers and students in mutually intellectually satisfying relationships:

> There is, I think, no point in the philosophy of progressive education which is sounder than its emphasis upon the importance of participation of the learner in the formation of the purposes which direct his activities in the learning process, just as there is no defect in traditional education greater than its failure to secure the active cooperation of the pupil in construction of the purposes involved in his studying. (p. 67)

A student's experiences outside the formal educational setting, in other words, should play a significant role in defining the purpose of the educational enterprise. "A student-centered pedagogy asks students to work within their own cultures and discourses by using experimental forms to learn actively from one another and to engage with the world around them," reflects Mary Hocks (2003). Like Dewey, she, too, believes that starting with students' experiences is a pathway into literacy instruction:

> Visual rhetoric—when understood as the dialogical processes of critique and design in contexts that deconstruct the visual world and the technologies surrounding us—goes much further in helping us teach students the rhetorical and compositional abilities that they can use for years to come. (pp. 214–215)

In this collection, the authors do not argue that digital technologies (such as audio and visual composing) and an emphasis on multimodal composition are going to be a catalyst in revolutionizing writing instruction. Instead, we argue that *opportunities to think and compose multimodally can help us develop an increasingly complex and accurate understanding of writing, composition instruction, and text.* It is only teachers' learning about new approaches to composing and creating meaning through texts that will catalyze changes in composition classrooms.

Before teachers can begin to explore the possibilities of multimodal composition classes, they must reflect on their pedagogical assumptions about writing instruction generally. What is the goal for composition instruction? With what knowledge/experience/skills/strategies do they want students to leave class? Which meaning-making arenas—academic, civic, private—should they consider for classes? If teachers believe that composition instruction should help students develop and fine-tune the meaning-making strategies and skills they bring with them to classrooms; if they believe it important to teach students to be stronger communicators and meaning makers; if they focus instruction on the many communicative genres, approaches, and forms that people communicate with and through, within and outside the university, then they already share many of the theoretical positions informing multimodal composition instruction. Thinking about multimodality often involves teachers in deep, careful thinking about composition instruction and what matters to communicators in the 21st century.

FIVE KEY QUESTIONS

Thoughtful teachers who are seriously considering whether or not they should expand the range of modalities that characterize their composition assignments do face some realistic concerns—as well as many new possibilities. These concerns are frequently focused on some variation—or combination—of the following five questions. We provide some responses here not to suggest definitive answers, but to offer perspectives that teachers can use as they formulate their own increasingly rich understanding of multimodal composing.

 When I teach multimodal composing, am I really teaching composition?

This question rests at the heart of many teachers' concerns about multimodal composing, so it's best to address it directly.

The classical basis of composition instruction involves teaching students how to use *all available rhetorical means* of communicating effectively. For oral cultures, this important phrase—all available means—focused on persuasive *oral* presentation; for Aristotle and later rhetoricians, *writing* provided an additional means of persuasive communication; for authors after Gutenberg, print text and images were among the resources that could be put to rhetorical use.

Some English composition teachers might argue:

- Composing with multiple modes takes attention away from writing concerns.

- Multimodal composing is just the newest trendy thing; it won't end up being a sustained concern for writing instruction.

- One semester is barely enough time to teach

At each of these particular points of history, people have expressed sincere concerns about the new technologies of communication and their effects on more conventional forms of literacy. In the *Phaedrus*, for example, Plato has Socrates express the concern that writing weakens the memory and can neither defend itself nor represent truth to others. Indeed, Socrates notes, people are naive if they "believe that words put in writing are something more than what they are" (p. 275). Similarly, in the 16th century, the Church considered the printing press to be a dangerous new communication technology—and one not to be trusted because it supported an increased flow of information to the masses and increasingly vernacular expression (Lea, 1902).

Today, many teachers of English composition worry about the effects of computers and the increasingly vernacular expressions of multimodality that digital environments have encouraged. Multimodality, however, is not limited solely to digital environments; rather, it has been encouraged over a much longer historical period by the advent of various nondigital technologies: engraving, film, photography, recording devices, animation, and television. Indeed, as Sullivan (2001) and Wysocki (2001) have pointed out, print text itself is *already*—at some level—multimodal, as any scholar familiar with Laurence Sterne's 18th-century novel, *The Life and Opinions of Tristram Shandy,* can attest. Print, in short, carries visual information as well as alphabetic information. This argument can just as easily be extended to other examples of multimodal communication from William Hogarth's 18th-century engravings of British life to Ira Glass' 21st-century essays on National Public Radio.

> students to write; how can I possibly also teach them audio and video composition?
>
> - I don't know how to use the technologies to create audio and video compositions; how can I be expected to teach it?
>
> - Audio and visual composing won't teach students important skills like how to construct correct sentences, consistent rhetorical theses, development or organization.
>
> - Literate composition is superior—intellectually, artistically, historically—to audio and video.

So, why *is* multimodal composition such a hot issue *right now*—especially if authors have had a long history of using multiple modalities (words, sounds, visual images) to make meaning, and if media technologies have supported such expressions long before the invention of computers and digital environments? One explanation lies in the convergence of *digital production technologies*. As composition scholars have noted (George, 2002; Wysocki, Johnson-Eilola, Selfe, & Sirc, 2004), the converging inventions of personal computers and the web; photo manipulation, audio-editing, and video editing applications; and digital recorders (still and video cameras and audio recorders) now make it possible for students in many schools to produce a variety of multimodal texts as well as to consume them.

These converging innovations—and the possibilities they help enable—have not gone unnoticed by professional organizations. The National Council of Teachers of English (NCTE), for example, has encouraged teachers to think in new ways about both the *production* and *reception* of multimodal texts. As early as 1996, for instance, the NCTE passed a resolution entitled "On Viewing and Visually Representing as Forms of Literacy," which acknowledged the importance of teaching students how to *produce* and *interpret* multimodal texts in print and nonprint contexts:

> To participate in a global society, we continue to extend our ways of communicating. Viewing and visually representing (defined in the NCTE/IRA *Standards for the English Language Arts*) are a part of our growing consciousness of how people gather and share information. Teachers and students need to expand their appreciation of the power of print and nonprint texts. Teachers should guide students in constructing meaning through creating and viewing nonprint texts.

And, by 2004, Randy Bomer, then President of the National Council of Teachers of English, had identified multimodal literacy as a key focus of the Council's attention:

> What can NCTE do to advance young people's learning about the multi-modal literacies that are becoming commonplace in a digital environment? How can we create resources that bring the widest possible range of teachers into this conversation? What public policy and public education will prepare the way for the rapid pace of change in these forms of literacy? (personal e-mail communication, October 19, 2004)

By 2005, and the writing of this book, faculty at institutions as diverse as Ohio State, Stanford, the University of Illinois, Michigan State, the University of North Carolina at Chapel Hill, Florida Central University, the University of Massachusetts-Amherst, Georgia Tech, Bowling Green State University, Michigan Tech University, Georgia State University, Kent State University, and the University of Colorado were experimenting with multimodal composition assignments in a variety of courses and curricula.

In each of these cases, organizations, institutions, and individual teachers acknowledge the realities of changing communication practices in which people—in business, science and research contexts, personal correspondence, community work—are increasingly exchanging information in online environments and using a variety of semiotic resources and systems to make meaning as they compose: not only words, but also still and moving images, sound, and color among other modalities. The exigence for changing educational approaches, in other words, has been the recognition that composition instruction must change if it is to remain relevant and fulfill the goal of preparing effective and literate citizens for the 21st century.

 Why should English composition faculty teach multimodal composing? Shouldn't we stick to teaching writing and let video production faculty teach video? Art and design faculty teach about visual images? Audio production faculty teach about sound?

As we have pointed out, a central goal of contemporary education within U.S. colleges or universities is the preparation of literate graduates—intelligent citizens who can both *create meaning in texts* and *interpret meaning from texts* within a dynamic and increasingly technological world. No collegiate unit bears the responsibility for achieving this goal more directly than do composition programs.

Historically, composition teachers have met this responsibility by grounding their instruction firmly in rhetorical theory: making sure that all students are taught how to use *all available means* to communicate in productive ways and that they are provided a range of strategies and techniques for reaching different audiences, achieving a variety of purposes, and using accepted genres effectively. The belief is that students can take these basic strategies into any disciplinary arena, build on them in more specialized ways, and put them to good use during the remainder of their collegiate programs.

Today, in a world that communicates increasingly via multimodal texts—web sites that include video clips, scientific texts built around visual data displays, radio commentaries, online reference collections—basic composing strategies have changed. Professionals in every discipline—math, physical education, health and medicine, education, science, engineering, the military—are communicating information via multimodal texts: PowerPoint presentations, video tutorials, data displays and animations, educational web sites, and they are expecting students to understand basic strategies for reading and composing such texts. In this context, basic composition instruction, too, must change in order to provide students an introductory, rhetorically focused introduction to a wider range of semiotic resources.

This situation does not mean that English composition teachers, especially in first-year courses, must now assume the responsibility for providing specialized or advanced instruction in animated data displays, video production, art and design, or audio production. Such advanced work, typically, remains solidly grounded in disciplinary contexts in which knowledge of design, production, and exchange is shaped by specialized expectations. The changing nature of communication does suggest, however, that the teaching of rhetorically based strategies for composition—the responsibility of introducing students to *all available means* of communicating effectively and productively, including words, images, sound—remains the purview of composition teachers.

 When you add a focus on multimodality to a composition class, what do you give up?

One of the main concerns of composition teachers considering the addition of multimodal composition assignments in their courses is that the instruction involved in such projects may take valuable time away from more fundamental instruction on the written word, instruction that many teachers feel is sorely needed among contemporary students.

We, too, would argue that writing is of vital importance to educated citizens. Indeed, it is clear that alphabetic writing—and the ability to express oneself in writing—retains a special and privileged position in the education of contemporary citizens. The fact that alphabetic literacy remains a key responsibility of composition educators is difficult to refute. So, it is not our purpose to suggest that composition teachers should abandon this belief or the practices it suggests. Throughout this book, readers will find that the authors include numerous opportunities for written composition, even within the context of projects that focus on multimodal composition.

The authors of this collection do, however, recognize that other communication modalities—among them, images (moving and still), animations, sound, and color—are *in the process of becoming increasingly important*, especially in a world increasingly global in its reach and increasingly dependent on digital communication networks. We hold that responsible educators will not want to ignore these changes. And we know that in many disciplines, including composition, educators are adapting their instruction to the exigencies of a world characterized by multimodal communication.

We also believe that teaching students to make sound rhetorically based use of video, still images, animations, and sound can actually help them better understand the particular affordances of written language—that such instruction can, moreover, provide students additional and instructive strategies for communicating in writing. For example, teaching students how to compose and focus a 30-second public service announcement (PSA) for radio—and select the right details for inclusion in this audio composition—*also helps teach* them specific strategies for focusing a written essay more tightly and effectively, choosing those details most likely to convey meaning in effective ways to a particular audience, for a particular purpose. In addition, as students engage in composing a script for the audio PSA, they are motivated to engage in meaningful, rhetorically based writing practice. Further, as students work within the rhetorical constraints of such an audio assignment, they learn more about the particular affordances of sound (the ability to convey accent, emotion, music, ambient sounds that characterize a particular location or event) and the constraints of sound (the difficulty audiences have in going back to review complex or difficult passages, to convey change not marked by sound, to communicate some organizational markers like paragraphs). Importantly, students also gain the chance to compare the affordances and constraints of audio with those of alphabetic writing—and, thus, improve their ability to make *informed and conscious choices* about the most effective modality for communicating in particular rhetorical contexts.

In short, whether instructors teach written composition solely or multimodal composition, their job remains essentially the same: to teach students effective, rhetorically based strategies for taking advantage of *all available means* of communicating effectively and productively, to multiple audiences, for different purposes, and using a range of genres.

 If I teach multimodal composition will the focus on technology detract in significant ways from a focus on rhetorically based composition instruction? Will I have to become a technology expert?

First, we note that multimodal compositions are *not dependent* on digital media (although digital tools can often help authors who want to engage in multimodal work). In Chapters 3 and 9, we suggest multimodal assignments that students can undertake in nondigital environments.

Second, in cases in which multimodal composition *does* entail the use of digital communication tools and teachers are concerned about the effects of technology on a course, we suggest that teachers start *slowly and small*—designing courses that make multimodal composition an option for *one assignment* during a term or creating assignments that make multimodal responses an option *only* for those students who have access to digital equipment (either their own or borrowed from friends) and some experience in using this equipment. These small experiments can help instructors gauge what kinds of assignments are best adapted to multimodal responses; which tasks are most effective in both providing rhetorical instruction and engaging students' interests; how much (and what kind of) assistance students are likely to need as they compose in multiple modalities; and how the teachers' process-based deadlines, conferences, and feedback need to be modified to meet students' needs in such cases.

Third, all teachers have to seek their own level of comfort in digital communication environments. We hope, however, that composition teachers are willing to respect the full range of literacies that students bring to classrooms and build effectively on these literacies, expanding them whenever possible. We also hope that composition teachers serve students as role models in life-long learning—especially with regard to literacy. Teachers who hope to accomplish these goals, we believe, will also accept some level of responsibility for preparing students to communicate in an increasingly global world and one increasingly dependent on networked digital environments.

 Does my school have the digital equipment that a composition class might need for multimodal assignments? Can I get access to this equipment?

Each teacher has to answer these questions individually and within the complex and overlapping contexts of their instruction, program, department, institution, and community.

By now, readers should know that multimodal composing tasks are *not dependent* on digital media (even though digital tools can, often, help authors who want to engage in multimodal work). Later in this collection, we suggest multimodal assignments that students can undertake in nondigital environments (see Chapters 3 and 9). So every teacher, we believe, even those who teach in schools that have very little access to computer technology and digital equipment like video cameras and audio recorders, can still modify some assignments to allow a multimodal option.

Those teachers who *do* want to work in digital communication environments need to make an early survey of the local instructional resources to which they have access: computer labs within which classes can be scheduled; campus programs or offices that have digital video or audio equipment for loan; informed personnel who might be persuaded to help with instruction; online tutorials and materials available on the web; students who have access to digital equipment or expertise in using such equipment; or community members willing to help. Teachers might also want to read Chapter 13 in this collection: Sustaining Multimodal Composition. In this chapter, Richard Selfe writes about how to form tactical alliances with colleagues, staff, students, other units, and programs in the service of designing not only instructionally effective but also *sustainable* efforts in multimodal composition.

HOW THIS BOOK IS ORGANIZED

This book is composed of three major sections. Part One leads instructors through the preliminary stages of theorizing how and why multimodal composition will enter their classrooms, then through the planning stages of extending composition assignments beyond the limits of conventional print essays—offering two sample assignments (one for an audio essay and the other for a video essay) that will be referenced throughout the book. Part Two offers material that helps turn teachers' attention toward composition processes and pragmatic pedagogical concerns as they begin to construct assignments—focusing on scheduling collaboration, rhetorical thinking, experimentation, response, and assessment. Part Three explores productive approaches to problem solving and trouble shooting, ways to connect with writing centers, and strategies for sustaining multimodal composing efforts.

Within the three primary sections, each chapter is written by a teacher, or a team of teachers, who have personal experience with both conventional and multimodal composing. As a group, this team of authors represents a talented and knowledgeable ensemble. Throughout this book, the pronoun "we" is used to refer to these authors collectively. Our use of this pronoun, we hope, will also imply our solidarity with, and inclusion in, the broader community of multimodal composition teachers and scholars around the world—a group to which we are proud to belong and committed to supporting.

At the end of this book, we have included a series of Appendices, to which we refer throughout; a Glossary, containing technical terms that teachers may run across in the teaching of multimodal composition; a complete list of the resources (print and digital) that we have identified in the various chapters; and a DVD with a number of student essays—both audio and video—that were composed in response to variations in the sample assignments. Also on this DVD are digital copies of all the Appendices for the book. Teachers can use these files when they want to modify the various sample documents to better suit their own classes and situations. *Indeed, we encourage readers to make these changes—experimenting with revisions designed to tailor materials more specifically to their particular needs and those of students within their classes.* We know that none of the assignments, directions, instructions, checklists, and handouts that we have designed for use with the students in our courses, programs, and institutions will be exactly right for use with students in other places; no teachers' digital equipment will be exactly like our own; no hardware and software will work exactly like that we now have in our classrooms. Each teacher and class will have its own set of resources that will need to be accommodated in some way—so *we encourage teachers to revise these materials according to their needs.*

What we hope to accomplish throughout this book is to explain to colleagues *how* and *why* we go about engaging with students, with their efforts to compose meaning, with the technologies they use for this purpose—and why we enjoy it so much—in our own classes and institutions. We hope that colleagues find the processes of reading, experimenting, and composing on the following pages just as engaging and enjoyable and satisfying as we have.

REFERENCES

Boxer, S. (2005). Digital 'Antigrafitti' Peels Away the Years. Web site review 'Graffiti Archeology,' Arts Section. *The New York Times.* Accessed 22 June at <http://www.nytimes.com/2005/06/21/arts/design/21boxe.html?ex=1120017600&en=a03801f5a29ef085&ei=5070&emc=eta1>.

Cope, B., & Kalantzis, M. (2000). *Multi-literacies: Literacy learning and the design of social futures.* London: Routledge.

Daly, E. (2003, March/April). Expanding the concept of literacy. *EDUCAUSE,* pp. 33-40.

D.C. Comics. (2005, June). *Harper's Magazine,* p. 22.

Dewey, J. (1938). *Experience and education.* New York: Touchstone.

Fraser, H. (2001, February 27). Hooked on classics. *Hamilton Spectator.*

Gee, J. P. (2003). *What video games have to teach us about learning and literacy.* New York: Palgrave Macmillan.

George, D. (2002). From analysis to design: Visual communication in the teaching of writing. *College Composition and Communication, 52*(1), 11-39.

Hocks, M. (2003). Teaching and learning visual rhetoric. In P. Takayoshi & B. Huot (Eds.), *Teaching writing with computers: An introduction* (pp. 202–216). Boston: Houghton Mifflin.

Hull, G., Mikulecky, L., St. Clair, R., & Kerka, S. (2003). Multiple literacies: A compilation for adult educators. A report of the Center on Education and Training for Employment, The Ohio State University, Columbus OH. Retrieved 26 June 2005, from <http://www.cete.org/>.

Kalantzis, M., Varnava-Skoura, G., & Cope, B. (Eds.). (2002). *Learning for the future: New worlds, new literacies, new learning, new people.* Altona, Victoria, Australia: Common Ground Publishers.

Lankshear, C., & Knobel, M. (2003). *New literacies: Changing knowledge and classroom learning.* London: Open University Press.

Lea, H. C. (1902). *The eve of the reformation.* In A.W. Ward, G.W. Prothero, & S. Leathes (Eds.), *The Cambridge Modern History* (Vol. 1, pp. 653-692). New York and London: The Macmillan Company.

New London Group. (1996). A pedagogy of multiliteracies: Designing social futures. *Harvard Educational Review, 66,* 60–92.

On viewing and visually representing as forms of literacy. (1996). A resolution published in the Web site of the National Council of Teachers of English. Retrieved 28 June 2005, from <http://www.ncte.org/about/over/positions/category/literacy/107573.htm>.

Plato. (1956). *Phaedrus* (W. C. Helmbold and W. G. Rabinowitz, Trans.). Indianapolis, IN: Liberal Arts Press.

Selfe, C. (2004). Toward new media texts: Taking up the challenges of visual literacy. In A. F. Wysocki, J. Johnson-Eilola, C. Selfe, & G. Sirc (Eds.), *Writing new media: Theory and applications for expanding the teaching of composition* (pp. 67–110). Logan: Utah State Press.

Sullivan, P. (2001). Practicing safe visual rhetoric on the world wide web. *Computers and Composition, 18*(2), 103-122.

Tufte, E. R. (1990). *Envisioning information.* Cheshire, CT: Graphics Press.

Tufte, E. R. (2001). *The visual display of quantitative information* (2nd ed.). Cheshire, CT: Graphics Press.

Tufte, E. R. (2003). *The cognitive style of PowerPoint.* Cheshire, CT: Graphics Press

Wysocki, A. F. (2001). Impossibly distinct: On form/content and word/image in two pieces of computer-based interactive multimedia. *Computers and Composition, 18*(3), 207-234.

Wysocki, A. F. (2003). With eyes that think, and compose, and think: On visual rhetoric. In P. Takayoshi & B. Huot (Eds.), *Teaching writing with computers: An introduction* (pp. 182–201). Boston: Houghton Mifflin.

Wysocki, A. F., Johnson-Eilola, J., Selfe, C. L., & Sirc, G. (Eds.). (2004). *Writing new media: Theory and applications for expanding the teaching of composition.* Logan: Utah State University Press.

IMAGES

WPA Classroom: Writing Lesson. New Deal Network
http://images.google.com/imgres?imgurl=http://newdeal.feri.org/images/l43.gif&imgrefurl=http://newdeal.feri.org/library/l43.htm&h=381&w=500&sz=80&tbnid=Fq-2dui9l7sJ:&tbnh=96&tbnw=125&start=23&prev=/images%3Fq%3Dwriting%2Bclassroom%2B%26start%3D20%26hl%3Den%26lr%3D%26ie%3DUTF-8%26sa%3DN

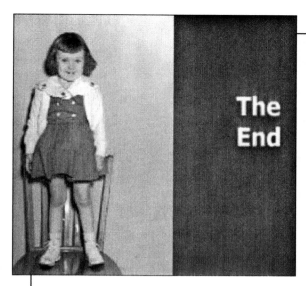

Literacy and Public Transportation, Elizabeth Powell

CHAPTER 2
Words, Audio, and Video: Composing and the Processes of Production

Cynthia L. Selfe
Stephanie Owen Fleischer
Susan Wright

As we have said, this book is designed to help teachers expand the modalities that students draw on for tasks of composing, to go beyond the limits of texts that rely primarily on words, and to explore the affordances—the special capacities—of video, image, and sound.

In this chapter, we compare the basic production processes of each of these modalities. For the purpose of focusing the discussion, we trace these processes as they are often played out by authors working in digital environments—even though neither alphabetic nor multimodal composing, clearly, are limited to digital environments. Later sections of this chapter introduce two sample multimodal assignments (one audio essay and one video essay) that serve as touchstones throughout the book. The student essays that we include on the DVD at the back of this book were composed in response to variations in these two sample assignments. Readers will want to explore this DVD and its contents before completing the chapter. We close this chapter with some information about hardware, software, and digital recording equipment, as well as a few words about the more specialized vocabulary often associated with multimodal composing.

COMPOSING WITH WORDS

Most teachers reading this book are familiar with composing extended alphabetic texts in digital environments—academic essays, reflections, and research papers, among others—and the broadly recursive production processes associated with creating these texts: brainstorming, planning, and taking notes (often in digital environments); citing and documenting copyrighted material; typing a draft (often using a computer keyboard); creating a new document by combining parts of old documents; using an outline or a diagram to create a plan for (or a representation of) an essay; organizing and arranging parts of a text; sharing texts with others and engaging in peer-review (often online); using a word-processing application to revise or edit text; assessing texts, printing texts, and distributing them; and reflecting on texts and the learning that accompanies their production. A basic representation of these broadly recursive processes is represented in Figure 2.1.

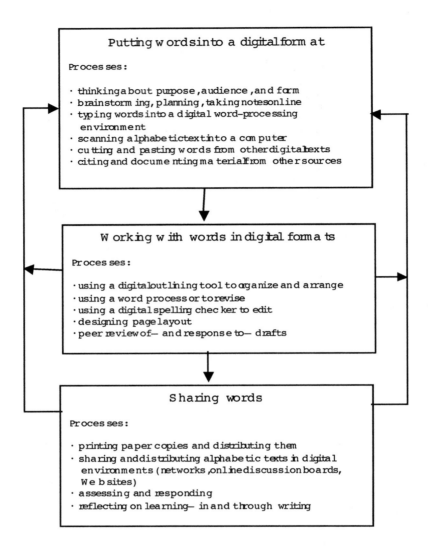

FIGURE 2.1 Composing with words

COMPOSING WITH SOUND

Relatively few composition teachers, however, assign students the task of creating extended audio essays—texts like Sonja Borton's essay about the role that music has played in her family's lives over the past three decades, or Daniel Keller's essay on computers and the challenges they have introduced into our lives. Take a few minutes to listen to these essays—all of which are included on the previously mentioned DVD.

Audio texts like these use the modality of sound as a primary semiotic channel. Composing these texts involves a series of broadly recursive production processes that—in some ways—resemble those involved in more conventional alphabetic composing: brainstorming and planning audio essays (often in writing or using a planning diagram); finding, citing, documenting, and requesting permission for copyrighted audio material to include in a text; putting sound into a digital format (recording original material or downloading copyrighted material); selecting, arranging, and organizing audio segments; engaging in peer review, revising, and editing of audio texts; experimenting with versions and drafts of audio texts; and assessing, sharing, distributing, and reflecting on audio texts (often using writing). These processes are represented in Figure 2.2.

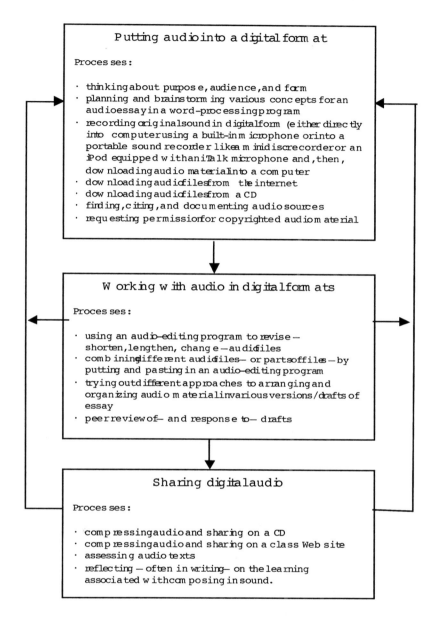

FIGURE 2.2 Composing with sound

COMPOSING WITH VIDEO

English composition teachers also often underutilize video as a composing modality. Few teachers, for example, assign students the task of creating video essays—texts like Elizabeth Powell's essay about the literacies her mother practiced on the bus as she was growing up in Nashville, a video text composed almost entirely of still photographic images, or Kara Alexander's essay about the literacy environment of one child. Readers may want to take a few minutes to view to these video essays—which are included on the DVD.

Video texts like these use the modalities of moving and still images and sound as primary semiotic channels. Composing these texts involves a series of production processes that—in some ways—

resemble those involved in more conventional alphabetic composing and sound essays: brainstorming and planning (often in writing or using a planning diagram); finding, citing, documenting, and requesting permission for copyrighted video and audio material to include in a video document; putting video and sound into a digital format (recording original material or downloading copyrighted material); selecting, arranging, and organizing video segments and the accompanying audio tracks; engaging in peer review, revising, and editing of video documents; experimenting with versions and drafts of video texts; and assessing, sharing, distributing, and reflecting on video texts (often using writing) that are represented in Figure 2.3.

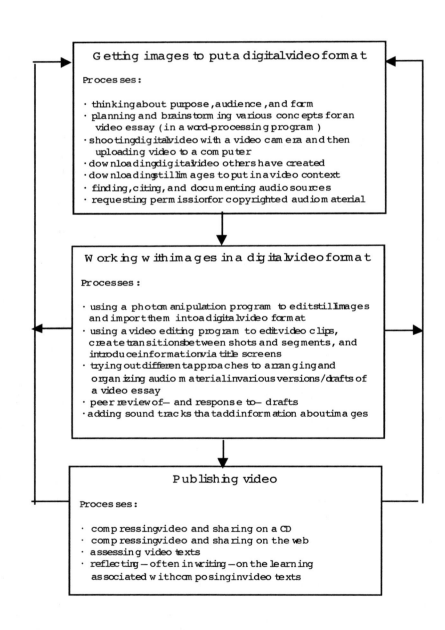

FIGURE 2.3 Composing with video

THE SPECIAL CHALLENGES OF TEACHING WITH AUDIO AND VIDEO

As this chapter has indicated, in some ways, teaching students to compose multimodal texts that contain video, still images, or audio is much like teaching them how to compose more conventional alphabetic texts: teachers must challenge students to take on a task that involves thinking about purpose and audience and exploring a topic; gathering materials and resources, documenting and citing sources; organizing elements around a theme; composing; selecting the appropriate semiotic channel in which to convey pieces of information; revising and editing material; sharing the results of composing in some format so that others can enjoy and respond to texts; and assessing and reflecting on texts. Teachers and students are both used to dealing with these tasks as they compose essays with words, therefore such tasks pose a series of familiar challenges.

It is also true, however, that teaching students to compose audio or video essays also poses new and unfamiliar challenges to many teachers and students. For instance, teachers who assign only alphabetic essays can anticipate that students have considerable experience choosing topics for written essays. In contrast, teachers assigning multimodal compositions must help students think about, choose, and focus on topics that take advantage of the particular capabilities of sound, video, or still images—what we will call their *affordances*.

Similarly, teachers who assign only alphabetic essays can anticipate working with students who have a basic familiarity with composing word texts and considerable experience locating alphabetic materials in libraries, downloading them from the web, and documenting sources (although students' skills often need to develop and refine these tasks). In contrast, teachers who assign multimodal essays will encounter many students who need considerable help using digital equipment (audio recorders, video cameras, microphones, still cameras, and computers with video and audio capabilities); understanding new vocabulary (e.g., framing, ambient sound, title screens, gain); and locating, downloading, and documenting appropriate video or audio clips from online sources.

Further, teachers who assign alphabetic essays can anticipate students who understand the various ways in which texts can be saved, shared, and distributed. Many students, for instance, have experience with printing or photocopying their essays and distributing them within a peer-review group, attaching a digital copy of their papers to e-mail messages, and publishing essays on web sites or in blogs. Teachers who assign multimodal essays, however, will encounter students who are less familiar with the constraints associated with storing large video and audio files and processes of compressing these memory-intensive files so that they can be shared via various digital channels.

In addition, teachers who assign alphabetic texts deal with students who have acquired a relatively robust understanding of written English—both from their natural immersion in language environments and through direct instruction in genres of written language—and who can put this knowledge to work in their alphabetic compositions. In contrast, teachers who assign audio and video essays may well be dealing with students who—although they have been immersed in media-rich environments—may not have had any *direct* instruction in the genres of multimodal composing or the compositional elements that make up such genres (e.g., shots, segments, frames, transitions, fades, soundtracks).

Finally, teachers who assign alphabetic essays can generally count on their students being familiar with, and having access to, some common forms of writing technology: pencils, pens, computers and word-processing programs. Teachers who assign multimodal composing, on the other hand, may encounter students who have only a limited knowledge of, and access to, those technologies associated with multimodal composing within digital environments: digital video and still cameras, digital sound recorders, photo-manipulation software, or audio- and video-editing software.

These differences, which represent only some of the distinctions between teaching conventional written essays and multimodal composing, are represented in Table 2.1.

TABLE 2.1
THE SPECIAL CHALLENGES OF TEACHING AUDIO AND VIDEO ESSAYS.

TEACHING STUDENTS TO COMPOSE WITH WORDS	TEACHING STUDENTS TO COMPOSE WITH IMAGES AND SOUND
Students have considerable experience choosing topics for written essays—although their skills need developing and refining.	Students may need to learn how to think about, choose, and focus on topics in ways that take advantage of the particular affordances of sound, video, and still images.
Students have a basic familiarity with composing their own word texts, locating alphabetic materials in libraries, downloading materials from the web, and documenting sources (although both need development and refinement in these tasks).	Students may need a great deal of help operating digital equipment (audio recorders, video cameras, still cameras, and computers with video and audio capabilities). Students may also need help understanding new vocabulary (e.g., framing, ambient sound, title screens, gain); locating, downloading, and documenting appropriate video or audio clips from online sources.
Students generally know how to save, print, and photocopy their alphabetic essays, and how to share them in digital environments.	Students may need help in saving large audio and video files and *compressing* final drafts of their texts to a manageable size so that they can be shared in environments.
Students have acquired a great deal of semiotic, syntactic, and grammatical understanding of English and can put this knowledge to work in writing alphabetic essays.	Students may have little understanding of, or instruction in, the semiotic, syntactic, or grammatical understanding of elements that make up sound or video essays.
Students are generally familiar with, and have access to, some common forms of writing technology: pencils, pens, or computers and word-processing programs.	Students may have only a limited knowledge of, and access to, those technologies associated with multimodal composing within digital environments: digital video and still cameras, digital sound recorders, photo-manipulation software, or audio- and video-editing software.

Subsequent sections and chapters of this book will help teachers respond to these special challenges.

TWO SAMPLE MULTIMODAL ASSIGNMENTS

To help teachers think about assignments that call for multimodal composition, we offer the following two sample assignments. These sample assignments are also referred to in subsequent chapters and are reproduced in Appendices 1 and 2 at the end of this book.

- an audio autobiography that asks students to explore the role of sound in their lives and the notion that they are literate users of sound (sample assignment #1)

- a video biography that asks students to explore some aspect of a family member's or friend's literacy practices and values (sample assignment #2)

These two assignments were originally conceived for a first-year composition course that focused on the theme of literacy and was later modified for a range of advanced composition courses, undergraduate teacher-education courses, and graduate courses on the study of literacy. Attached to each assignment is an evaluation rubric consisting of assessment items the teacher considered essential to the composition. These rubrics serve at least three major purposes:

- First, because they are handed out along with the assignment itself, they provide students with a clear understanding of the criteria on which their final audio and video projects will be assessed.

- Second, while students are in the process of working on multimodal compositions, the rubrics provide students with a guide for both informal feedback sessions among peers and the more formal studio-review sessions discussed in Chapter 8: Responding and Assessing and Chapter 9: More about Reading, Responding, and Revising.

- Third, the rubrics are designed to be used by teachers to assess students' final products. In this role, they provide a common point of reference for all members of the composition classroom.

SAMPLE ASSIGNMENT #1
AUDIO AUTOBIOGRAPHY: SOUND AND LITERACY

DIRECTIONS

Compose an audio essay that explores the role of sound in your own personal literacy history and that will help class members gain a broader understanding of your literacy practices and values.

This project should not simply record and reproduce sounds. Rather, it should use sound to tell a story, make meaning about, create some commentary on, offer some insight into your literacy practices and values. Most importantly, it should help listeners reflect on what they are hearing. Your essay can take the form of a sound portrait, soundscape, audio documentary, or sound reflection.

Other than these requirements, the assignment is wide open—and purposefully so! I want you to exercise your own creativity in the service of teaching us all something about literacy.

In class, we will listen to the audio essays below to explore sound. Listen to them yourself as well.

- **sound portrait:** an audio essay that focuses on some aspect of a person's life. It is often bio-graphical.

     "Willie Young Rabbit Hunter" (sound portrait, 1:37)
     <http://www.soundportraits.org/on-air/rabbit_hunter/>

     "Reggie Jones, Lifeguard" (sound portrait, 3:45)
     <http://www.soundportraits.org/on-air/lifeguard/>

- **audio documentary:** an audio essay that records the sounds of an important event or time in history when something momentous is happening, some change is taking place, or some trend/pattern is observed in society.

     "Woolworth's Lunch-Counter Waitress" (audio documentary about the original civil rights sit-in at a Woolworth's lunch counter, 4:58)
     <http://www.soundportraits.org/on-air/lunch-counter_waitress/>

     "Street Dogs" (audio documentary about dogs who live with street people, 12:06)
     <http://www.transom.org/shows/2001/200108.shows.streetdogs. perrywarga.html>

- **soundscape:** an audio on-location essay that tries to portray the aural nature, spirit, or essence of a particular place.

     "The Streets of a Holy Hindu City," by Alex Chadwick
     <http://www.npr.org/templates/story/story.php?storyId=4980828

     "The Sound of the World Cup," by Smily Harris
     <http://www.npr.org/templates/story/story.php?storyId=5543566

Now, create your own audio project—on some aspect of literacy. It should be about 5 minutes in its final edited form—but this criterion is flexible and provided only so that you have some idea about my expectations.

Your audio project should have the following characteristics:

—The project should employ the affordances (capabilities) of the medium and mode(s) in effective rhetorical ways.

—The project should lend insight to our study of literacy, information value to our discussion of literacy issues/themes.

—The project should have some meaningful connection with your own literacy practices or values.

For this assignment, you may need to do quite a bit of **writing**: taking notes, making outlines, writing a script, reflecting on your draft for completed essays.

For this assignment, you will need to **record some sound** on digital sound recording equipment. See me to check out a digital audio recorder and microphone. You will need time to learn how to work with this equipment. We will practice with the minidisc recorder in class. You will also need to buy a set of inexpensive headphones.

Finally, you will need to **edit the sound** you record, cutting out the parts that you don't need, re-arranging the parts that you do need, and changing the volume or gain of your audio file. For this purpose, you will be using the program called Audacity. Documentation on Audacity is available at <http://audacity.sourceforge. net/ docs1.1/contents.html>. **SAVE OFTEN—AUDACITY IS A FREEWARE PROGRAM AND CAN PROVE UNSTABLE WITH LARGER FILES.**

HINTS FOR SUCCESS

- Make sure to plan for your sound project. Writing will help you here and you should hand in all the written materials that support your project. For example, be sure to keep a written production log of the time you spend on your project. Here is a sample entry for that log:

    > 27 November 2006
    >
    > 9:40-11:00   In class, spent 40 minutes uploading audio and 40 minutes editing audio according to plan. PLAN FOR NEXT SESSION: Continue to edit audio.

Other written documentation will also come in handy. Careful written documentation will help your teacher understand how much work you have put into your project. Here are some suggestions for the documentation you should be keeping:

   —storyboard your audio essay or write a scene-by-scene outline

   —write out interview questions beforehand and share them with the person(s) you are interviewing.

   —make a list of sounds/people/activities you need to record

   —record citations for the audio clips you download from the web

   —write a reflection on a draft

- Make sure you know how to use your recording equipment! Read the documentation that comes along with the digital sound recorders!

   —always wear isolating headphones so that you can hear what you are recording

   —whenever possible, connect the audio recorder to a power source with an adapter; batteries fail at the worst possible times.

   —make sure you are not recording sounds (e.g., air conditioning hum, a lawn mower going by, a nearby source of electrical power, ambient noise in a room) that will obscure or contaminate the sounds you want to capture

- Schedule more time than you think you need for editing with Audacity—it always takes much much longer than the original recording!! Before you begin editing, be sure to go through the Audacity tutorial on the SourceForge web site <http://audacity.sourceforge.net /help/> or the Audacity overview at the Transom web site <http://www.transom.org/tools /editing_mixing/200404.audacity.html>.

- Before you edit—draw a visual plan of how you want the essay to be structured—what anecdotes go where, where you are going to include soundmark, signal sound, keynote sounds, silence, music, narration, etc. Identify when and where you are going to layer these sounds to create a rich texture for your project.

- Make sure to provide some kind of focused reflective frame for your audio project—some way of helping listeners understand what they are hearing, why it is significant, and what you are trying to convey about your subject. (Read the excerpt from Abel and Glass, *Radio: An Illustrated Guide*.)

- Select/edit/winnow! Make sure your sound composition is tightly and effectively composed. Cut everything that doesn't directly contribute to your intended message. (Read *Radio: An Illustrated Guide*.)

- Make sure your sound project effectively takes advantage of the specific affordances (capabilities) of the medium. What can sound capture best (e.g., tone, emotion, accent)? What escapes the affordances of sound (e.g., a wink, a hand gesture, a facial expression).

- SAVE OFTEN, SAVE OFTEN, SAVE OFTEN!!!

- BACK UP YOUR WORK, BACK UP YOUR WORK, BACK UP YOUR WORK!!!

- **See the attached evaluation sheet for the criteria on which this assignment will be graded.**

EVALUATION SHEET
AUDIO AUTOBIOGRAPHY: SOUND AND LITERACY

| 1 | 2 | 3 | 4 | 5 |

Little evidence of careful planning/ <---> Lots of careful planning/
composing/producing   composing/producing

COMMENT:

| 1 | 2 | 3 | 4 | 5 |

Reveals very little about <--> Reveals a great deal about
role of sound in life   role of sound in life

COMMENT:

| 1 | 2 | 3 | 4 | 5 |

Lack of reflective focus on personal <--> Great reflective focus
literacy practices   on personal literacy practices

COMMENT:

| 1 | 2 | 3 | 4 | 5 |

Ineffective use of affordances <---> Effective use of affordances
of audio   of audio

COMMENT:

| 1 | 2 | 3 | 4 | 5 |

Ineffective attention to audience/<---> Effective attention to
purpose   audience/purpose

COMMENT:

| 1 | 2 | 3 | 4 | 5 |

Less than careful approach <---> Very careful citation and
to citation, documentation, copyright, licensing   documentation, copyright,
                                                                                      licensing

COMMENT:

| 1 | 2 | 3 | 4 | 5 |

Less than careful approach <---> Very careful approach
to permissions/releases   to permissions/releases

COMMENT:

| 1 | 2 | 3 | 4 | 5 |

Poorly written documents/supporting materials <--------------> Excellent written documents/supporting materials

COMMENT:

| 1 | 2 | 3 | 4 | 5 |

Less creative/insightful <---> Very creative/insightful

COMMENT:

GRADE:

SAMPLE ASSIGNMENT #2
VIDEO BIOGRAPHY: LITERACY VALUES AND PRACTICES

DIRECTIONS

Compose a video text about literacy (using Video Studio, I-Movie or some similar software that you have access to) that provides an insightful representation of the literacy issues/themes we have identified thus far in this course.

In your video, combine still images, video, music, written words, narration, and/or sound to compose **a narrative documentary. You can use one or more of the following focus ideas:**

- an individual's or group's interesting or unusual literacy practices/values practices/values
- an interesting or unusual place in which this individual practices, or values literacy
- an individual who practices an interesting or unusual literacy that represents a larger trend
- a person that practices an interesting or unusual kind/type/genre of literacy

Your literacy video text should have the following characteristics:

- Some video or still images, some narration or voice over, and some music that adds significant information about the topic.
- Information that is valuable to our class discussion of literacy issues/themes.
- **A title screen** for your video.
- **A credit screen** that include full citations for video clips, images, music that you download and use.

The project should employ the affordances (capabilities) of the media you are using in effective rhetorical ways. It should be characterized by careful design that helps to convey meaning. The project should be both instructive and creative.

The project should do more than simply depict a literacy practice/value/issue/place/event/genre—it should help readers/viewers reflect on/gain insight into the subject of the video.

For this assignment, you will probably need to do several of the following tasks:

- **Record some video** (use a digital video camera).
- **Use some digitized images** (shoot your own video or download video clips from a collection on the web).
- **Use some music, and sound/narration/voice over** (use a digital sound recorder to capture sound and or download music/sound from the Internet). This will involve cutting out the parts that you don't need, re-arranging the parts that you do need, and layering these semiotic elements in Video Studio. You may also need to edit your sound using Audacity.
- **Write** supporting materials and documents.

If you don't have access to your own digital camera, see me to check out a digital video camera or a digital still camera. I can also help you check out a digital audio recorder and microphone. You will need time to learn how to work these pieces of equipment, so plan ahead to read the documentation.

You will also need to buy a set of inexpensive headphones.

I will demonstrate in class how to use digital cameras and edit video at various times, but you can also follow the directions for using Video Studio at <http://www.ulead.com/learning/vs.htm> and those I have written in the Downloading Sound and Images handout.

Want to see some sample student-made videos? Look at some of the examples on the DVD at the end of this book.

EVALUATION SHEET
VIDEO BIOGRAPHY: LITERACY VALUES AND PRACTICES

1   2   3   4   5
Little evidence of careful planning/composing/ <---> Lots of careful planning/
producing   composing/producing
COMMENT:

1   2   3   4   5
Teaches viewers very little <---> Teaches viewers a great deal
about literacy   about literacy
COMMENT:

1   2   3   4   5
Ineffective attention to audience/ <--> Effective attention
purpose   to audience/purpose
COMMENT:

1   2   3   4   5
Lack of reflective focus on literacy <---> Great reflective focus
practices   on literacy practices
COMMENT:

1   2   3   4   5
Ineffective use of affordances <--> Effective use of affordances
of video and audio   of video and audio
COMMENT:

1   2   3   4   5
Less than careful approach to citation, <---> Very careful citation and
documentation, copyright, licensing   documentation, copyright, licensing
COMMENT:

1   2   3   4   5
Less than careful approach <--> Very careful approach
to permissions/releases   to permissions/releases
COMMENT:

1   2   3   4   5
Few written documents/supporting <--> Extensive written documents/
materials   supporting materials
COMMENT:

1   2   3   4   5
Less Creative/insightful <--->Very Creative/insightful
COMMENT:

GRADE:

The chapters that follow talk more about these two sample assignments and provide suggestions for teachers who want to try out similar tasks in their classes. We also provide readers with additional, nondigital variations of these assignments (see Appendix 3 and Chapter 9, Figure 9.1).

We also encourage teachers to modify these two assignments or invent entirely new multimodal composing tasks that suit the needs of their particular classrooms and student populations. For example, teachers may want to consider the following suggestions:

Collaborative projects: Teachers may want to design multimodal assignments that require students to work in groups of 2-3. As we note in Chapters 4 and 7, collaboration can help stretch scarce resources (e.g., digital video cameras and audio recorders), spread out the workload of composing in new modalities, and provide students with important emotional support.

Sequencing assignments in different modalities: Some teachers may want to sequence assignments so that they call on different modalities (words, audio, and video) and build on one another. For example, students could begin with an *initial* assignment that involves writing a conventional alphabetic essay in which they reflect on their own literacy practices and values. For a *second* assignment, students could then compose an audio essay focused more specifically on the literacy values their parents or grandparents passed along to them. Then, for a *third* assignment, students might digitally scan snapshots (or video footage of themselves as children) to create a *video essay* about their family's literacy values—one that that builds on the insights of the original alphabetic essay (Assignment #1) and uses the audio essay (Assignment #2) as a soundtrack for the video essay (Assignment #3).

Writing about audio and video projects: Some teachers may want to assign an audio or video essay and then have students complete several pieces of alphabetic writing in, around, and about this assignment. For example, students could be asked to write conceptual descriptions of their audio or video projects, scripts for their audio or video projects, progress memos about their essays addressed to teachers, or reflections on their projects after they are done.

Audio and video as an individual alternative: Teachers may want to start slowly with work in audio and video—allowing only one student or a small group of students who already have experience in digital recording to try composing an audio or video alternative to one conventional alphabetic assignment during a term.

SOME NOTES ABOUT SOFTWARE, HARDWARE, EQUIPMENT

As we have noted, multimodal assignments can be done in both digital and nondigital environments. Chapters 3 and 9 provide examples of multimodal assignments that can be completed in *nondigital* environments. The *digital* audio and video assignments in this book can be completed on various computer platforms (Mac or PC), and they are designed to be completed with very inexpensive computer programs and a minimum of video or audio equipment.

For example, to record material for an audio essay, students can use computers that have built-in microphones and sound cards, or a digital minidisc recorder and microphone (and then download the recorded material to computer for editing), or an iPod and a Griffin iTalk Voice Recorder (and then download recorded material to computers for editing). Similarly, if students don't have access to a video camera, they can compose a video essay using still photographic images that they download from the web.

Some software, hardware, and recording equipment will be necessary, however, for multimodal assignments that are designed to be completed in digital environments.

To record audio and video, for instance, teachers or students will need some access to digital recording devices. Depending on the assignment, a class might need to find access to still cameras that take digital photographs (unless students download all still images from the web), video cameras that capture digital video and have a microphone input jack (unless students download all video clips from the web), or digital audio recording devices with a microphone input jack, such as a mini-disc recorder or some other digital audio recorder attachment (unless students download all audio clips from the web).

The compatibility of recording devices, editing programs, and computers can be a challenge in the multimodal classroom. Video camera manufacturers, in particular, have improved their interface with computers in recent years. So, for example, the video on older, nondigital cameras (e.g., 8mm, Hi8, and VHS) are not always immediately compatible with computers and video editing software. In contrast, video on newer, digital cameras (e.g., miniDV, digital 8) is quite easy to download. The compatibility issue will prove especially important for teachers who allow students to use their own video cameras for multimodal composing. Teachers should check the documentation for all video and audio recorders to make sure that the files gathered on recording devices can be downloaded to computers and used by the audio- and video-editing software applications. Recording formats are not necessarily readable in all editing programs.

After video or audio is recorded in a digital form it generally has to be downloaded to a computer so that students can edit the material they have collected—separating key information from the unnecessary information, arranging and organizing segments, adding transitions and music. Most up-to-date computers will handle audio and video editing, but, as composition faculty know, schools don't *always* offer such up-to-date equipment and composition teachers don't *always* have access to such equipment when it *is* available. Hence, teachers will want to find access to personal computers with processors fast enough to handle audio and video work (2 gigahertz or faster); audio and video cards (so they can process the necessary media files); drives that can read and write DVDs and/or DVDs (so that audio and video files can be compressed and saved on these more portable media); sufficient random-access memory (RAM) to handle audio and video editing (at least 1 gigabyte); local hard drives with sufficient capacity to store large video and audio files (250 gigabytes recommended, unless students have individual jump drives for this purpose); USB and/or firewire ports for connecting cameras, recorders, portable hard drives; headphones jacks, built-in microphones, and speakers (so that students can record sound and hear their projects without bothering others around them); and easy-to-learn software programs for editing audio and video (for instance, Audacity or Garageband for audio work, Movie Maker or iMovie for video work).

Finally, depending on the assignment, teachers or students will need access to some peripheral equipment: microphones (cartiod or hypercartiod, see p. 27) that plug into digital recording devices; headphones that plug into computers so that students can hear sound as they edit; and, possibly, personal jump drives (also known as flash memory) or portable hard drives large enough to accommodate students' video and audio projects.

These suggestions are summarized in Figure 2.4, and readers are encouraged to talk to the technical support staff at their own institution about the available technology in advance of implementing multimodal assignments. More advice about the importance of making these connections between faculty and staff are detailed in Chapter 12: Sustaining Multimodal Composition.

A WORD ON TECHNICAL VOCABULARY FOR MULTIMODAL COMPOSING

Each teacher who reads this book will have to decide how deeply into the specialized vocabulary of audio and video production a composition class should delve. For those teachers who find terminology useful in conceiving production strategies and techniques, we provide a glossary at the end of this book that contains many of the key terms used in the chapters that follow.

In general, however, our goal is to keep the specialized technical vocabulary of audio and video production to a minimum. Teachers of English composition should not have to become audio or video specialists in order to design effective multimodal assignments or undertake explorations of such assignments with students. When we do introduce more technical terms in the chapters that follow, we have tried to define them in context as well as in the glossary.

COMPUTER HARDWARE

- Personal computers with the following items
    - —processor speed 2 gigahertz or faster
    - —sound and video cards
    - —drives that can read and write CDs and/or DVDs
    - —at least 1 gigabyte of RAM
    - —250 gigabyte hard drives (or individual jump drives for students)
    - —USB and/or firewire ports
    - —microphone input jack

COMPUTER SOFTWARE

- video-editing software (inexpensive programs like i-Movie, VideoStudio, Movie Maker)
- sound-editing software (freeware programs like Audacity or inexpensive programs like GarageBand)

PERIPHERAL EQUIPMENT

- microphones that hook up to both video cameras and audio-recording devices.
- isolating headphones to monitor sound recording
- personal jump drives

PORTABLE RECORDING EQUIPMENT

- digital video cameras (which can be shared by students) and cables needed to download video to computer
- digital still-photography cameras (which can be shared by students) and the cables needed to download photographs to a computer
- digital audio recording devices (for instance, minidisc recorders and microphones, or other digital audio recorder attachments, or laptop computers and microphones) and the cables needed to download audio to a computer

N.B. Many video cameras and laptop computers have built-in microphones that will record sound. However, because most of these microphones are omni-directional, they pick up *all* the sound in a location, not simply the targeted sound. In addition, these built-in microphones are often of poor quality and, thus, produce muddy or distorted sound. If at all possible, use a good quality microphone that can be plugged into recording devices and *aimed* at the targeted sound. These microphones are known as *cartiod* or *hypercartiod* depending on their pattern of pickup:

A *cartiod* mic is sensitive to audio input from the front of the mic. It also has good sensitivity on the sides (at 90°, 6 decibels less than the front), and good rejection of sound from the rear (180°). The pick-up pattern of these mics is like a heart (hence, the term "cartiod"). cartiod mics are good in eliminating a narrow source of sound directly to the rear of the mic and focusing on one source of sound in front of the mic.

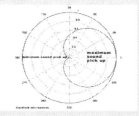

A *hypercartiod* mic is also sensitive to audio input from the front of the mic. They differ from cartiod mics in that their point of least sensitivity is from 150°-160° and 200°-210° (not directly behind the microphone as in a cartiod pattern). hypercartiod microphones are used to eliminate a wider pattern of sound sources in the rear of the mic and to focus on a sound source located in the front of the mic.

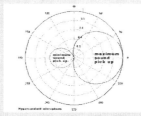

FIGURE 2.4 Digital hardware, software, and equipment for multimodal composing

CONCLUSION

Our five primary goals in this chapter were the following:

- provide an overview of the general processes associated with creating alphabetic, audio, and video compositions
- show how these processes are similar to and different from each other
- identify some of the special challenges associated with multimodal composing
- offer two sample assignments that might be used in a multimodal composition classroom
- identify some of the basic computer hardware, software, and recording equipment that teachers and students will need for creating multimodal compositions

We hope that teachers, after reading the "Get Ready" section of this book, have learned more about why some scholars consider multimodality so important a concept for composition classrooms and why they encourage teachers to integrate multimodality into their own assignment sequences. We hope, as well, that readers have formulated an increasingly clear picture of how multimodal assignments might fit into their own classrooms, composition curricula, and institutional contexts.

Subsequent chapters in the "Get Set" section that follows will help teachers design and schedule effective multimodal assignments (including assignment variations that can be done without digital composing environments), encourage students' collaborative efforts on such projects, think rhetorically about multimodal assignments, retain an experimental frame of mind about such assignments, and formulate effective response and assessment practices in connection with such assignments.

REFERENCE

Abel, J., & Glass, I. (1999). *Radio: An illustrated guide*. Chicago: WBEZ Alliance Inc.

CHAPTER 3
Composing Multimodal Assignments

Mickey Hess

Susan Wright, *From To Write, With Love*

The goal of this chapter is to help teachers plan for and undertake assignments that can yield not only print essays, but also audio projects, video projects, and projects that combine the modalities of sound, image, and word. It extends the discussion begun in Chapter 2 by offering a third sample assignment that leaves the choice of composing modality (and medium) open to students.

One of the most important reasons to design assignments for multimodal composition is to *expand* students' thinking about composing and how this complex set of processes works. Thus, the multimodal assignments we suggest in this book attempt to provide some productive structure for composing, but avoid adding too many constraints. Effective composing assignments, we believe, involve students in reflection about not only the processes, but the products of composing. Finally, and perhaps most important, effective assignments count on the fact that each student contributes ideas and approaches, interests and perspectives, skills and understandings that change composing tasks and personalize composition.

Teachers who compose the best assignments, then, don't outline a step-by-step procedure for students to follow; instead, they create assignments that prompt writers to think in new ways. With that goal in mind, this chapter also includes several opportunities for reflection. Whether these reflections take a written form or are articulated in individual or peer conferences or in class discussion, the idea is to get students thinking and talking about what they're doing as they compose. Assignments that are less directive may be more productive in that they can help students to develop their own perspectives and theorize how they came to a particular composing approach and *why* it fits their project.

In composing an open–ended assignment, teachers will want to keep in mind three elements that are crucial to composing pedagogy, as indicated in Figure 3.1: theory, structure and choice, and circulation. Teachers should not experiment with multimodal composing assignments in the hope of getting students to produce perfect video or audio projects, any more than they should expect students to write a perfect alphabetic essay in more conventional composition courses. Rather, we encourage both teachers and students to undertake such work with the goal of thinking about what humans can accomplish when they use different modalities—and *all available rhetorical means*—to communicate as effectively as possible.

THEORY: Faculty need to think not only about *why* they want to integrate multimodal assignments into their classes, but also about *which* assignments are amenable to the affordances of different modalities. Once teachers have made a decision to try a multimodal assignment, they will want to think about *how* such an assignment can complicate or expand the goals for their courses, and *when* they can most effectively schedule such an assignment.

STRUCTURE AND CHOICE: Multimodal composition can expand the range of choices students make, but these same choices can also overwhelm students with a range of rhetorical considerations for composing audio and video projects.

The instructor's job, then, is to leave plenty of room for choices within a structure that outlines the goals and objectives for student work. Faculty can, for instance, make a point of asking questions in assignments, prompting students to think about what they *can* do, rather than telling them what they *must* do.

CIRCULATION: Multimodal composing projects should *go* somewhere. They should have authentic audiences and purposes that extend beyond the walls of the classroom. When assignments are designed in this way, students and teachers will want to show their work outside the classroom.

FIGURE 3.1 Elements of multimodal composition assignments: Theory, structure and choice, circulation

Revising and Testing Composing Theory

For teachers, one of the greatest benefits of experimenting with multimodal composing—composing audio and video essays as well as alphabetic essays—is the opportunity to *re-think* what they know about composing: to test, evaluate, and expand the theories of composing they have developed when teaching alphabetic writing and get students to do so as well. Ideally, multimodal composing tasks will help *both* students and teachers arrive at what James Zebroski (1994) cites as the composition classroom's primary goal: theory revised and realized. Multimodal assignments, however, must *also* fit within *existing* systems of pedagogy; teachers will want to consider how—or if—multimodal composing fits their instructional approaches and goals for students. Making such connections, even if this theorizing isn't represented in the finished text of assignments, will influence the way students communicate about the purpose of composing, the modalities they use to compose, and the confidence with which they experiment.

Balancing change and convention is not an easy task, of course. Even the most innovative composition classrooms are complicated by existing conceptions of academic discourse and student writing. Most composition teachers, for instance, are faced with the complex task of helping students use the more conventional forms of discourse that they encounter in school and the workplace, while—at the same time—encouraging young people to develop their own voice and approaches to composing.

Given this context, multimodal composing can be useful in providing teachers and students opportunities to extend their thinking about both conventional and unconventional forms of discourse. Teachers, for instance, can use multimodal composing to encourage students to think about existing modalities and genres of academic discourse and why they have developed as they have. Similarly, students and teachers may find that multimodal compositions provide interesting ways to re-think more formulaic approaches to composing—what to do and what not to do when they write a paper. And although both teachers and students come to the classroom with prior experience in, and habitual approaches to, composing alphabetic essays, it would be unusual for them to have had similar extensive experience, or developed such sedimented habits, with video and audio composing. Thus, assignments that ask students to compose in multiple modalities can encourage both teachers and students to take creative approaches to making meaning. Finally, multimodal assignments—when designed by skillful teachers—can help students compare the affordances of audio, image, and video with the affordances of words. Through these comparisons, students can develop conscious strategies for choosing and applying the most effective composing modalities for making meaning within a given rhetorical context.

John Trimbur (2000) argues that composition classrooms isolate composing from systems of distribution and delivery—that they separate the act of composing from the act of reception by an audience. Changing the style of composing, Trimbur continues, does not solve the problem of connecting composition to circulation. Experimenting with multimodal composing, however, can provide teachers and students an opportunity to re-think this connection. Because video and audio are more popularly based forms of communication, students have a great deal of experience in receiving and interpreting such communicative forms—much more than they may have, indeed, in reading and interpreting academic genres. Students know how video and audio messages are delivered and distributed differently for different purposes and different audiences. These understandings can enliven and enrich composition classrooms—whatever modalities, or combinations of modalities, are used for making meaning.

Erika Lindemann (1987) reminds writing instructors that successful assignments must take into account at least five rhetorical factors:

- student engagement with the subject

- purpose of composing

- audience

- student role in relation to subject and audience

- form of discourse

At least three of these factors change dramatically when the assignment invites students to experiment with additional modalities of composing. Given the nature of contemporary media, Western society associates the modalities of video and audio *primarily* with efforts to entertain an audience rather than with efforts to inform. In contrast, we associate the modality of alphabetic writing *primarily* with the purpose of informing readers. Theorizing the purpose of a rhetorical task, then, is crucial to helping students engage with multimodal composing and take advantage of revising opportunities with different audiences and their expectations in mind.

TYPES OF STRUCTURE, TYPES OF CHOICE

This chapter discusses a sample assignment (see Appendix 3) in which students are encouraged to choose the genre (essay, comic, 'zine), the medium (print, radio, computer), and the modality (words, still images, video images, sound)—or combination of modalities—that will best accomplish their rhetorical purposes. Hence, the assignment can be done—depending on students' choices— in non-digital as well as digital environments. As students engage with such choices, they are encouraged to think rhetorically about audience, purpose, form, and delivery. With such choices, teachers can help anchor students' composing firmly in the realm of rhetorical decision making.

For teachers who are just beginning to explore multimodality or those whose classes have limited access to digital cameras and audio recorders, this kind of assignment is particularly useful. Rather than starting experimentation with an assignment in which *every* student in a class uses audio or video, teachers can use an open-ended assignment that provides students a choice of both medium and modality. If several students choose to work in multiple modalities, teachers can encourage them to participate in collaborative projects and involve them in peer-group studio reviews.

To design an assignment that provides an effective balance of structure and open-endedness, teachers can consider the following points:

- Allow for choice of composing modalities. Students need to learn how to decide what modalities best suit their purpose, audience, and information—whether the purpose, audience, and information associated with the piece they want to compose is best presented in audio, video, print, or some combination of these modalities. This decision should also take into account the particular affordances of specific modalities—considerations of not only what they do well, but what they do not do well (Table 3.1).

- Allow options for group work. Collaborative efforts provide the opportunity for students to become a community of learners who rely on each others' different technical and composing expertise. Collaboration itself, however, can provide drawbacks for some students and in some conditions. Compulsory group work can limit students' choices and may involve them in projects that do little to encourage individual investment or commitment. Students often find, moreover, that collaborative work on multimodal projects suffers from the uneven involvement of group members and that coordinating the contributions and meetings of group members adds an additional—and unwelcome—layer of complexity to a project. Finally, students who work effectively or efficiently by themselves may find collaborative projects to be less flexible in terms of management. One person might easily abandon or restructure a collaborative project; however, changing the direction of a collaborative project can be more difficult and might require more time and consultation. Chapter 4 offers a more detailed look at collaboration among students.

- Allow for exploration and questions. Because multimodal composition remains a relatively new approach within college composition classrooms, students will and should question if what they're doing really *counts* as composing. These conversations—which should be encouraged rather than avoided—present outstanding opportunities for students and teachers to talk about rhetorical concerns like purpose, audience, genre, and circulation; review the instructional goals of the composition course; and talk about professional communication practices. Whether or not teachers formally sponsor and take part in these conversations, assignments should encourage discussion along these lines.

TABLE 3.1
AFFORDANCES OF AUDIO AND VIDEO

COMPOSING FOR AUDIO	COMPOSING FOR VIDEO
Examples	**Examples**
Sonja Borton's "Legacy of Music," in which we hear her family's voices as well as their music. Daniel Keller's "Lord of the Machines: Reading the Human Computer Relationship," in which Daniel uses a sound effect to computerize his voice, making it sound as if a machine narrates the piece.	Elizabeth Powell's *Literacy and Public Transportation*, a video in which her mother recounts her childhood literacy practices on city buses in Nashville, Tennessee.
Affordances	**Affordances**
Projects dealing with music, dialect, and accent, or sonic environments are particularly well suited for the affordances of sound. The absence of visual print or images makes us hear essays differently and focus on the experience of listening. Audio may not be particularly good in images.	Projects dealing with history, a temporal unfolding of events, physical movement, or facial expressions may be suited to video, which can show historical artifacts, and convey motion and body language. Video can be combined with still photos, title screens, and voice-over narration to create a well-rounded presentation using sound and alphabetic text along with visuals depicting silent movement or gesture. Video may not be particularly good in depicting people's internal thoughts.

- Provide structure and strategies for success. As we suggest elsewhere in this book, faculty will want to spend some time creating their own multimodal texts as they design and finalize assignments. Through this activity, instructors can better gauge the support that students will need as they compose the text of their projects, the directions and documentation required by the assignment, the time required for students to complete certain tasks, and the challenges students may run into as they begin composing. If nothing else, such practice means that teachers will be better prepared to answer students' questions.

- Include written reflection. Reflection encourages critical thinking and deepens the learning that multimodal assignments demand. In addition, reflection allows students the opportunity to articulate the personal connections they establish with their work and their subject matter. Some of the prompts in Figure 3.2 may help teachers think about how to phrase such reflective tasks.

- Explain the choice of composing modalities that you are using in your project. Why is video, audio, or alphabetic writing best suited to your purpose? Audience? Subject matter?

- What does your audience expect from your chosen modality? What are its conventions, affordances, expectations? How does your composition consider or address such matters?

- Consider your composing processes. In what ways is it different from or similar to the processes you use in composing alphabetic texts?

- Why did you choose to compose with a group, or, alternatively, as an individual? If you're working with a group, what roles have you and other team members taken on? What have you learned about composing from each other? If you're composing individually, what have you learned about your own composing processes, and how will you extend your understanding to help classmates?

- Consider your revision processes. If you are working on a video or audio text, consider if the revising you have done differs from what you do for printed word essays. If so, how? Why??

- Consider your own skill in—and understandings of—alphabetic texts, video texts, and/or audio texts. Which skills and understandings are your strongest? Which do you need to develop further?

- How will this text be circulated? How does the method and circumstances of circulation affect your composing?

FIGURE 3.2 Prompts for student reflection during composing

CIRCULATION

Questions about the circulation of a completed project can also play an important role in the design of an assignment. Where will students' projects be seen or heard or read? Who will be their audience? What is the project's purpose?

Many of the papers students write in school settings circulate in very limited environments and among few people. Print essays, for example, often circulate within a classroom, but seldom outside the academy; similarly, they often circulate among classmates and teachers, but infrequently within a broader public audience or a specialized audience who has a particular interest in their content. Indeed, these papers are generally of very limited interest to audiences outside an academic setting—and often for good reason. The genres, language, and subjects of such papers are often artificial, inauthentic, or forced; the language is aimed at teachers of composition; the writing is formulaic. They do not respond seriously and creatively to the needs of different audiences in terms of information, explanation, or example.

Multimodal compositions, in contrast—because they are rendered in vernacular media and communicate in images and sounds, as well as words, in popular and familiar forms—are much more likely to be circulated by students outside the classroom and shared with audiences other than teachers. These essays may appeal to different audiences who enjoy listening to the radio, watching television, or reading newspapers. They can also serve to expand the kind of work students do and the ways authors can engage with different groups of listeners and viewers.

In other chapters throughout this collection, we address how teachers can help students generate and pursue creative ideas for multimodal projects, think rhetorically about such texts, experiment with various strategies of making meaning, solve problems, and collaborate with others on such texts. Teachers can increase the circulation of students' multimodal projects by *archiving* and *showcasing* them. Both of these strategies have the benefit of expanding the audiences for students' work. Before teachers or students make a decision to take work outside the classroom, however, they should make sure that students have cited and documented all material that is not original to the author, and have requested and obtained clearance from the owners of any copyrighted materials (images, audio material, or video) that are contained within multimodal essays. Teachers and students should also make sure that all people who appear in, or are heard in, students' projects have signed written release/consent forms (see Appendix 6). See Chapter 6 for more information on copyrighted material (*Chapter 6: Saving, Sharing, Citing, Documenting, and Publishing Multimodal Texts*).

Once teachers have informed themselves and students about constraints on copyrighted material, students' original multimodal compositions can be made available in digital venues available to the public so that other people can locate, listen, and view the essays. Students can also archive their own digital video and audio work on university web spaces if these are available, and they can create hyperlinks to bring traffic to their sites. Teachers can use class, departmental, and school Web sites to archive students' work—again after informing themselves about copyright law. University libraries may also archive video, audio, or bound publications produced by students. Academic departments may be interested in obtaining copies of such projects as well. Departmental archives provide a resource for students and instructors interested in working with multimodal compositions, and they provide the public a place to see and listen to the finished projects of students who represent their programs.

Showcasing multimodal essays during the semester can provide students additional opportunities to get the reactions of various audiences. Showcasing—which usually goes beyond peer and instructor feedback—uses public displays of students' original texts. Teachers can, for instance, organize a public showing of students' final multimodal projects. In connection with such showings, students can be involved in the process of composing press releases for student newspapers and the local media. Students can also be involved in designing posters, flyers, and written invitations to individuals in a department, institution, or community. Teachers can help research these opportunities, but they shouldn't do the work themselves. Rather, their primary focus should be on encouraging students to make contacts inside and outside the university and seek new venues for publication of their original work.

DESIGNING ASSIGNMENTS FOR THE MULTIMODAL CLASSROOM

With theory, structure, and circulation in mind, teachers can help an assignment take shape. However, the curricular contexts within which assignments exist and the material conditions in which they are assigned will also affect how students approach assignments. Thus, teachers need to consider how assignments fit into both curricula and course schedules. In many cases, although not all, they must also coordinate resources so that students will have access to the digital cameras, digital audio recorders, and the computer hardware and software they need to complete multimodal assignments. Without devoting careful attention to some of the nuts-and-bolts matters, teachers may be asking students to do the impossible when they compose multimodally. Here's a to-do list for teachers preparing multimodal assignments:

 Devise a timeline. Consider how much course time to devote to multimodal composing within the classroom and curriculum. Such considerations will be shaped by teachers' understanding of how—or, indeed, *if*—multimodal assignments feed into, enhance, or extend other assignments and instructional efforts. *Chapter 7: Experimenting with Multimodal Texts* offers more thinking about scheduling assignments. Of course, for most teachers, the first multimodal assignment is the hardest, so plenty of time should be set aside for the experience the first time around. See Appendix 4 for a sample of one timeline for a multimodal assignment.

 Devote attention to the technical side of production—especially in classes using digital environments. A class needs to establish a common technical vocabulary for students as they learn to compose in multiple modalities, especially if they are depending on digital tools and environments. The *Glossary* at the end of this collection identifies a list of terms that teachers may want to consider using. The best assignments, of course, integrate this kind of vocabulary learning into the rest of the course instruction in meaningful ways. They also give students opportunities to experiment with digital equipment. Appendices 21 and 22 provide directions for two preliminary workshops that teachers can use to introduce students to digital audio recorders, video cameras, and the vocabulary they need in order to work both kinds of equipment.

Teachers might also want to involve students in creating homemade, customized documentation for important technical processes, such as downloading student-recorded video from a video camera to a computer or downloading images from the web to a project folder. In Appendix 7, we provide an example of such a homemade documentation project—one focused on downloading still photographs from a digital camera to a computer. We remind readers, however, that *this text will not be immediately applicable in their own labs or classrooms. Indeed, this kind of documentation is valuable specifically because it is so local and customized.* Such documents arise from the immediate composing needs of particular class members, are specific to the software and hardware resources at a specific institution, and are directed at an audience whose members have developed a shared technical vocabulary. Readers *are* encouraged to *assign* such customized mini-documentation projects to students in their own composition classes or partner with the teachers of other related courses—such as technical communication—to involve different groups of students in such projects.

 Invite knowledgeable consultants to work with students for a class period. Teachers can invite guests to the classroom—experienced students; instructional technology staff members; faculty members who teach film, radio, or design classes; other instructors who work with multimedia on a more regular basis; or community members—to help students learn more about working effectively in digital environments, with hardware and software, or with equipment. Teachers might also want to invite guests willing to serve as expert consultants on other matters connected with the assignment. For instance, an instructor might invite students from a partnering class on technical communication to create—or user test—documentation for video- or audio-editing software. These same people might also enjoy being asked back later in the semester to attend a showcase of class projects.

 Design assignments with peer response in mind. Effective revision of multimodal compositions depends, to some extent, on useful peer and teacher feedback. Teachers will want to schedule the time for studio peer reviews at various points throughout a unit on multimodal composing. Among the considerations for such sessions are how and when they should be conducted, what feedback listeners and viewers will be asked to provide, how to ensure that feedback is productive, and how much time students will have to revise their projects (see *Chapter 8: Responding and Assessing* and *Chapter 9: More about Reading,*

Responding, and Revising).

 Remind students to incorporate writing into their process of composing an audio or video essay and in their theorizing of how multimodal composing works. For some English composition teachers, a multimodal assignment remains incomplete until it involves students in writing. Students can be asked to pause at various stages of a project in order to reflect on

- the processes involved in composing in different modalities

- their role as author/composer

- the content of their project

- the effectiveness of their project

- the affordances of different modalities that they use

- which aspects of their projects work well and which need additional attention

 Help students identify and engage with opportunities for research. Most teachers want students to engage in assignments as opportunities for research and learning as well as for composing. Some teachers, for example, may want to ask students to keep an annotated bibliography of all sources they use as they compose their projects (see Chapter 6: Saving, Sharing, Citing, and Publishing Multimodal Texts for more about citation and documentation). In the case of the sample assignment outlined in Appendix 3, students are asked to study documentaries with a critical research eye to determine how narratives are constructed. Students are also asked to compare narrative and rhetorical structures in film, audio, and print, and to interview subjects as part of the assignment. Some guidelines for interviewing are provided in Appendix 5. If students are conducting research, teachers should check their school's research guidelines on the use of human subjects to make sure that students are not violating university or federal regulations. Appendix 6 provides a sample release/consent form for students to use when interviewing.

REFERENCES

Lindemann, E. (1987). Making and evaluating writing assignments. In *A rhetoric for writing teachers*, (pp. 191-224). New York: Oxford University Press.
Trimbur, J. (2000). Composition and the circulation of writing. *CCC, 52*(2), 188-219.
Zebroski, J. (1994). *Thinking through theory: Vygotskian perspectives on the teaching of writing*. Portsmouth, NH: Boynton/Cook.

Annee-Marie Pederson and Carolyn Skinner

CHAPTER 4
Collaborating on Multimodal Projects

Anne–Marie Pedersen
Carolyn Skinner

Collaborating on audio and video projects involves benefits and challenges similar to those involved in collaborating on alphabetic compositions. Audio and video projects can reshape collaboration, however, by asking authors to draw on a broader knowledge base than is necessary for alphabetic composition. For example, the composition of audio or video projects relies on collaborators' combined knowledge of the project's topic, its dominant modalities, the technology used for recording and editing, the medium in which the project is read or circulated, and the conventions or expectations of audiences.

The sample assignments in *Chapter 2: Words, Audio and Video: Composing and the Processes of Production* and *Chapter 3: Designing Multimodal Assignments* offer opportunities for meaningful collaboration. In connection with audio and video projects, such collaboration efforts work best under certain circumstances, such as those described in the left-hand column of Table 4.1, but nearly every multimodal classroom context can benefit from the sharing of ideas and techniques among students. Our advice assumes that all students in a multimodal course are collaborating at some level, either within—or across—groups in a class. Some of our suggestions apply to whole-class collaboration, and some address small-group collaboration specifically.

THE BENEFITS OF COLLABORATING ON AUDIO OR VIDEO PROJECTS

For students, many of the benefits of collaboration may be intangible; for example, the emotional rewards and the learning that occurs when group members discuss ideas that are difficult to quantify or trace back to their sources. There are, however, some steps teachers can take to facilitate productive collaboration—and ways they can encourage the learning and negotiations that accompany the development of a complex composition. In an effective collaborative environment, students learn about the project, composition, *and* collaboration (see Table 4.2).

TABLE 4.1 COLLABORATING ON AUDIO AND VIDEO PROJECTS	
WHEN TO COLLABORATE ON VIDEO AND AUDIO PROJECTS	
Indicated	Contra-indicated
Students share content ideas: Students choose topics based on shared backgrounds or common interests.	**Students explore personal or idiosyncratic content:** Students compose on topics based on individual experiences and knowledge, which makes it difficult for all group members to contribute meaningfully. (View Sonya Borton's video project on this book's DVD as an example.)
Class meets regularly and has access to a computer lab: Students will have ample opportunity to meet with their group members.	**Class does not meet regularly and students have little scheduled lab time in common. Access to computer lab is sporadic:** Students may have trouble scheduling time to work together on the project. Certain distance learning situations may hinder students' ability to collaborate successfully; others may encourage sharing in virtual environments.
Teacher wants to assess students' ability to work with technology in teams: In the work world, most audio and video texts are composed by teams, and collaborative projects help teachers evaluate students' potential to succeed in a real-world environment.	**Teacher wants to assess students' ability to work individually with technology:** To judge the students' ability to produce audio and video texts alone, teachers should assign solo projects.

 Students can draw on shared knowledge of technology and of audio and video composition.

Today's students bring a range of technological experiences and expertise to the classroom, creating a context in which students can learn from one another. This learning can be about the technology that students employ to compose audio and video projects or about different modalities they call on to complete such projects. For example, some students have extensive experience with technology from home computer use, whereas others may have little technology experience but a keen ear for music or an eye for visual design. Collaboration allows students to learn from each other and synthesize what they know about various modes and the digital technologies that are often used to compose them.

In Appendices 21 and 22, for example, we have included the directions for two discovery workshop sessions in which the members of small student teams help each other discover how to use a digital video camera and a minidisc recorder—with the dual aim of conducting short practice interviews with each other and learning how to use some digital equipment properly. The key to this activity is that students learn by helping each other in a collaborative effort. In this activity, students quickly realize that their collective knowledge is often far greater and more useful than their individual experiences—especially with unfamiliar technologies. We encourage teachers to refocus this activity (and to revise the direction sheets included on the book's DVD) on different pieces of equipment, hardware, or software programs in order to accomplish similar goals.

To encourage students to draw on each other's knowledge, teachers can also set up a class listserv through which students can share problems and solutions. They can also set aside class time in the computer lab during which students can ask each other questions. Teachers may also want to survey students about their experiences and knowledge working with technology, especially in connection with audio and video (see Appendix 8). Teachers can use the survey responses to create a class Expertise Grid on which students identify their experience with a variety of programs. Students can then use this Expertise Grid to find out who might be able to help them with questions or problems (see Appendix 9). Teachers can also use survey responses to achieve effective combinations for collaborative groups, mixing students who have various levels of expertise with technology or familiarity with composing modalities.

 Students can support and encourage each other.

Collaboration can alleviate the frustration of learning a new technology and can boost student morale. For example, seeing collaborators' contributions to a project can be exciting and can inspire renewed interest in the project. Collaborators can also give each other the emotional and intellectual support needed to persist in working with new modes and technologies. In groups in which everyone is a novice, experimenting with nonprint modes and new software feels less overwhelming. Even when students are familiar with the technology, working with it can be frustrating: software can crash or create unexpected problems or delays. Teachers can encourage students who become frustrated by the technology to hand off the work to another group member.

All collaborative projects require good communication among collaborators, and this is especially true for audio and video projects, in which students often work with technology in unfamiliar contexts. Teachers can encourage good communication by asking students to leave notes for each other in the form of collaborative project logs (Appendix 10) and by providing a safe place for students to leave these notes and other shared materials. Recording achievements, however small, allows students to see their progress and can boost morale.

Teachers might also want to provide the opportunity for the class as a whole to discuss the file-sharing techniques that various collaborative teams find useful. Some collaborative teams, for example, may find it useful to transfer project drafts via portable memory devices that are increasingly inexpensive and accessible to students. Other teams may prefer to work on projects only during a time when all members can be present in the same computer lab and in person. Still other teams may rely on their project logs to provide members with direction for their revising efforts. In such whole-class sessions, collaborative teams may also be able to share valuable information about file-naming conventions, useful recording and editing techniques, and hints for arranging and using server space in increasingly effective ways.

 Students can use time, space, and technological resources effectively.

Because most schools have limited resources, finding the technology, lab space, and class time to devote to audio or video composition can be difficult. Collaboration is a good option for teachers with limited resources. In collaborative projects, students can share available resources such as computers, headphones, recording devices, and server space.

Even though students are working collaboratively and sharing resources, they may not use the resources simultaneously. Because computers are designed for one user at a time, students may need simple and relatively inexpensive devices like headphone splitters that allow two or more students to listen to the same project on their own headphones. To facilitate effective use of group lab time, teachers can give students calendars to schedule times to work on their projects individually and simultaneously. Teachers may also want to provide a sign-up sheet to coordinate the dates and times that audio and video equipment will be checked out to student teams.

Students who have busy or rigid schedules, however, may still find it easier to work on these projects at different times—thus making the most effective use of available hardware and accommodating the schedules of various team members. Teachers can support this pattern of work by encouraging the effective use of collaborative project logs (Appendix 10) by all team members, and by identifying a safe place for students to leave their shared materials.

 Students can learn by articulating composition principles.

To produce a coherent project, collaborators need to articulate to other team members their ideas for developing and revising a composition. Because working in modes other than print text will be unfamiliar to some students, talking about audio or video composition may prove difficult for them, but it is also a crucial part of the learning associated with composing these texts. Collaborators must come to agreements about what is working *well* in a text, what's *not working* well, *why* things are working or not, and *what they should do to improve the composition*. Although more formal, peer–review studio sessions (Chapters 8 and 9) may provide some of this information (and provide students a venue in which to practice using the new vocabularies of multimodal composition and production), collaborative team members must also do their part to articulate their own understanding about the team's composition as it is and as it could be. Without defining the characteristics of the composition, the collaborators cannot compose or revise in ways that produce a unified composition.

To facilitate consensus on these matters, teachers can provide students with heuristics that prompt discussion about multimodal projects. These heuristics can list the key compositional elements for an assignment—and touch on the affordances of sound, image and video—so that collaborative groups can better determine how to manipulate those elements and affordances in their projects (see Appendix 11). Teachers can also ask groups to diagram their projects, giving special emphasis to the key points and duration of segments in their projects. These planning diagrams should prompt discussion on what the groups hope to accomplish and how they will achieve these ends (see Appendices 12 and 13).

TABLE 4.2

THE BENEFITS OF COLLABORATING.BENEFITS	STRATEGIES FOR COLLABORATING ON AUDIO AND VIDEO PROJECTS
Students can draw on shared knowledge of technology and of audio and video composition.	**Class Listserv:** Set up a class listserv through which students can share problems and solutions. **In-class Workshop:** Set aside class time in a common computer lab during which students can ask each other questions. **Student Expertise Grid:** Survey students about their experiences and knowledge of working with technology, especially in audio and video modes. From survey responses, create and distribute a chart that lists students by areas of expertise (see Appendices 8 and 9). **Student Groups:** Use survey responses to group students in ways that mix members' technology strengths and familiarity with modalities. Some teachers also find it useful to designate student groups that form around an interesting project, a shared expertise, or some other factor.
Students can support and encourage each other.	**Forums to Boost Morale:** Provide forums such as collaborative project logs, email updates, or space to leave messages (bulletin boards, chalkboards, mailboxes) for students to share accomplishments and encouragement. Recording achievements, however small, allows students to see their progress and can boost morale (see Appendix 10). **Relay Work:** Reduce frustration by limiting the length of any one student's work session. Suggest that students who become frustrated by the technology hand off work on the project to another group member.
Students can use time, space, and technological resources effectively.	**Division of Labor:** Give students calendars to schedule times to work on the project individually and simultaneously. **Division of Time and Resources:** Provide a sign-up sheet to coordinate the dates and times that audio and video equipment is checked out to students.
Students can learn by articulating composition principles.	**Heuristics To Prompt Discussion:** List key composition elements and key affordances of sound and video, and ask students to discuss in their groups how they will use these elements and affordances in their projects (see Appendix 11). **Planning Diagrams:** Ask students to diagram their projects (Appendices 12 and 13), giving special emphasis to key points and duration of segments. Use these planning diagrams to prompt discussion about what the groups hope to accomplish and how they will achieve their goals.

POTENTIAL CHALLENGES IN COLLABORATING ON AUDIO AND VIDEO PROJECTS

Collaborating on audio and video projects is prone to many of the same difficulties as collaborating on traditional alphabetic projects. Interpersonal conflicts, unfair distribution of work, and struggles to match busy schedules don't go away just because the projects are more high-tech. In fact, the technology itself sometimes presents obstacles to effective collaboration. Despite these obstacles, our experiences collaborating on audio and video compositions suggest that the benefits of collaborating on these projects outweigh any potential drawbacks. Teachers who anticipate and address the most common challenges to collaboration on audio and video projects can increase the effectiveness of these projects. Below, and in Table 4.3, we list potential challenges and strategies for responding to them.

 **Students may find that the limitations of the technology prohibit working simultaneously.**

One factor teachers might consider when planning group projects is access to production resources that class members will have. For example, if teachers have access to only one video camera but want to incorporate video composition into their classes, they might consider forming large teams of collaborators. Teachers might even want to involve an entire class on collaboratively planning, shooting, and editing one short video.

Technology design can also present limitations. Because computers are designed for use by one person, input devices for editing multimedia (mice, touch pads, etc.) can often be operated by only one person at a time. For example, when working on an audio project, students may need access to headphone splitters so that they can both listen simultaneously. Other students may prefer to take turns on a project—working with each other in a relay fashion—and periodically sharing what they do.

Despite the extra time commitment that alternately editing and sharing requires, editing collaboratively does not necessarily inconvenience students. Those with busy schedules may welcome the flexibility that working collaboratively, but not simultaneously, allows. Teachers should encourage students who compose at different times to communicate frequently with their group members about changes they've made when working individually (see Collaborative Project Logs, Appendix 10).

Students who do want to work simultaneously can use headphone splitters. These splitters allow collaborators to listen to audio and video projects simultaneously without disturbing others around them.

 **Students may choose to work only on parts of a project.**

For various reasons (different levels of familiarity with digital technology, personal preferences for auditory or visual modalities, mismatched working styles) students on a collaborative project may want to divide work so that each does what he or she is most comfortable—or interested—in doing. Although dividing the project this way may be efficient, it can also diminish the range of students' learning. If teachers do not pay careful attention to groups' work habits and dynamics, for example, they may find that a technologically savvy group member on a team has done all the technological work and the other group members have learned very little about new software, editing, or multi-modal composing.

To ensure that groups fulfill their intended educational purpose, teachers should refer to the technology expertise surveys and grid when assigning students to groups (see Appendices 8 and 9). If teachers want students to draw on each other's strengths in technology and composing in non-alphabetic modes, they may want to group students with unlike skills together. On the other hand, if teachers are worried that students will only do what they're comfortable with, they may want to group students will like skills together so team members will be forced to work outside their comfort zones.

To optimize learning, teachers may also want to require all students to try all aspects of a project or challenge students to work on those parts of a project with which they are least familiar—and document how they managed such a challenge. To gauge such efforts, teachers can check project logs. Teachers can also ask students to evaluate their own contributions and the contributions of their group members (Appendices 14, 15, and 16).

Creating groups for collaborative projects is a context-specific process with no clear-cut rules. Teachers should consult their own instructional goals for multimodal composing and exercise their own best judgment about when and how to group students and when to allow students to select their own team members.

 **Students may struggle to create a shared vision for the project.**

One of the most challenging aspects of working collaboratively on multimodal compositions involves formulating shared visions of a project's rhetorical purpose, audience, and form. The difficulties associated with these tasks may be exacerbated by students' lack of familiarity with the affordances and genres associated with different composing modalities or combinations of modalities. Both audio and video compositions, in addition, involve the added difficulty of dealing with digital tools and multiple channels for conveying information—all of which have to be accounted for in a group's vision for a project. Consistency in such projects depends on the success the team has in focusing on content and imagining the ways various digital and nondigital technologies can be employed. Personal preferences and tastes can sometimes hinder the coherence of a final composition.

Teachers need to remember that team members must not only complete a project, but they also must be able to spend a good deal of time together—discussing, explaining, and understanding their rhetorical goals—especially when planning multimodal compositions. Teachers can offer students help on these efforts by encouraging teams to budget adequate time for planning and discussing the ongoing development of projects. To facilitate these efforts, teachers can provide heuristics that prompt discussion on (and reflection about) projects (purpose, audience, and focus), as well as on the affordances of various modalities and media. Teachers might, in addition, want to ask teams to diagram the layering and sequencing of various elements, segments, or events within projects. Appendices 11, 12, and 13 provide sample documents that will help on such tasks.

The challenges associated with creating a shared rhetorical vision decrease over time, as the initial sketchiness of a composition gets filled in and group members become more comfortable working with each other. However, all class members participating in collaborations need to be encouraged to check in with their partners via different communication channels—face-to-face meetings, collaborative project logs (see Appendix 10), written notes, and email—during every stage of a project, and especially during the time when their shared rhetorical vision is first being developed and instantiated.

TABLE 4.3	
THE CHALLENGES OF COLLABORATING	
POTENTIAL CHALLENGES	**HOW TO MINIMIZE CHALLENGES**
Technology limits collaboration.	**Headphone Splitters**: Purchase headphone splitters so that collaborators can listen to audio and video projects simultaneously without disturbing others around them.
	Collaborative Project Logs: Because some technology inhibits composing by all group members simultaneously, ask students to communicate frequently about changes they've made when working individually (see Appendix 10).
Students work only on parts of a project.	**Group Makeup:** Refer to technology expertise survey and grid when assigning students to groups (see Appendices 8 and 9).
	Participation Evaluations: Check the collaborative project logs to confirm that students are working on all parts of the project. Also, ask students to evaluate their own contributions and the contributions of their group members, especially in terms of the affordances and technologies associated with audio and video projects (see Appendix 10).
Students may struggle to create a shared vision for a project.	**Heuristics To Prompt Discussion:** By coming to a consensus on the application of key rhetorical principles to their audio or video project, students develop a shared vision (see Appendix 11).
	Planning Diagrams: Ask students to discuss and diagram the general shape of their project. These diagrams should prompt discussion on what the group hopes to accomplish and how they will achieve their goals (see Appendices 12 and 13).
	Channels and Vehicles of Communication: Provide multiple channels for, and vehicles of communication—collaborative project logs, email updates, or space to leave messages (bulletin boards, chalkboards, mailboxes)—so that students can communicate about changes and how these contribute to a developing rhetorical vision (see Appendix 10).

CONCLUSION

To collaborate successfully on multimodal composing projects, students need not only access to the appropriate tools but also guidance on how to use these tools. Teachers do *not* need to be experts on technology, however, to support students as they work. In fact, a teacher willing to experiment with and learn about technology—and willing to explore the complexities of multimodal composing—along with the class can foster a truly collaborative environment. In a classroom with no clear teacher-expert, students can become their own experts on technology and teach other class members what they've learned.

In our collaborating experience, explaining how we wanted a project to develop; describing the project's progress to each other; coming to agreements about rhetorical effectiveness, style, consistency, and scope; and sharing both dread and excitement about large-group studio sessions forced us to be explicit about otherwise intuitive composing processes. Students who collaborate on audio or video projects, regardless of their age or educational experience, may similarly benefit from the critical thinking needed to articulate this metaknowledge about complex rhetorical tasks.

From "Reading the Face" by John Branscum
and Dan Keller

CHAPTER 5
Thinking
Rhetorically

Daniel Keller

Given a familiarity with the conventions of alphabetic texts, English composition teachers recognize when such texts are rhetorically effective and know the strategies to pursue to help students become more persuasive writers. For example, instructors encourage students to use specific details, offer relevant examples, provide guideposts for readers, and avail themselves of figurative language. Composition teachers also know how to advise students writing persuasive texts. They help students, for instance, craft appeals that address an audience's emotions (pathos), rest on a logical argument (logos), or appeal to an understanding of ethical behavior (ethos). We also recognize that such appeals often overlap and blend their effects. But how do visual compositions persuade? How do *logos*, *pathos*, and *ethos* apply to aural texts? How can our rhetorical understandings be applied to multimodal projects?

The audio and video assignments in Chapter 2 provide opportunities to think rhetorically across different modalities, to explore and understand the possibilities of multimodal compositions as rhetorical texts. In exploring the potential for such assignments in their own classrooms, readers will want to examine their own motivations—there is little reason to make radical changes in classroom or curriculum simply for the sake of keeping pace with technology. However, there is good reason to try multimodal assignments in order to learn more about how individuals are communicating and persuading through different modalities, and to examine the rhetorical possibilities of various kinds of texts, including traditional print-based texts. With calls for 21st-century literacies assuming urgency in schools at all levels, with conventional lines between media shifting and blurring with increasing regularity, exploration of a wider range of texts can only help improve our own teaching and students' abilities to make meaning—alphabetically, aurally, visually.

This chapter focuses on rhetorical principles familiar to teachers of conventional alphabetic essays, and we will use them to build bridges to the study and composition of multimodal texts.

COMMON RHETORICAL PRINCIPLES APPLIED IN PRINT AND MULTIMODAL TEXTS

TABLE 5.1 COMMON RHETORICAL PRINCIPLES APPLIED IN PRINT AND MULTIMODAL TEXTS		
LOGOS: **Appeal to Logic**	**PATHOS:** **Appeal to Emotion**	**ETHOS:** **Appeal Based on the Character of Author**
Factual data and statistics	Expressive, vivid language	Fair-minded, honest tone
Quotations and citations of scholars	Emotional narratives	Correctness in formal features, vocabulary, and grammar.
Informed arguments	Figurative language	Authoritative and credible response.
Rational, balanced responses	Emotional responses	

To be most effective, the study and creation of multimodal texts should focus not only on how each modality is different or what affordances each brings to the task of making meaning, but also on the rhetorical uses authors can make of media and modalities and the ways in which both medium and modality can be employed to make a rhetorical appeal—or, more likely, some combination of appeals—to a specific audience.

By examining the rhetorical possibilities of different media and modalities, teachers can help students accomplish several instructional goals important to most composition classrooms:

- expanding the ability to author a wider range of texts

- learning how to read a wider range of texts with critical understanding

- gaining a better understanding of how to interpret and effectively respond to texts involving different modalities

- exploring the boundaries between various kinds of texts (audio, visual, and print)

- achieving additional understanding about the rhetorical potential of modalities and their various combinations

TEACHERS WITH RHETORICAL EXPERIENCE

Teachers of composition need to realize that they *already* have valuable rhetorical knowledge and experience that will help them approach the teaching of multimodal texts.

For example, teachers of composition may already be aware of many of the visual elements that shape a paper composed primarily of words—the type of paper, margins, typeface, font size, placement of white space, use of headings. Using a very traditional font and printing on paper with a high rag content, for example, might be just the ticket for an attorney or investment banker who wants to convey information about his firm's conservative values, financial health, and longevity—all of which contribute to their ethos. Similarly, in using both a bold font and white space to emphasize the following headings on annual statements (Barnhardt, 2005) mailed to citizens, the U.S. Social Security Administration hopes to focus readers' attention on specific information about the fund's continuing security and its role in the future of this country—to convey the ethos, in short, of the federal government and its programs:

> **Social Security is for people of all ages . . .**
> **Work to build a secure future . . .**
> **About Social Security's future . . .**

Clearly, the visual features of text (font, placement, white space, layout), far from being simple matters of aesthetics or elements that reveal students' abilities to follow formatting rules, actually communicate meaning and shape the rhetorical effectiveness of a text as Stephen Bernhardt (1986), Elizabeth Keyes (1993), and Anne Wysocki and Johndan Johnson-Eilola (1999) have said.

Composition teachers also know that when they can help students pay special attention to such features *and* make rhetorically effective choices about type font and size and style, the use of white space and bulleted lists and columns, the placement and formatting of text, students can be more effective in communicating to a specific audience, for a particular purpose. In effect, then, composition teachers who pay attention to such matters *are already helping students to think rhetorically about texts that are visual as well as alphabetic.*

Similarly, most teachers of composition already encourage student writers to think about their alphabetic essays in aural terms—discussing how to bring out the author's voice in an essay or suggesting that students read their work out loud to check on how effective the content and argument might be with a particular audience. In student-teacher conferences and peer-review sessions, composition teachers frequently encourage students to read their papers aloud, not only so that the authors themselves catch errors, but also so an audience can "hear" the rhetorical moves of juxtaposition and comparison-contrast at work. Many teachers also ask students to read their work aloud as a way of focusing on emphasis and word choice, repetition, and clarity. By paying attention to such matters composition teachers *are already helping students to think rhetorically about texts that are aural as well as alphabetic.*

In Appendix 17 at the end of this book, we provide an assignment that should help teachers—and students—build a conceptual bridge from thinking about *rhetorical effectiveness in alphabetic essays* to thinking about *rhetorical effectiveness in multimodal contexts.* We encourage teachers to modify this activity to meet the needs of specific students, assignments, courses, programs, and institutions.

THESE YOUNG KIDS TODAY, WITH THEIR HOVERBOARDS AND MULTIPLE MODALITIES . . .

By now, most teachers of composition have encountered students in their classes who seem to know a great deal about technology. Indeed—although computers are still unevenly distributed within the United Stated and the world—it is not uncommon to meet students who are involved with various media, whether through maintaining their own Web sites (combining print, audio, and visuals); creating and editing music and movies; programming computer games; or reading film and music in sophisticated ways. Indeed, even students without direct experience in *composing* multimodal texts often know a great deal about *reading and interpreting* multimodal texts as a result of being bombarded daily with television commercials, magazine and billboard advertisements, hundreds of cable channels, cell phones with text-messaging and gaming options, news websites that borrow elements from both print and televised news, and video games that feature popular music and attempt to recreate the visual style of film.

It is also true, however, that although many students are familiar with composing and reading texts in various modalities, they also lack the rhetorical skills necessary to be reflective and critical about these texts—especially in sustained ways. Operating from the base of rhetorical theory and practice, teachers of composition can help students gain critical perspective on the purpose and intended audiences of multimodal documents, as well as the appeals employed within these texts. In exchange, students can help teachers become familiar with a wider range of rhetorical texts and learn some of the skills required for producing such texts. When this reciprocal exchange happens, composition classrooms can become dynamic and engaging places where teaching takes place on multiple levels.

ARE YOU THINKING RHETORICALLY?

Part of thinking rhetorically about multimodal texts involves learning the language of video and sound. In the Additional Resources listed at the end of this book, we provide readings that can help composition teachers and students acquire some of this language; and in the Glossary, we define many of the more common terms associated with audio and video production. However, although a focus on developing vocabulary might be reassuring—in that it offers a patch of solid ground in an uncertain terrain—it often proves less important than a focus on the *rhetorical* possibilities and approaches of multimodal texts.

To help teachers *balance* the focus on specialized vocabulary and rhetorical effectiveness, we suggest the approach of identifying only a short list of specialized terms (Fig. 5.1) and encouraging stu-

---

KEY TERMS

Point of View: The perspective from which events are presented within a video.

Camera angle: The direction from which events are shot by a video camera and recorded.

Title Screen: A screen in a video that uses alphabetic text to convey information about the video.

Soundscape: A context—social, cultural, historical, natural, artificial—characterized by a particular set of sounds (Schafer, 1997).

Keynote: A sound that serves as a fundamental tone, orienting the audience to a piece's overall meaning. A keynote may not always be heard consciously, but it adds meaning to the surrounding tones (Schafer, 1997).

Signal: Foreground sounds that are given direct attention. These are hard to ignore: bells and sirens (Schafer, 1997).

Soundmark: A sound that has a unique meaning to a community (Schafer, 1997).

Establishing Shot: Visual images that establish the location of a story or sequence of events.

Voice over: Audio commentary, explanation, or interpretation added by the author in a video or audio essay.

Fade Out and Fade In: Paired terms that apply to both the audio and video. To make the transition to a new subject or theme, authors can make images gradually appear on the screen and/or gradually increase the volume (gain) of sound (fading in). To signal the end of a sequence or episode, authors can make an image gradually disappear and/or gradually decrease the volume (gain) of the audio (fading out).

Affordance: The capabilities of different media and modalities.

FIGURE 5.1 Specialized terms for audio and video analysis

dents to practice using these terms as they engage in rhetorical analyses of multimodal texts. To demonstrate how this process might work, in the following section we offer sample analyses of Beth Powell's video essay "Literacy and Public Transportation" and Dan Keller's audio essay "Human-Computer Interaction." Both focus on rhetorical principles and introduce a series of four key terms specific to multimodal compositions.

These analyses are not meant to be exhaustive, and our sample reading of these two texts should not suggest that we believe all readers will approach them in the same ways. Different readers, with different experiences and backgrounds, we know, will read and respond to texts in very different ways. Nor are the analyses we offer meant to suggest that a focus on rhetorical appeals—specifically logos, pathos, and ethos—is the *only* way that teachers and students might want to approach these texts. Teachers and students, we hope, will apply a range of analytical tools to such texts. Rather, we hope these short sample analyses provide one concrete, if limited, example of how teachers can introduce a small handful of specialized terms within the context of a discussion of rhetorical effectiveness.

BETH POWELL'S "LITERACY AND PUBLIC TRANSPORTATION"

For her video documentary, "Literacy and Public Transportation," Beth Powell interviewed her mother, Mary Reeve, about the literacy practices she encountered on buses as a child in Nashville, Tennessee. In the introduction to the video essay—roughly, the first minute of the piece—Beth took on the task of establishing an authorial ethos that was both playful (in keeping with the theme of childhood) and serious (in adding insight about the cultural contexts of literacy). Faced with this dual challenge, Beth decided that she needed to maintain a focus on her mother's generally positive memories but place these recollections within a more serious historical context and connect them, in some informed and knowledgeable way, to scholarship on literacy.

Beth did not want to make her composition seem too weighty or suggest that viewers were about to watch something as serious as *Roots* or Ken Burns' *The Civil War*. She did, however, want to intimate that the subject mattered. To properly orient her audience, in short, Beth needed to balance appeals to ethos (in part, by establishing her own credentials as a person knowledgeable about literacy), logos (in part, by connecting her mother's memories to scholarship on literacy), and pathos (by linking childhood memories and selected historical events). How did Beth try to accomplish these tasks for the viewers/readers of her text?

Beth's piece opens with video taken from inside a moving bus set to the music of Willie Nelson's "On the Road Again." Beth then combines Nelson's jaunty song, which suggests a nostalgic sense of the past, with historical black-and-white video footage. This footage is shot from a **camera angle** that recalls the point of view of a passenger looking out the window of a moving bus. Using this combination of sound and image, Beth is able to establish the primary **point of view** in the movie—that of her mother, Mary Reeve, as a school-aged child—and evoke a sense of nostalgia and pathos. With the formal title screen at the end of this sequence, "Literacy and Public Transportation," Beth cues the audience to the focus of the video. The formal diction of this screen (the diction choices of "literacy" rather than "reading and writing" and "public transportation" rather than "bus") helps to establish Beth's scholarly ethos (0:00-0:20). Beth continues the work of establishing a scholarly ethos with three static shots of buses, taken from different camera angles outside the bus, suggesting that these vehicles are objects worthy of study and observation (0:23-0:31). With the title screen at 0:33, "Specifically literacy practices on the bus," Beth narrows the focus of her video subject for the audience.

At 0:37, Beth introduces a new theme in the video—the historical context of her mother's bus rides—with an audio **signal**: Buffalo Springfield's "For What It's Worth," music introduced dramatically against the backdrop of a black screen, to indicate an important new section of the video. The song by Buffalo Springfield—used in countless Vietnam War-era films—also helps the audience place themselves back in the **soundscape** of America in the 1960s. Importantly, for the ethos that Beth wants to establish (as a scholar she wants to place her subject in a historical context) and the pathos she wants to evoke (associated with the nostalgia of her subject matter), this song serves as a **soundmark** of American culture. Although the song might evoke different feelings for each viewer, its lyrics point directly to the political awareness that characterized the 1960s as a historical era in which civil rights issues predominated. Beth chose this music to set the stage for the historical images of Rosa Parks and the Freedom Riders that follow (0:43-1:02) (Figure 5.2).

Although Beth has used no voice over commentary at this point in the essay, she has employed the music and black-and-white images in effective ways to convey meaning—especially in conjunction with accompanying alphabetic messages. As the music identifies the historical theme of political activism in the 1960s, for instance, the visual images and the alphabetic information within these images (e.g., the image of Rosa Parks on a bus juxtaposed with the words "How I Fought for Civil Rights"; an image of a charred bus juxtaposed with the words "Freedom Riders bus set on fire by the KKK"; and the image of a newspaper clipping with the headline "Bus Mixers are Beaten") combine to provide a textured sense of the political scene in the South during this period.

FIGURE 5.2 Historical images of the civil rights era in the 1960s

With these **establishing shots,** Beth manages to situate her mother's story in the South and in the 1960s, providing a historical context for her mother's literacy experiences on buses. She also indicates that she considers the story of her mother's literacy practices on buses to be a narrative about social action, one linked to the 1960s themes of political awareness and democratic involvement. These black-and-white images also carry a great deal of authority as historical artifacts, a move that contributes to the logos of Beth's project, and their arrangement in the video sets the stage for the narrative that is about to follow.

Teachers who want to conduct this kind of rhetorical analysis of Beth's video essay may also find it useful to note all the work that gets done within this minute and a half of video time and ask students to consider how the composition might have been different if it used only the modality of audio. Beth could have retained the music by Willie Nelson and Buffalo Springfield, for example, but she would have had to add additional audio soundmarks from buses themselves—sounds of buses driving, doors opening and closing, horns honking, and so on—to properly orient her audience. She might have also needed to create audio voice over to establish her subject, which she does in her video in a more expedient fashion with a combination of images and title screens. For the segment on Rosa Parks and the Freedom Riders, which helps establish historical context and logos, Beth could have included sound bites from interviews and news reports to locate her mother's story within the context of political action.

The main subject of the video is Beth's mother, Mary Reeve. At 1:02, Beth uses a series of audio and video moves that complement each other to provide viewers with a rhetorically effective transition from the context-setting work she did in the video's introduction to the main subject of Mary's story. During this series of moves, she simultaneously **fades out** a photograph of Freedom Riders looking at the charred remains of a bus to a black screen (visually signalling the end of the history segment) *and* **fades out** the Buffalo Springfield song to a moment of silence (providing an auditory signal that the sequence is ending). Next, Beth **fades in** visually on a title screen announcing the new topic ("My Mom, Mary Reeve, b. 1952, Nashville, TN (1:03) *and* **fades in** to a new auditory **soundmark**—a special version of "I Get Around" (artists, Brian Wilson and Gary Usher), performed by a chorus of children at the Wix-Brown School in Langley, British Columbia, and a segment of **voice over** narration provided by Beth's mother. With these carefully coordinated rhetorical transitions, Beth ends one segment of the video and begins another. The visual fade-to-black and the auditory fade-to-silence serves as the equivalent of white space in a print document—it demarcates segments of the video and signals the importance of the material to come. Beth uses these rhetorical devices to signal the importance of her mother as the primary narrator of the video. With the "I Get Around" music that fades in, Beth refocuses the audience's attention on the theme of *childhood* memories. The song serves as another soundmark of the 1950s and 1960s, and the lyrics help establish a rhetorical coherence with the theme of buses as a form of public transportation and mobility.

Mary's narration opens with her looking back on her childhood: "When I was a little girl, my mother worked for the National Transit Company . . . so my sister and I got to ride the bus for free." In this opening, viewers hear Mary's Southern accent and her laughter. These auditory elements help create rhetorical coherence in the essay by reminding viewers of Beth's visual establishing shots (of the Southern civil rights movement) and reasserting the lighter tone associated with the theme of childhood memories suggested by the Willie Nelson music in the introduction. These auditory elements of laughter and accent, clearly, would be difficult to convey adequately using only the modality of print. Throughout this segment of the video, Mary's diction and recollections sound both natural and unforced. As the author of the video, Beth has refrained from editing out the slight stumbles and pauses of her mother's recollections. This decision helps establish a sense of authenticity in the essay and shapes Beth's rhetorical ethos as a documentarian of history and literacy. The **affordances** of sound in this multimodal essay make it possible for the audience to get a sense of Mary's speech patterns, her Southern accent, and the timbre and speed of her voice. These qualities would be difficult to convey in an essay that was composed only of words printed on a page.

As the video essay continues, Mary recalls how she and her sister rode the bus as children, and Beth uses several video clips of buses on city streets (1:03-1:36) to provide an illustrative scene. These brief video sequences (Fig. 5 3) are clearly modern, but Beth has rendered the video clips in black and white to suggest historical authenticity and, thus, further support an appeal to logos.

Beth has also used these video scenes to create a sense of rhetorical coherence in her video essay. All these bus scenes, for example, are recorded from street level and the same side of the street— a **camera angle** that suggests the **point of view** of a bus rider. The sequence of scenes, moreover, mirrors Mary's narration of the daily routine that her bus riding takes (1:07-1:36)—starting in the morning and ending in the evening. The repetition of bus images helps to emphasize, in a rhetorical sense, the central theme of buses as sites for public literacy practices.

As Mary continues to narrate her stories about practicing literacy on buses (1:37-4:04), Beth employs an appeal to logic in her composition—using specific images to provide visual evidence for the observations her mother makes: among these images, a bus billboard, an advertisement, and a picture of a Nashville landmark (Fig. 5.4).

FIGURE 5.3 Rhetorical coherence and consistency

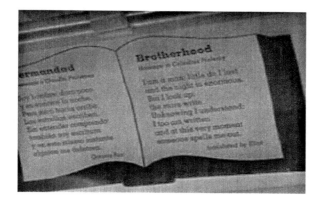

FIGURE 5.4 Visual evidence of Mary Reeve's claims about literacy

The conclusion of Beth's video essay can also provide some interesting points of rhetorical analysis. In alphabetic compositions, the conclusion often "zooms out" from a series of detailed points to focus on some larger implications. In the conclusion of this video essay, when her mother has finished with her recollections, Beth's video similarly "zooms out" from a personal story to re-establish the importance of the bus as a site of public literacy. During this final segment, Mary talks about the sense of community she felt on the bus: "It was a fact, and you never thought about not doing it: If an older person got on the bus and there were no seats, you got up and you gave that person your seat—race, color, gender, did not matter." This sentence both resonates with and complicates the earlier visual and aural references to political activism, public transportation, and the Civil Rights movement in the South during the 1960s—establishing, once again, a coherent set of themes within the essay. Beth underscores her point with more songs that serve as **soundmarks** of the 1960s— the Youngbloods' "Get Together," which includes the lyrics, "Come on people now, smile on your brother. Everybody get together, try to love one another right now." As Mary speaks, and the music plays, the audience also sees video images of people getting on and off the bus. These scenes (Fig. 5.5) are shot from the **point of view** of a rider inside the bus, situating the audience as part of the community (3:30-3:45) being referenced—an effective rhetorical appeal to pathos.

As Mary's narration fades, Beth finalizes the importance of her subject using quoted material from literacy scholars Brian Street (4:05) and Kathleen Rockhill (4;37), and a summary of her own thinking about the social and literacy practices Mary Reeve observed—and participated in—on the bus (4:49). These statements are displayed in white text on black screens, an aesthetic decision that, for some readers, lends a sense of authenticity (through a connection with things that are old) and a sense of authority (though a connection to scholarly expertise) to their content—thus, appealing to ethos and logos. The video ends with a picture of Mary Reeve standing on a chair as a child, one last appeal to pathos.

FIGURE 5.5 Buses as "a place for community"

DAN KELLER'S AUDIO ESSAY "HUMAN-COMPUTER INTERACTION"

In this audio essay, Dan explores the relationships humans have with computers through daily interaction and media representations. The composition itself refrains from taking an argumentative stance; instead, it functions as a cross between a sound performance and a sound documentary. The narrator's voice is presumed to be that of the author, but this is complicated by the fact that the voice is inhuman, mediated by a text-to-speech computer program like that employed by physicist Stephen Hawking. This **voice over** commentary serves both as a **soundmark** that references the information age of the late 20th or early 21st century and as a **signal** in representing the complex and dependent relationship between humans and machines. It also complicates the notion of ethos—listeners may be unsettled by the cyborg-ian voice, but they also understand that a person, at least in part, helped generate the voice. This realization could prove thought-provoking (logos) or novel (pathos) to the audience.

Dan introduces his essay with the sounds of several technologies, organized roughly in historical order: pages being flipped, alphabet letters being recited ("A, B, C"), a pen scribbling, typewriter keys tapping, a telephone ringing, binary code being recited ("1,0,1,0"), and, finally, a computer modem dialing and connecting to a network (0:21). These **signal** sounds focus the audience's attention on the related themes of technology and its effects on the lives of humans—a primary subject of the audio essay. The sounds may also encourage the audience to reflect on the commonsense narrative of technological progress. Dan uses an audio clip from Pink Floyd's song "Welcome to the Machine" (0:29-0:31) to complete this segment of his audio essay. The song serves as a **keynote** reference to the technological age—interrupting the modem connection sounds with overpowering vocals and industrial sounds. In this context, Pink Floyd's inhuman "welcome" to the age of information technology strikes the audience as either ironic or menacing (0:29)—or both. The "welcome" is followed by brief silence—an auditory marker that signals a transition to a new segment.

The next segment of the essay (and the second segment of the introduction) begins with the cyborg narrator's **voice over**:

> A 1999 study by software company Symantec Corporation reveals that 33% of computer users have physically assaulted a computer. Over 70% admit that they curse at computers. I fall into the 70%. At least once a month, I curse at my printer—and that's if it's a good month. (0:29-0:59)

This opening line of this segment lends itself both to the appeal of logos (the use of statistics) and pathos (most listeners will be able to relate to similar feelings toward technology). When the voice admits that it curses at its printer, the audience realizes that the voice speaks for all human beings who maintain a vexed relationship with technology. The humor of this segment is underscored by the mechanical delivery of the cyborg voice and an audio clip of a man ranting about the "paper jam" message that appears on a photocopy machine (an audio clip from the film *Office Space*). The man's accent implies that troubled relationships between humans and machines are increasingly widespread in a global context.

In most print essays, the rhetorical goals of an introduction involve establishing a purpose, focusing on a topic of exploration (often, but not always, expressed as a thesis), and giving some preview of what is to come. In this second segment of the introduction to his audio essay, Dan accomplishes much of this same work—articulating the topic he will explore ("our relationship with computers" 1:15) and his thesis ("many people fear what the wired world is doing to our society" 1:27). He also indicates—with the Pink Floyd music, the cyborg voice, the audio clip about the paper jam, and his choice of statistics—that his intention is to undertake a seriocomic exploration of this thesis. In the introduction, Dan also makes another important move. From 1:45-2:07, for instance, the cyborg narrator observes that people's fears of computers and the Internet are reflected in popular culture, an observation followed and underscored with music (Elliott Smith's haunting "Can't Make a Sound," containing the lyrics "Nobody knows what he's doing"), and several audio clips from film (*Office Space* and *Sneakers*, 2:17-3:00). With this carefully crafted sequence, Dan actually forecasts and demonstrates the organization of subsequent segments of the essay. He previews how—in each segment—the narrator will introduce a particular point of view on the human-computer relationship and then provide popular culture examples taken from television and film to support the claim. Within the rhetorical structure of this audio essay, then, Dan has structured it so that the cyborg narrator articulates the claims, and a series of popular culture examples provides evidence of each claim.

In a subsequent segment (4:17-5:14, Fig. 5.6), for example, the cyborg narrator makes the claims that humans are "worried about becoming machines" and they are concerned with maintaining their humanity within an increasingly technological world. Dan provides evidence for this claim with a series of audio clips from a television show (*Six-Million Dollar Man*) and two movies (*Robocop* and *Star Wars*). Dan also **fades in** a song ("AntiStar") by Massive Attack—written in a minor key (4:25-5:14)—to provide a subtle sense of the anxiety characterizing the postmodern information age, thus underscoring the concern and worry addressed more directly and explicitly by the narration and contributing to a sense of pathos.

The rhetorical effects of this carefully constructed sequence will vary from person to person, of course—just like the rhetorical effects of a more conventional alphabetic essay will differ with each reader. Some listeners, for instance, may be unfamiliar with the original source of the clips and, thus, will listen to them primarily as **signal** sounds, understanding the direct commentary on the relationship between humans and computers. Other audience members will be familiar with the original context of the clips. For these individuals, the excerpts may serve as **soundmarks** that locate the

Narrator:

Not only are we concerned about our relationship with machines, but we are also worried about becoming machines.

[Audio clip: Running sound from TV show *Six-Million Dollar Man*; Background music track: Massive Attack's "AntiStar"].

Narrator:

The question seems to be: Do we maintain our humanity as we depend more upon technology?

[Audio from the *Six-Million Dollar Man*: "We have the technology. We have the capability to make the world's first bionic man. Better than he was before—better, stronger, faster."

Robocop audio: "Robo? Excuse me, Robo? [robotic gear noises] Any special message for the kids watching at home?"

"Stay out of trouble."

Star Wars audio: [Darth Vader breathing]

FIGURE 5.6 A short segment of Dan's layered audio essay

essay's claims more precisely in a system of signification associated with a specific film or television show and the historical context within which it occurred.

For example, some members of the audience will immediately recognize the audio clip Dan placed from 4:36 to 4:52 as coming from *The Six-Million Dollar Man* television series. For these individuals, the audio clip works both as **signal** (commenting directly on the beneficial aspects of the human-computer relationship) and as **soundmark** (referring to one of the first television shows to deal with the subject of humans being augmented with robotic technology). Other individuals, however, may *not* be familiar with the series. These individuals may nonetheless perceive this audio excerpt as an important **signal** sound because it occurs during a pause in the narration and, thus, foregrounds commentary on the relationship between humans and machines. Similarly, people familiar with the movie *Robocop* may recognize the original source of the audio clip that Dan includes from 4:53 to 5:00.

THINKING ABOUT AFFORDANCES

Many readers will have noticed, by this point, how difficult it can be to describe the effects of a multimodal composition—like a sound essay or a video essay—with words alone. A discussion of even a short excerpt takes a great deal of space and time. Moreover, in print, references to music and sound clips (which are laden with meaning and reference in an audio essay) or video clips (which render movement and sequence so dynamically) can come across as one-dimensional and flat given the affordances of alphabetic text. We do not want to suggest with this observation that one modality is better than another in all cases. But each modality does have certain affordances—capabilities of representing meaning in particular ways and in certain contexts. We have, for example, chosen alphabetic text as one modality to convey information in this book. Words, after all, are a common modality familiar to teachers, and they work well in representing the propositional logic familiar to most educators. We have also, however, chosen to include visual images in this book and a DVD with video and audio essays. Each modality and medium we use allows us to take advantage of different affordances. Video, for example, is extremely efficient and effective in representing movement and the passage of time. Music can convey emotion and tone with great efficiency and effectiveness.

Teachers can help students explore the affordances of media and modalities by comparing how different modalities do the work of creating meaning and talking about the possibilities of representing meaning in different ways. Teachers might want to show Beth's video to students first *without* any sound. The class could talk about the essay and the meaning conveyed both by the alphabetic title screens and the video clips and still images before seeing the project again—this time with the sound. After this second showing, a productive discussion might focus on the specific ways in which sound adds meaning to this essay and the ways in which sound combines with still or moving images to create meaning in dialogue with these modalities. With Dan's essay, teachers might want to explore how the essay would come across to readers/listeners if the cyborg voice were changed to a normal human voice. For some readers, this change might affect the meaning conveyed by the author or his effectiveness in communicating through the text of his audio essay.

Another productive classroom activity might be to imagine what kind of work it would take to transform an essay that employs one modality into an essay that employs another modality or a combination of modalities—for example, what would be involved in transforming Dan's audio essay to a video essay. It is clear that some of the work involved in such a transformation would be relatively easy: video clips from the television shows and films could replace the audio clips. The visuals might even make the composition's length (over 12 minutes) more palatable to audiences. Because some of the films and television shows "quoted" within the audio composition are obscure (e.g., *Six-Million Dollar Man* and *Office Space*), visual accompaniment would assist audiences to more easily connect with some of the examples. But some of the advantages of audio might be diminished: the surprise of hearing Darth Vader's breathing would be lost, for instance. Also, would audiences be able to focus on the difficult cyborg voice—already competing for attention among an array of other sounds—if images were present? If this were the case, then the cyborg voice might not be a feature of a video composition. Making such adjustments is a crucial part of learning the affordances of each modality.

Finally, after talking about affordance from various perspectives, teachers might want to work with their classes to identify a more explicit categorization of the affordances associated with video and sound as modalities: conceptual, presentational, or scholarly affordances, for example. In Chapter 2, we suggested that the audio and video assignments be sequenced and combined so that students can use the same material for two different modalities.

As teachers and students assess multimodal compositions, both may become overwhelmed by how technologically impressive the pieces may seem. Although the overall quality should be something to take into account in assessment, we would also recommend that a key factor in assessment should be what the students have learned about multimodal rhetoric (see Appendix 14 for an example of a self-evaluation sheet and Appendix 15 for a sample of a group-evaluation sheet). Less emphasis on what students produce and more emphasis on what students have learned will not only engender experimentation in the students' compositions, but also ease teachers' minds by providing them with familiar assessment tools.

STOP THINKING SO MUCH. GET TO WORK!

This chapter provides teachers with a brief introduction to thinking rhetorically about multimodal texts. Students will need to practice this kind of thinking as well. They will need help not only in learning some of the specialized terms involved in working with video and audio essays, but also, more importantly perhaps, in understanding and using this vocabulary within a framework of rhetorical effectiveness.

Teachers can best encourage this work by giving students multiple opportunities to rehearse this work in class:

 Before they begin their own multimodal compositions, students can benefit from viewing and listening to multimodal compositions created by others, and then discussing the structural elements of specific works using a short list of specialized vocabulary (e.g., camera angles, points of view, soundmarks, signal sounds, keynotes) *within a framework of rhetorical effectiveness.* See Appendices 18, 19, and 20 for in-class activities that can be used for this purpose. We encourage teachers to modify these activities to take advantage of their own special expertise, as well as meet the needs of specific students, assignments, courses, programs, and institutions.

 As they are engaged in creating their own multimodal compositions, students can benefit from both formal and informal opportunities (e.g., studio-critique sessions, informal showings, peer-review sessions, reflection logs) in which they analyze their own projects. In these sessions, students can rehearse ways to talk and write about the structural elements of their projects, use some specialized vocabulary, and focus on *rhetorical effectiveness.* See Chapters 8 and 9 for further information about assessment.

 As they are engaged in the work of creating their own multimodal compositions, students can benefit from opportunities (e.g., small group demonstrations, mini-teaching sessions, team work sessions) to collaborate with others. In these collaborative efforts, students should be encouraged to focus on sharing specific technical strategies they have learned (e.g., camera shots, interviewing techniques, video- or audio-editing strategies) for creating pieces that are increasingly effective in rhetorical terms (see the Collaboration Checklist, Appendix 16).

 After they have finished their projects, students can benefit from opportunities to assess their own or others' projects. In doing this work, students should be encouraged to talk and write about the structural elements of their projects, use some specialized vocabulary, and, most importantly, focus on the *rhetorical effectiveness of compositions* (see Chapters 8 and 9).

REFERENCES

Barnhardt, J. B. (2005, March 31). Sample Statement Page 1. Sample statement from the web site of the U.S. Social Security Administration. Retrieved July 5, 2005 from, <http://www.ssa.gov/mystatement/ sample1.htm>.

Bernhardt, S. (1986). Seeing the text. *College Composition and Communication, 37,* 66-78.

Keyes, E. (1993). Typography, color and information structure. *Technical Communication, 40*(4), 638-654.

Schafer, R. (1997). *The soundscape: Our sonic environment and the tuning of the world.* New York: Knopf.

Wysocki, A. F. & Johnson-Eilola, J. (1999). Blinded by the letter: Why are we using literacy as a metaphor for everything else? In G. E. Hawisher & C. L. Selfe (Eds.), *Passions, pedagogies, and 21st century technologies* (pp. 349-368). Urbana: University of Illinois Press.

RESOURCES

Print:
Hill, C. A., & Helmers, M. (Eds.). (2004). *Defining visual rhetorics*. Mahwah, NJ: Lawrence Erlbaum.
Kress, G., & van Leeuwen, T. (1996). *Reading images: The grammar of visual design*. London: Routledge.

Internet:
The Language of Film and Video
      <http://english.unitecnology.ac.nz/resources/resources/film.html>
Revised and Improved: Rhetorical Figures in Sound.
      <http://www.americanrhetoric.com/rhetoricaldevicesinsound.html>

CHAPTER 6
Saving, Sharing, Citing, and Publishing Multimodal Texts

Iswari Pandey

Chapters 2, 3, and 4 have covered the processes of planning and developing multimodal projects using multiple modalities. This chapter is divided into two major sections. The first discusses the practical and pedagogical issues connected to saving, sharing, archiving, and publishing multimodal texts. The second focuses on issues related to intellectual property (e.g., video, audio, and images) that students use in their multimodal projects. In this chapter, we focus on how these processes and issues compare with those in classrooms that focus primarily on producing alphabetic texts.

SAVING AND SHARING

Educators trained in rhetoric and writing instruction know the value of composing, saving, and publishing alphabetic-print texts. We value these processes and repeatedly remind students to compose with a specific audience and purpose in sharp focus; to save drafts of written work on a regular basis; and, often, to include this writing in a composition portfolio at the end of a semester. Because these processes occupy such important roles in composition classrooms, it is important to pay attention to how they might change when composing becomes multimodal.

Saving words. When composing is done in word-processing environments, composition teachers encourage students to save their texts on a regular basis, archive various drafts of their compositions, and maintain systematic approaches to naming, storing, and retrieving these drafts. Unless these systems work effectively, students will lose what they write. For most teachers, this means that when we assign print essays to students composing within digital environments, we remind them to save their projects and also back up their files on a separate disk or memory device (e.g., a jump drive, a portable hard drive, or another server). Often we include suggestions about giving documents descriptive titles (attending to the file-naming conventions of different computer platforms) and organizing them logically in folders where they can be found. Similar approaches will serve students well in saving sound files, video files, and image files.

✔ **Saving and sharing sounds and images.** In some ways, saving sound files, still image files, and video files is not much different from saving words. There are, however, additional factors that teachers will want to consider. Figure 6.1 summarizes some of the similarities and differences associated with saving and sharing both word documents and multimodal projects.

SAVING AND SHARING	
SAVING/SHARING WORDS	SAVING/SHARING SOUNDS AND IMAGES
• Name documents with descriptive titles.	• **Name sound, image, or video files with descriptive titles**. Make sure that suffixes are identified for each file: alphabetic documents (.doc, .rtf), sound files (.wav, .aiff, .mpeg, .ra, etc.), image files (.jpg, .tif, .gif), and video (.mov, .wmp, .mpg).
• Organize files by placing them in folders, also with descriptive titles.	• **Organize files by placing them in folders (also with descriptive titles) stored where you can find them.** This is crucial to audio/video projects as a single project contains numerous files and misplacing any one of them can result in malfunctioning of the entire project.
• Document all material not original to author in a bibliography. Save this information with the primary file.	• **Document all sources of words, images, sound files, video clips not original to the author.** Create an annotated bibliography of both the source of materials and the address *of the* information copyright holder. Save this information with the primary file. • **Obtain signed release/consent forms from all individuals who appear in a video/audio essay.** File these documents in a safe place.
• Cite all sources appropriately within the text of the paper.	• **If project is to be published outside the confines of a class, request and obtain permissions from all copyright holders**. In all cases, cite sources appropriately in credits (video) or in an attached annotated alphabetic bibliography (audio).
• Save documents and any changes on a regular basis.	• **Save files and changes on a *frequent* basis—even more frequently than with word-processing files.** Because audio and video projects involve large files and complex operations, they may crash more frequently than word-processing files.

FIGURE 6.1 Saving and sharing word, sound, and image

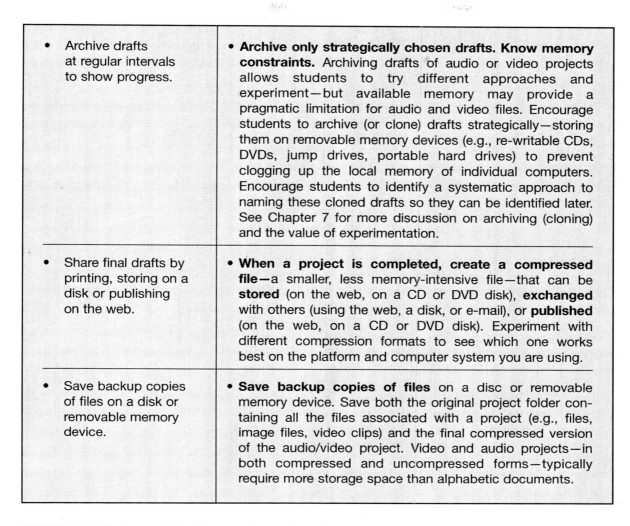

• Archive drafts at regular intervals to show progress.	• **Archive only strategically chosen drafts. Know memory constraints.** Archiving drafts of audio or video projects allows students to try different approaches and experiment—but available memory may provide a pragmatic limitation for audio and video files. Encourage students to archive (or clone) drafts strategically—storing them on removable memory devices (e.g., re-writable CDs, DVDs, jump drives, portable hard drives) to prevent clogging up the local memory of individual computers. Encourage students to identify a systematic approach to naming these cloned drafts so they can be identified later. See Chapter 7 for more discussion on archiving (cloning) and the value of experimentation.
• Share final drafts by printing, storing on a disk or publishing on the web.	• **When a project is completed, create a compressed file**—a smaller, less memory-intensive file—that can be **stored** (on the web, on a CD or DVD disk), **exchanged** with others (using the web, a disk, or e-mail), or **published** (on the web, on a CD or DVD disk). Experiment with different compression formats to see which one works best on the platform and computer system you are using.
• Save backup copies of files on a disk or removable memory device.	• **Save backup copies of files** on a disc or removable memory device. Save both the original project folder containing all the files associated with a project (e.g., files, image files, video clips) and the final compressed version of the audio/video project. Video and audio projects—in both compressed and uncompressed forms—typically require more storage space than alphabetic documents.

FIGURE 6.1 Saving and sharing word, sound, and image (continued)

SAVING, ORGANIZING, AND MANAGING MULTIMODAL COMPOSITIONS

Coordinating a class of students as they work with multimodal assignments has its challenges—among them teaching students how to store their files safely, organize and manage files, work with files of different formats, and compress projects for sharing with others. The following sections provide some key points for teachers to consider.

Storing and archiving multimodal assignments requires a great deal of computer memory. For this reason, audio- and video-editing programs are often installed locally on individual computers rather than stored on a central machine and served over a network. This arrangement offers the benefit of speed because the large files involved in video and audio editing remain resident on individual computers and do not have to travel over a networked system. The downside of such an arrangement, however, is that individual machines must have considerable memory storage and processing speed to handle the media files. Fortunately, many newer computers are designed to handle both video and audio editing—they have video and sound cards, high-speed processors, headphone jacks, speakers, and lots of memory. However, teachers will want to check with an information technology specialist about suitable computers for multimodal projects.

 The memory space needed to store audio and video projects represents a major concern for most information technology specialists, and composition teachers need to understand why this is so. Unlike most word-processing files that students create in response to conventional assignments asking for an alphabetic essay, the audio and video files that students create in response to multimodal assignments are huge. One way of predicting the memory space that a student's audio or video project might use in a class is to multiply **minutes of raw video or audio times 1 gigabyte**. Thus, if a student records and downloads 60 minutes of raw video in preparation for creating a 5-minute finished project (a situation not unusual for beginning video authors), the raw video is likely to occupy 60 gigabytes of storage space on the computer. If files of this size are stored locally on individual computers, they quickly use up all the available memory or storage space.

In many collegiate computer labs, this situation can become a problem. In some facilities, students have only limited memory space allocated for their personal use and so they cannot store large files. In other facilities, the local hard drives of computers are erased once a week to avoid cluttered memory spaces. In either case, teachers planning multimodal assignments need to be aware of where students should back-up and store large media files. There are several options. Some departments or teachers can afford to purchase portable hard drives that teachers can check out for a semester and use to back up students' audio or video files at the end of every class session. These portable memory devices are fast and relatively sturdy. To calculate how big a portable hard drive might be needed, teachers can use the following formula:

> Length of raw (uncompressed) audio and video project (in minutes)
> X 1 (gigabyte of memory)
> X number of projects to be produced in the class
> = total gigabytes of storage needed

For example, if there are 15 students in a class and each of them has collected 20 minutes worth of raw audio and/or video material for editing into short 5-minute multimodal projects, the class will need a minimum of 300 gigabytes of storage (20 minutes X 1 gigabyte X 15 students = 300 gigabytes of storage needed). If students store several drafts of their projects, the storage requirements will increase. And if students are working on more than one such project, the space requirement will also grow accordingly. Having students work in collaborative groups, however, can reduce demands for both memory and storage.

Teachers who do not have portable hard drives available might ask each student in their classes to purchase re-writable DVDs (if computers have the capability of writing on such media) or portable jump drives (as long as these have sufficient memory) on which to store their own back-up files. Other teachers find it useful to request that a portion of each computer's local hard drive be partitioned and set aside for the audio and video files that students create. In all cases, teachers will want to talk to information technology specialists in advance of their class so they can give students clear directions.

 During the early stages of multimodal assignments, teachers may need to slow down and deal explicitly with issues of file management that will help students save time and avoid frustration at later stages. Effective file management and organization strategies are necessary whenever projects include a number of different files from a number of different places—and audio and video projects *almost always* combine a large number of files—interviews, music, sound effects, still images, video clips—collected from many sources.

As Figure 6.2 indicates, student-made multimodal projects may include some or all of the following elements:

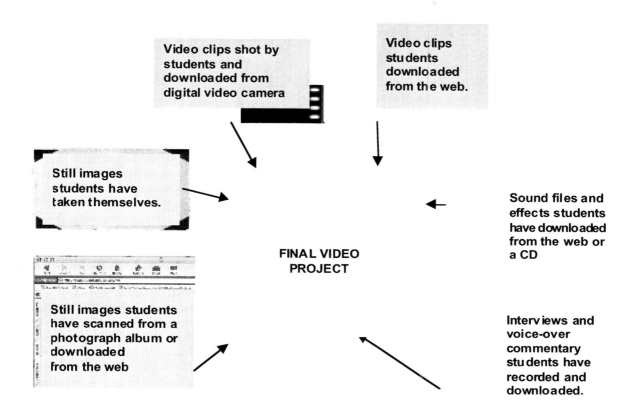

FIGURE 6.2 Assembling files from multiple sources for a multimodal video project

- interviews that students have recorded and downloaded onto a computer
- audio files they have downloaded from the web
- photographs students have taken with a digital still camera downloaded onto a computer
- still images or photographs students have downloaded from the web or scanned from a personal photograph
- video files students have shot with a digital video camera and downloaded on a computer
- video clips students have downloaded from the web.

Given this range of texts, teachers will want to use some class time to discuss strategies for organizing these materials—which will later be imported into audio- or video-editing programs. Although audio- and video-editing programs such as Audacity and iMovie do some organizing of files for students (e.g., automatically generating a primary project folder), students may need to discuss some initial file-naming and file-organization strategies—working from their own planning and conceptual documents (Appendices 11, 12, and 13). In many cases, students will be able to identify pragmatic strategies that serve them well in assembling the pieces that will make up their multimodal compositions. In other cases, working from an understanding of the assignment goals, teachers might be able to identify different organizational strategies that can help. With some assignments, for instance, teachers might suggest organizing files *hierarchically*: creating a central folder for assembling the whole range of files that will go into a multimodal project and then creating subfolders for each type of file (e.g., images, video clips, audio clips). For other assignments, teachers might want to suggest organizing files *sequentially*: creating a central folder for assembling the segments that will comprise a multimodal project and then creating subfolders for each segment of a longer project.

 It is important to teach students to take advantage of online help files, print documentation, and web information to learn about technical concepts and explore specialized technical terms. It is also important to ask them to teach other students what they know and what they have learned. For example, audio files, still image files, and video files, come in different **formats** that are appropriate for different uses and different computer systems. Figure 6.3, Figure 6.4, and Figure 6.5 list some of the most frequently used formats for audio files, still images, and video files, respectively. Understanding the concept of file formats and their uses is important for both teachers and students working with multimodal compositions. Thus, teachers might find it useful to ask student teams to conduct some valuable research for themselves on this topic, using online help files or printed documentation texts to determine which formats can be readily imported and used by the editing programs they plan to use for their multimodal projects.

SOME COMMON FORMATS FOR SOUND FILES

AIFF: Audio Interchange File Format (.aiff) was developed by Apple and is a very flexible file format, especially for cross-platform audio, as it allows the specification of arbitrary sampling rates, sample size, number of channels, and application-specific format chunks. AIFF-C is AIFF with compressed samples.

Windows WAVE (.wav): Created by Microsoft and IBM, this format has different compression formats. IMA and MS ADPCM provide a 4-to-1 compression ratio.

QuickTime Movies (.mov): a popular compression and presentation format for both audio and video. It was created by Apple, but its accompanying media player is available for both Mac and PCs.

RealAudio (.ra, .ram, .rp): a popular format that uses various compression algorithms depending on the type of audio to be encoded (speech-music-type of music-bandwidth consideration, etc.). The RealAudio encoder can be downloaded for free and will encode digital audio from a file (.wav, .au, or raw .pcm format), or from any live source input including audio CDs. RealAudio files are good in quality and small in size.

MPEG Audio (.mpg): MP3 or MPEG-3 files have become the standard for music files on the Internet. They provide excellent quality but are larger than most of the above formats. These audio files can be either layer I, II, or III—the higher the layer the more complex the format. Files can be in stereo or mono. Typical MPEG compression rates are about 10-to-1.

Windows Media Audio (.wma): Microsoft's equivalent to RealAudio and QuickTime. Windows Media Audio is popular and better quality than .WAV files and can be streamed by a Windows Media Server. It is generally poorer than RealAudio at lower bandwidths but better in quality at higher bandwidths.

For an excellent introduction to compression (reducing the size of sound files to a length and format that can be more easily stored and accessed) see Ashley Holmes' and Martin Francis' Web site on Audio Production and Contemporary Culture at <http://webfuse.cqu.edu.au/Courses/2002/T3/MMST12016/course_site/tut%203.htm>

FIGURE 6.3 Common formats for sound files

SOME COMMON FORMATS FOR DIGITIZED STILL IMAGES

TIFF (Tagged Image File Format): TIFF is probably the most widely used bitmapped file format. Image-editing applications, scanning software, illustration programs, page-layout programs, and even word processing programs support TIFF files. This format works for all types of images. TIFF is also a cross platform: applicable versions are available for the Mac, PC, and UNIX systems.

BMP (Short for BITMAP): The BMP format has been adopted as the standard bitmapped format on the Windows platform. It is a basic format supported by most Windows applications and is considered a very efficient format.

GIF (Graphics Interchange Format): Created by CompuServe, this format may be listed as CompuServe GIF. It is one of two standard formats used on the Web without plug-ins (the other is JPEG). It is the method of storing bitmaps on the Web.

PICT/PICT2 (Short for picture): PICT/PICT2 formats are for the Macintosh and are generally used only for screen display. Some Mac programs can only import images saved as either PICT or EPS.

JPEG (Joint Photo4graphic Experts Group): JPEG creates a very compact file. Because of its small file size, it is easy to transmit across networks, and is one of two major graphic file formats supported by the World Wide Web without plug-ins (the other is GIF). However, pixels will be removed from the image during compression, and, as a consequence, the pictures may not be as sharp.

FIGURE 6.4 Common formats for digitized still images

SOME COMMON FORMATS FOR COMPRESSED VIDEO FILES

MPEG-1 (.mpg)—a very good format for (a) delivery over the Internet, (b) storage on CD-ROM, and (c) output to VHS tape. MPEG-1 files can be read by almost all machines. There are also many free programs for playing mpeg files. These files are handled by QuickTime players on the Mac and Windows Media Players on PCs by default. Still, may not be a very good medium for storage and editing unless you have a separate good-quality editing system.

MPEG-2 (.mpg)—the standard video format for DVDs. It requires a fast computer system and a CD-ROM or DVD drive. The file size and data rate in this format are much larger than in MPEG-1. This format is known for excellent quality.

QuickTime (.mov)—Created by Apple, it is an excellent format for delivery over the Internet and storage on CD-ROMs. QuickTime contains many useful features for educational applications such as multilingual text tracks, hotspots, pausing for user input, and integration of links, jumps to specific times, and the ability to call other movies.

RealSystem (RealMedia/Realplayer) (.rm, .ram)—It is usually appropriate for delivery of material over a network. The video can also be streamed if the host machine has a RealServer. Many online news and other media outlets (for example, BBC, CNN, etc.) use this format or its variant.

Windows Media (.wmp)—Windows Media is the multimedia format supported by Microsoft. It can be streamed using a Windows Media Server and allows text tracks, URL links, and calling other movies, although some users feel it currently has fewer features than RealSystem and QuickTime.

FIGURE 6.5 Some common formats for compressed video files

This approach also works well in helping students to define the many important technical terms they run across as they read about audio- and video-editing. Teachers might want use some class time, for instance, to have student teams collaborate on mini-research projects—exploring technical terms like **file compression** and then explaining the terms in short presentations to the other members of the class. (See the Glossary at the end of this book for this and other useful terms.) In a mini-research project, for example, students could learn that file compression is a process used to bring down the size of video and audio files, reducing the space these files occupy on a disk/drive and the time they take to download from the web. Most of the video and audio files students will locate on the web, for example, are already compressed versions of a larger project. File compression is a useful technology, although it is not loss-immune. Compressing a project results in a slight loss of data and, therefore, quality—a kind of tradeoff for having more manageable file sizes.

Once teachers have had students research and teach technical terms using online help, print documentation, and web resources, they may also want to ask them to explore the same concepts (such as compression) using rhetorically based questions like those provided in Figure 6.6. The best way to teach students about compression is to focus on rhetorical choices. Just as word choice, tone, and other formal features are determined by such considerations as purpose, audience, genre, and expected methods of circulation, the specific compression format of a multimodal project can best be discussed in terms of who will view or listen to it, under what circumstances this will be done, and what purpose the piece is meant to achieve.

RHETORICAL CONSIDERATIONS FOR COMPRESSION FORMATS

- Will your audience view or listen to your compressed project by accessing it over the web with a modem? If yes, consider the format that reduces the file to the minimum size to ensure faster downloading.

- Are the audiences who view or listen to your compressed project using a computer with a broadband or fast Internet connection? If yes, consider using the format that retains the most data as downloading large files will not be a problem.

- Will the audience need to view or listen to your project on several different hardware platforms? If so, choose a compression format that works on well on both Macintosh and PC platforms.

- Will the audience need to view your compressed project using a projector and a large screen? If so, consider minimal compression to retain the highest quality.

- Does your audio project contain a number of layers of music and narration? Will the audience need high fidelity to make the most out of their listening experience? Consider minimal compression to retain the highest quality of sound.

- Do you want people from other countries and cultures to listen to or view your project on a range of different computers? Is your project a public service announcement that should be seen or viewed by people in the United States who do not have access to the fastest or the latest technology? If so, ensure a broader audience by using the most common compression formats and a format that reduces the file to the minimum size.

FIGURE 6.6 Rhetorically based questions about compression

SHARING MULTIMODAL COMPOSITIONS: INTELLECTUAL PROPERTY AND WORKING WITH SOURCES

Although the processes of gathering and using source materials for multimodal compositions has definite similarities to those employed with compositions that are alphabetic, there are also definite and important differences—particularly in the arena of intellectual property. For example, although digital tools have made it easy to copy and paste words from one document to another, most students have learned strategies for quoting, paraphrasing, and summarizing and have heard lectures about the responsible use of such material. In contrast, the ease with which students can download images, audio, and video from the web to their desktops—especially when combined with the confusing array of social practices surrounding the use, documentation, and citation of digital still images, video files, and audio files—is seldom balanced by careful discussions about when they must request permission from copyright holders and how to do so. Indeed, even many teachers confess to being confused by rapid changes in intellectual copyright law and the changing nature of fair use in a time when corporate interests and educational efforts so often seem to conflict. At the same time, contemporary media accounts suggest that students have little or no regard for others' intellectual property and may even conflate the legitimate use of intellectual property with acts of theft (cf. Educators, Entertainment Industry Team Up, 2005; Gantz & Rochester, 2005; Valenti, 2003).

Intellectual Property Instruction

Given the cultural context we have just sketched, it has become increasingly important for teachers and students in composition classes to discuss intellectual property issues in connection with multimodal compositions—especially those that include a complex array of materials taken from various digital sources. Teachers will need to help students clarify when it is necessary to record the source of digital files and how to do so, when students must seek permission to use copyrighted files, how they can determine copyright holders of digitized materials, and how to document and cite the sources of digital materials not their own (attribution).

In particular, teachers should discuss four key intellectual property topics that have a direct influence on the projects students produce within multimodal composition classrooms: copyright law, the doctrine of Fair Use, the concept of work in the public domain, and open-licensing. (See Figure 6.7 and the Glossary for further information about these topics.)

> **Copyright law:** the legislation designed to protect the rights and the economic interests of authors and artists. Copyright law applies to multimodal texts in ways that are both similar to and different from the ways they apply to print texts, and many of these laws are changing rapidly as the use of digital communication environments expand. Teachers should educate themselves about copyright law and its limits—before assigning multimodal essays to students—by reading some of the following Web sites. They might also assign students the task of browsing and making sense of such sites within the context of plans for their multimodal projects:

> "Rules of Thumb for Digitizing and Using Others' Work in Multimedia Materials for Educational Purposes," *Fair Use of Copyrighted Materials*, Georgia Harper, Office of the General Counsel, The University of Texas System
> <http://www.utsystem.edu/OGC/IntellectualProperty/copypol2.htm#mm>

> "Legal Issues; Introduction," Youth Media Distribution Organization Web site
> <http://www.ymdi.org/toolkit/archives/000484.php>

> "Learn More about Creative Commons," Creative Commons Web site
> <http://creativecommons.org/learnmore>

SOME INTELLECTUAL PROPERTY RESOURCES ON THE INTERNET

The Creative Common <http://www.creative commons.org>

<remix culture> a talk by Lawrence Lessig, Chair of the Creative Commons project
<http://netfiles.uiuc.edu/jlsolber/www/lessig/>

The Electronic Frontier Foundation <http://www.eff.org/>
Devoted to issues of individual rights in the digital environment

U.S. Patent and Copyright Office <http://www.copyright.gov/>
Has current laws governing copyright issues

Government information on copyright laws: The Basics
<http://www.copyright.gov/circs/circ1.html>

Information on Obtaining Copyright Permissions prepared by Ann Hemmens,
University of Washington
<http://lib.law.washington.edu/ref/copyright.html>

Obtaining Permissions Copyright Management Center
<http://depts.washington.edu/trio/train/howto/pieces/writing/permission.htm>

Crash Course in Copyright, Georgia Harper, The University of Texas
<http://www.copyright.iupui.edu/permhome.htm>

Youth Media Distribution (path: Legal Issues)
<http://www.ymdi.org/toolkit/index.php>

Stanford Law School's Center for Internet and Society
<http://cyberlaw.stanford.edu/>

FIGURE 6.7 Some intellectual property resources on the Internet

Fair Use Doctrine: the area of copyright law that allows for some limited uses of copyrighted materials in certain specified academic contexts—primarily for the purposes of parody and commentary, and for research—and under specific conditions. For more information on this topic, teachers might want to assign Section 107 of the Copyright Law of the United States <http://www.copyright.gov/title17/> and have students compare key definitions of Fair Use at the Answers.com Web site <http://www.answers.com/Fair%20Use> and the Copyright.com Web site <http://www.copyright.com/ccc/do/viewPage?pageCode=cr11-n#copyfaq7>. A fruitful classroom activity might have students identify the specific conditions under which the Fair Use doctrine might apply to the multimodal essays they create in class and the limitations on materials they could use under the Fair Use Doctrine.

Public domain: a part of copyright law that allows the public's use of materials not currently covered under copyright law. Teachers might ask students to work in collaborative groups to compare key definitions of public domain at the Answers.com web site <http://www.answers.com/topic/public-domain> and the U.S. Copyright Office web site <http://www.copyright.gov> or to research those factors that determine when audio, video, text, or images are considered within the public domain by reading a comic book about copyright law (*Bound by Law*) created for Duke University's Center for the Study of the Public Domain <http://www.law.duke.edu/cspd/comic/>.

Open-source licensing/the Creative Commons: Audio, video, word, or image files that have open-source types of licenses attached typically allow individuals to use protected material without paying the original author as long as the user adheres to a flexible set of conditions (with some rights reserved having to do with such things as attribution, commercial/noncommercial use, changes, sampling, and sharing); these rights are determined by the original authors/artists.

The Creative Commons Web site is influenced by the open-source movement. This site can be very useful in multimodal composition classes because it offers a wide range of free audio, video, and image files that students can use without charge in their own multimodal texts as long as they adhere to the artist's/author's conditions (as expressed by the Creative Commons license attached to a work). Teachers might want to ask students to explore the Creative Commons Web site to determine the range of materials offered there. Teachers might also encourage students to compare the processes of clearing permissions under traditional copyright law (see the Crash Course in Copyright Web site at The University of Texas <http://www.utsystem.edu/OGC/IntellectualProperty/permissn.htm> or the list of Frequently Asked Questions at the U.S. Copyright Office Web site <http://www.copyright. gov/help/faq/faq-fairuse.html> and under the licensing guidelines of the Creative Commons <http://creativecommons.org/licenses/by-nc-sa/2.0/>.

CITING AND DOCUMENTING SOURCES, OBTAINING PERMISSIONS FROM COPYRIGHT HOLDERS

In addition to providing instruction on the key concepts associated with intellectual property, teachers will also want to talk to students about pragmatic strategies for accurate attribution, citation, and documentation—explaining the importance of attributing creative work to its original authors and showing students how someone's work must be appropriately cited and documented in a bibliography that accompanies a final multimodal project. As in the print-based composition classrooms, it is important for teachers to use discussions of citation and documentation not simply as occasions to scare students about plagiarism or teach uncontextualized (and unrealistic) rules, but rather as opportunities to discuss how and why others' ideas and texts are important to our own composing efforts. Focusing only on plagiarism and legal battles without due discussion of authors' and artists' rights might induce an unnecessary paranoia that can paralyze even the most ethically conscientious students. Resources such as the Copyright Crash Course <http://www.utsystem.edu/ogc /IntellectualProperty/cprtindx.htm> and a talk entitled *remix culture* by Laurence Lessig, Professor of Law at Stanford University and Chair of the Creative Commons project <https://netfiles.uiuc.edu/ jlsolber/www/lessig/> can be exceptionally useful in helping students become aware of both their *rights* and *responsibilities* as authors and artists—people who both create texts and use the creative texts of others. The U.S. Patent and Copyright Office <http://www.copyright.gov/>, in addition, can be useful in making students aware of existing copyright laws. Using such sites, teachers can help students acquire an increasingly robust and responsible understanding of intellectual property rights and the conventions governing it.

As students begin working on multimodal projects, teachers can help them practice ethical composing habits by requiring them to keep lists of any elements that are not original—every video clip, audio clip, song taken from a CD, image and photograph, or poem or piece of writing taken from a published print-based work or the Internet. Each of these elements will need to be documented in two ways. First, the bibliographic information needs to be recorded (Fig. 6.8). Second, the intellectual property constraints associated with each nonoriginal element—whether the texts are protected by copyright, an open-source license, or in the public domain—must be identified.

Teachers can help students in this effort at two important stages. As the class begins conceptualizing and planning multimodal projects, teachers can encourage students to think about building multimodal projects from constituent elements (e.g., images, photographs, video clips, recorded audio) that are either original, available in the public domain, or part of collections like the Creative Commons, which grant various kinds of open-source licenses. This approach will save students a great deal of time and effort—especially if they hope to publish final multimodal projects at some later point or even put their projects on the web in a publically available site. Second, as students undertake the process of assembling the elements of their multimodal projects, teachers can require them to keep running lists of source materials and check such lists at regular intervals. In collaborative teams, students can keep team lists of source materials.

SAMPLE CITATIONS FOR IMAGES, AUDIO, AND VIDEO

The art of citing online sources continues to evolve. We suggest that teachers provide students with sample citations from which to work and that the goal of this citation work be identified as giving credit to the artists/authors. Citations should be complete enough to lead a reader/viewer to the source of material if that is at all possible within the dynamic space of the Internet.

The sample citations we include below follow, roughly, the guidelines of the Modern Language Association (MLA) and the American Psychological Association (APA). We have, however, changed minor elements to better suit the documentation of online sources, and we encourage teachers to revise these samples to meet the needs of their own classes.

Online Image or Photograph (MLA)
Evans, Walker. Penny Picture Display. 1936. Museum of Mod. Art web site, New York. 25 Oct. 2004. Retrieved 2 February 2005 from <http://www.moma.org/collection/photography/pages/evans.penny.htm>.
Smith, Greg. "Rhesus Monkeys in the Zoo." No date. Online image from the Monkey Picture Gallery web site. Retrieved 12 Oct. 2004 from <http://monkeys.online.org/rhesus.jpg>.

Online Video/Film or Film Clip (MLA)
Murnau, F.W., dir. Nosferatu. 1922. The Sync web site. Retrieved 16 Oct. 2004 from <http://www.thesync.com/ramnosferatu.ram>.

Online Audio (MLA)
Edelman, Lee, Sara Suleri Goodyear, and Stephen Nichols. "Love Poetry, Volume 2." What's the Word? 2001. Modern Language Association web site. 20 Sept. 2002. MLA. Retrieved 17 Oct. 2004 <http://www.mla.org/>. Path: Radio Program; Browse Shows and Listen; 2001 Program Topics.

Online Image or Photograph (based on APA)
Evans, Walker. (1936). Penny Picture Display. Museum of Mod. Art web site, New York. Retrieved Oct. 25, 2004 from <http://www.moma.org/collection/photography/pages/evans.penny.htm>.
Smith, Greg. (No date). "Rhesus Monkeys in the Zoo." Monkey Picture Gallery web site. Retrieved Oct. 23, 2004 from <http://monkeys.online.org/rhesus.jpg>.

Online Video/Film or Film Clip (based on APA)
Murnau, F.W., dir. (1922). Nosferatu. The Sync web site. Retrieved Oct. 16, 2004 from <http://www.thesync.com/ramnosferatu.ram>.

Online Audio (based on APA)
Edelman, Lee, Sara Suleri Goodyear, and Stephen Nichols. (20 Sept. 2002). Love poetry, volume 2. *What's the Word? 2001*. Modern Language Association web site. Retrieved Oct. 17, 2004 from <http://www.mla.org/>. Path: Radio Program; Browse Shows and Listen; 2001 Program Topics.

Commercial CD (based on APA)
Jones, Norah (26 February 2002). The long day is over. Come Away with Me. New York, NY: Bluenote Records.

FIGURE 6.8 Sample citations for images files, sound files, and video files

If students are going to publish their multimodal projects or circulate them widely beyond the walls of a classroom—and especially if they hope to sell their creative work—they must go beyond documenting and citing sources; *they must request and obtain written permission from the copyright holders of all images, audio material, and video material that is not students' original work.*

Unfortunately, the process of obtaining permission to publish other people's music, video, or images is a bit harder and sometimes more opaque than obtaining permissions to use written texts. Students can usually find a range of resources and texts on the web, for instance, but finding essential information about the copyright holder may be more difficult. Teachers can help by showing students how to locate information about copyright holders and request permission to publish copyrighted materials from these individuals. Teachers can also help students learn both how to read and honor open-source licenses. Productive class time, for instance, can be spent teaching students how to locate and read the "permissions" or "legal" section of potential resources (e.g., images, music, video clips) they plan on using within their projects *before* they decide to use these resources. Teachers will find instructional materials on finding copyright holders and requesting permissions at the *Crash Course in Copyright* web site <http://www.utsystem.edu/OGC/Intellectual Property/permissn.htm> and on adhering open licensing agreements at *Creative Commons* <http://creativecommons.org/licenses/by-nc-sa/2.0/>.

When students turn in projects for evaluation, teachers should be clear about the requirement to document any nonoriginal elements just as meticulously as with conventional alphabetic texts — using a bibliography for this purpose. For audio essays, students can include a list of such materials on the CD or DVD that contains their essay. For video projects, students can provide citation credits at the end of the project. This bibliography requirement, we believe, should be identified as part of any assessment rubric attached to assignments, so that students know such ethical practices are both important and required. Most college writing manuals and handbooks include information on citing audio, video, interviews, photographs, and similar materials, and we have provided some sample citations for such materials in Figure 6.8. We encourage teachers to revise these samples to meet the needs of their classes. For more detailed information on documenting such sources, teachers can also direct students to those web-based resources indicated in Figure 6.9.

To teach students the value of intellectual property from the perspective of authors and artists, teachers can also encourage students to publish their multimodal projects—registering for copyright protection through the U.S. Copyright office <http://www.copyright.gov/> or for a Creative Common's license at <http://creativecommons.org>, after they have cleared all appropriate permissions for elements that are not their own.

WEB RESOURCES FOR CITING DIGITAL MATERIALS

APA Style Guide for Citing Electronic Sources
<http://www.apastyle.org/elecref.html>

Purdue (OWL) MLA Style Guide for Citing Electronic Sources
<http://owl.english.purdue.edu/handouts/research/r_mla.html#Electronic>

Vanderbilt University Resources for Citing Sources: Online Style Sheets, prepared by
Larry Romans <http://www.library.vanderbilt.edu/romans/polsci/evalweb.html>

**International Federation of Library Associations and Institutions' list of Online Style
Guides (MLA, APA, Chicago)**
<http://www.ifla.org/I/training/citation/citing.htm>

UC Berkeley's Media Resource Center
"How to Cite Media" <http://www.lib.berkeley.edu/MRC/mla.html>
Good for help with citing multimedia such as film, TV, etc.

Landmark's Citation Machine, David Warlick, Landmark Project
<http://www.landmark-project.com/citation_machine/index.php>

Documenting Sources, Diana Hacker
<http://www.dianahacker.com/resdoc/humanities/list.html#M>

FIGURE 6.9 Sample citations for images files, sound files, and video files

Informed Consent and Release Forms

As teachers and students take advantage of the rich affordances multimodality offers, we need to make sure to behave in informed and ethical ways. Thus, another area of ethical behavior related to intellectual property that teachers will want to help students navigate has to do with informed consent. Students should know that any person they want to record in a video or audio text, or in a still photograph, should, first, be asked permission and told about the context of the project and its uses. Such people—if they are recognizable by their voice or image should also be asked—to give their informed consent to being recorded and to sign a release form. Students should also know they need written parental consent for anyone under 18 years of age.

Similarly, students should know that they need to request permission to record in a specific place or location—if it is recognizable. If students have plans to record in such a location they should identify the person in charge of the location, tell them about their project, and ask them to sign a release form for places such as the one provided by the Youth Media Distribution organization at <http://www.ymdi.org/toolkit/archives/000492. php>

Teachers can help in this effort in a number of ways. They can emphasize both the ethical and legal responsibilities involved in digital recording and matters of informed consent by talking to students about people's right to privacy and their own image. Teachers might also talk about release/consent forms as legal documents that protect both students (by proving that they obtained an individual's permission before recording them) and the people they record (by informing them about being recorded and the purpose of the recording). Students may also need help in learning to deal respectfully with individuals whose culture, religion, or personal beliefs do not permit such recordings. A good classroom activity at this point might be to have students write about a time when they have had their picture taken *without* permission and used for purposes they did not approve.

Teachers can also help by providing students with samples of release/consent forms for people (like the sample included in Appendix 6) and places. If students plan to shoot or record in a public place and there is a possibility that many people's images or voices might be recorded and recognized as a result, they must post large signs that advise the public of recording efforts. The following example of such a sign is provided by the Youth Media Distribution organization <http://www. ymdi.org>.

> By entering this space, you are granting permission for your likeness/words to be included in the project "_____" by "_____." In such situations, students should be prepared to deal respectfully with individuals whose culture, religion, or personal beliefs prohibit such recordings.

Teachers can also help students write or revise their own series of consent/release forms that can be used by members of the class. Such writing projects—for which there is a real purpose, a real audience, and serious implications—are perfect opportunities for instruction. We invite teachers to use and revise the forms that we include or mention in this book—working with students to change these documents to meet their own particular needs and those of the class.

Finally, teachers can help by requiring students to collect and hand in signed consent forms for all multimodal projects that involve recordings of people or places—and specifying this requirement on all assignment assessment rubrics.

A WORD ABOUT THE SOCIAL NATURE OF TEXTS AND ACTIVISM

Most teachers of composition recognize that writing is inherently a social act: We write in order to connect with others, to respond to them. Multimodal compositions are also socially situated efforts. In fact, one of the primary goals for teaching multimodal composition is to help students become more than passive consumers of the sound and image bites saturating today's media-driven world. Many teachers feel a responsibility for helping students learn to *produce* media texts—to make meaning for themselves and others through these texts.

Teachers who focus on the social context of composing may want to emphasize this aspect of composing by having students create public service announcements for local not-for-profit organizations, create documentary pod-casts that can be downloaded from Web sites, or compose political campaign commercials that focus on issues about which they care deeply. For instance, teachers might want to consider having students create multimodal projects for public libraries; various literacy programs targeting refugee, immigrants, or similar other groups; local units of Red Cross, the Salvation Army, the United Way, or America Reads—as well as other programs that aim to educate people about health, legal, political, or environmental issues. Every community has some of these organizations or programs, and nonprofit organizations often depend on volunteers for a number of their activities. There are always opportunities for those who are interested. Students may, however, need help in learning to approach organizations with sensitivity, identify what multimodal communications may be useful or needed, and also decide if such projects are feasible given the available resources.

If teachers encourage students to publish their compositions outside the classroom, they should make sure that students are scrupulous about citing and documenting the intellectual property of others, clearing permissions for all copyrighted and licensed materials, and obtaining informed consent for all people and places that appear in their projects. There are several national venues that publish or archive audio and video projects in public collections (Fig. 6.10). Teachers can encourage students to submit their work if appropriate.

For graduate classes in composition and rhetoric, several scholarly journals have begun to publish multimodal texts and scholarly contributions. Some of these journals are identified in Figure 6.11.

PLACES TO SUBMIT AUDIO OR VIDEO ESSAYS

For audio contributions

- **Transom** is a web-based forum for showcasing audio work in the tradition of public radio. Transom.org is described as "an experiment in channeling new work and voices to public radio through the Internet, for discussing that work, and encouraging more." Information on submission can be found at <http//www.transom.org>.

- **StoryCorps** publishes great stories about ordinary people. Students can interview anyone at one of StoryCorps Story Booths or MobileBooths. They will receive a copy of this interview on CD and have the option of archiving the interview at the American Folklife Center at the Library of Congress. For more information on the procedures to follow, go to <http://story corps.net/participate/>.

For audio and video contributions

- **Youth Media Distribution** has a mission to improve the distribution of independent youth created film, video, radio, and new media. YMDi.org allows students to post "videos, radio projects, digital stories, flash animations, interactive websites, docs, fiction, satires, comedies, all of it!" <http://www.ymdi.org/index.php>.

- **The Veterans History Project** at the Library of Congress <www.loc.gov/vets/> has a large number of **audio** and **video** stories. Teachers and students can also contribute to the collection.

FIGURE 6.10 Some places to submit audio or video essays on the web

---

SELECT SCHOLARLY JOURNALS PUBLISHING MULTIMODAL ESSAYS

- Computers and Composition Online: The journal publishes contributions in the area of computers and composition. Its online edition accepts contributions also in audio, sound, video, and hypertext formats. See <http://www.bgsu.edu/cconline/>.

- KAIROS publishes in the intersections of rhetoric, technology, and pedagogy. See <http://english.ttu.edu/kairos/>

- Enculturation: A Journal for Rhetoric, Writing, and Culture is devoted to contemporary theorizations of rhetoric, writing, and culture. The journal accepts contributions in all media forms suitable for web-based publication, including conventional articles, hypertexts, and multimedia projects. See <http://enculturation.gmu.edu/>.

FIGURE 6.11 Scholarly journals that publish multimodal essays

CONCLUSION

Appropriate attention to intellectual property concerns is not simply a matter of ethics; it is also a matter of law. And, importantly, such attention represents a good faith effort to understand the complex balance between important freedoms and protections. Students, in particular, are often unfamiliar with their rights and responsibilities—especially within new digital composing environments—and this lack of information makes them vulnerable. Teachers can help students learn more about their rights and responsibilities when composing in multiple modalities—but we can not accomplish this goal unless we educate ourselves in the process.

REFERENCES

Educators, entertainment industry team up to fight peer-to-peer copyright piracy. *Patent Trademark & Copyright Journal, 65* (2003). Retrieved April 25, 2005, from <http://ipcenter.bna.com/pic2/ip.nsf/id/BNAP-5KA85M?OpenDocument>.

Gantz, J., & Rochester, J.B. (2005). *Pirates of the digital millennium: How the intellectual property wars damage our personal freedoms, our jobs, and the world economy.* New York: Prentice Hall.

Valenti, J. (2003). A clear and present danger: The potential undoing of America's greatest export trade prize. Ashburn, VA. Retrieved April 25, 2005, from <http://www.mpaa.org/jack/2002/2002_04_23b.htm>.

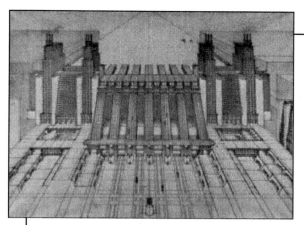

From *Reading Architecture*, by Aaron Toscano

CHAPTER 7
Experimenting with Multimodality

John Branscum
Aaron Toscano

Multimodal classes—at their best—can offer spaces for teachers and students to think in creative and intellectual ways about meaning and communication, rhetorical goals and rhetorical effectiveness, different modalities and their rich affordances. Not all classes, however, automatically accomplish these goals—sometimes teachers and students are distracted by the challenges inherent in new ways of learning and communicating and forget that these challenges also represent great possibilities for exploration and learning. Faced with unfamiliar digital technologies and a new set of literacy practices, teachers and students can sometimes forget why intellectual experimentation is so engaging; how creative work can feel so satisfying, even when it is hard; and how flexible we all need to be about learning and learning styles.

The benefits of experimentation, creativity, and flexibility, we believe, are important for several reasons. First, by modeling these strategies—by fostering these attitudes—teachers can help students discover the generative power of making meaning. Further, by teaching students to value creative and effective communication, experimental approaches to problem solving, and flexible responses to technology challenges, faculty help students develop those habits of mind they will need to succeed and thrive in the increasingly technological workplaces of the 21st century. In such environments, employees are responsible not only for generating and arranging alphabetic texts, but also for using other semiotic systems—when appropriate and needed—to communicate across linguistic and cultural borders. Medical and nonprofit organizations, gaming and entertainment industries, education and engineering and scientific fields, increasingly, have all begun to use and generate multimodal texts: not only the more conventional memoranda and reports, but also Web sites, video tutorials, public service announcements, pod-casts, and visual data displays,

In this chapter, we hope to provide some suggestions for maintaining a value on creative and experimental explorations of composing modalities and flexible learning—even when the class is exploring the use of new digital technologies that may be unfamiliar (Fig. 7.1). We want, in other words, to help teachers and students have some fun as they learn and as they undertake their initial experiments with multimodal composing.

SOME CHALLENGES OF MULTIMODAL COMPOSING

NEW COMPOSING FORMS
- soundscapes
- sound portraits
- audio essays
- video documentaries
- video poetry composed of still photographs and words, music and sound

NEW COMPOSING QUESTIONS
- Where do we find images? Photographs? Video? Sounds?
- How do we sequence images? Sounds?
- What are the copyright and licensing laws associated with downloading images, video, and sound files from the Internet?
- What rhetorical work can sound, video, still images accomplish?

NEW VOCABULARY
- multimodal
- jump drive
- burning CDs
- .jpeg
- .mpeg
- layering

NEW EQUIPMENT NEEDS
- digital video cameras
- digital still cameras
- microphones
- video-editing software (e.g., Ulead's VideoStudio or Apple's iMovie)
- audio-editing software (e.g., Audacity or GarageBand)
- battery charger

FIGURE 7.1 Some challenges of multimodal composing

THE BENEFITS OF STAYING FLEXIBLE AND EXPERIMENTAL

So how do teachers establish a classroom environment that is flexible and experimental, one in which students can thrive as they undertake assignments that demand creative explorations of new composing modalities? The successful teachers we know rely heavily on their own prior experience with teaching composition and a solid understanding of rhetorical theory. Thus, they approach new kinds of assignments with an underlying sense of **confidence**. They also plan for these assignments in ways that take advantage of both human and technological resources—and create some **compatibility** between the people in their classes and the digital composing environments within which they work. These teachers also seem to have fun with their teaching—thinking in **creative** terms about assignments and encouraging students to exercise their own creativity in response to composing tasks. Finally, the best teachers stay calm and **cool** in the face of technological challenges—perhaps because they keep their attention focused on the possibilities lying just on the other side of such difficulties. In Table 7.1, we identify these characteristics as the four Cs of staying flexible and experimental in multimodal classrooms.

TABLE 7.1 **THE FOUR Cs OF STAYING FLEXIBLE AND EXPERIMENTAL**	
FOUR Cs	**EXPLANATION**
Confidence	Have *confidence* in your teaching ability and your understanding of rhetoric and composition. Multimodal assignments must appeal to specific audiences, and they must have an identifiable purpose. They depend on effective organization, arrangement, and details. They are circulated in specific rhetorical and cultural contexts.
Compatibility	Survey the *compatibility* of human and technological resources before the term begins. Survey students about their technological expertise, interests, and concerns. Before the terms begins, try specific digital cameras and digital audio recorders to make sure they work with specific computers and software packages.
Creativity	Multimodal assignments are enhanced by *creativity*. In conventional composition assignments, teachers sometimes forget to focus on creativity as a key ingredient of successful student essays, and students, often concerned about mastering more formal aspects of writing, sometimes forget to deliver it. Multimodal assignments can reintroduce the importance of creativity by focusing students' attention on new genres and approaches. Showing examples of different kinds of multimodal projects can start the students' creative juices flowing.
Cool	Keep your *cool*. Technology isn't 100% predictable, so keep the focus on the creative possibilities that digital environments allow. Don't exacerbate problems by getting frustrated—instead, use the opportunity to try some problem-solving approaches and invite students to learn along with you. When everyone is stumped, take a deep breath, relax, and reboot!

✓ **Approach multimodal assignments with confidence—focus on rhetorical effectiveness.** What most teachers add to the process of composing multimodal assignments is a strong background in rhetoric—an understanding of purpose, audience, organization, arrangement, and form. We can test this claim with an experiment. Take a few minutes to look at the short video essay entitled "ham and eggs: una historia por antonio cruz nova," <http://edcommunity.apple.com/gallery /student/item.php?itemID=719>, composed by Rosa María Ruvalcaba and Elizabeth Ruvalcaba, two sisters at the University of San Francisco. This short video is composed of relatively simple components—a series of very short video clips, mostly of a man telling a story in Spanish; some music; and some words, primarily translations of the Spanish. The video was shot with a digital video camera and edited in a common video-editing program, *Final Cut Pro*. The title screens and translations were added during the editing process. The music was edited in an audio-editing program called *GarageBand* and then imported into the video.

It is not necessary, however, to be an expert user of either of these programs to analyze many of the rhetorical choices that the Ruvalcaba sisters made in their composition. In fact, teachers and students can learn a great deal about the piece and its strengths by considering the following rhetorically derived questions:

- **Who are the authors of this essay?** What can a viewer tell about the authors of this essay? What messages do they hope to convey? What do they consider important? Unimportant? How does the piece as a whole convey their point of view? Their values? What rhetorical appeals are they using? Why?

- **Who is the audience** for the Ruvalcaba essay? To whom are the sisters speaking? What aspects of the audio track indicate this? What aspects of the video? How do video and audio work together in an effective dialogue that exceeds the sum of their parts? What is the historical context within which this piece will be viewed/read/ understood by the audience? The sociocultural context? The economic context? The artistic/aesthetic context? What could be done to make the piece work even more effectively for the intended audience? Are there images, animations, or narrative images that should be removed? Added? Why?

- **What is the purpose** of the essay? What messages are the Ruvalcaba sisters trying to convey? What are you trying to do? What and how do the video clips help contribute to this purpose? The audio track? The use of words throughout the essay? What choices did the authors make about the subtitles? When and where are they placed? The font? The color? What choices did they make about the music? About the video images? What could be done to make the piece work even more effectively toward its intended purpose? Are there images or words that should be removed? Added? Why?

- **What organizational strategies** have the Ruvalcaba sisters used to accomplish their purpose with the intended audience? Of what parts is the video composed? How have the authors organized the video clips? Why? How have they set up the context for the narrative? Why? How are the shots framed? Why? From what perspective are the shots taken? Why? How have the authors used music and sound in relation to each other? Why? How have they focused readers' attention on the message they want to convey? What organizational strategies could be employed to organize the elements of this piece so that they work even more effectively?

Most teachers of composition can generate these kinds of rhetorically based questions. In some ways, they are similar to those we might ask students about an alphabetic essay. They also, however, acknowledge that the modalities of video and sound carry some of the meaning in this composition—along with the modality of words.

✔ **Deal early with compatibility issues—both human and technological—and plan time for working them out.** Compatibility isn't limited to equipment! Students, too, come to classes with different skills, experiences, literacies, and interests. Given this fact, we suggest that teachers begin their first multimodal assignment by surveying students about their expertise and experience with—as well as their interests in and concerns about—any digital equipment that a multimodal assignment might require. In Chapter 4, we included a digital Technology Survey (Appendix 8) and a Student Expertise Grid (Appendix 9) that can help teachers find out what digital literacies students bring to a multimodal class. These two documents can help teachers identify those students who are expert users of digital communication technologies and environments and those students who might need extra help in adapting to such environments. Employing the results of such a survey, teachers can adjust multimodal assignment requirements to meet the experience levels and concerns of students, as well as coordinate classroom resources.

Compatibility also refers to how different digital technologies work together. Because digital video and still cameras and digital audio recorders aren't always immediately compatible with computers and software packages, teachers are also well advised to test compatibility before the term begins and before giving a multimodal assignment to students.

The best way to approach this compatibility testing involves the teacher undertaking a *small* mini-project of the same kind that is to be assigned to students. These small pilot projects are important for several reasons. First, they are essential when teachers have minimal experience composing in unfamiliar modalities, with digital tools, or in digital environments. Without a minimum of such experience, teachers will find it difficult to help students address the challenges associated with creating a multimodal text. These mini-projects can be *very simple* and *very short, even one or two minutes*—just as long as they involve teachers in using the same equipment and programs as assignments required of students.

Second, because these mini-projects involve the same digital equipment and programs as students will use, they are also valuable in revealing compatibility problems: Will the digital cameras download video easily to the video-editing program? Do the microphones work with the digital audio recorders? What format should audio files be in so that they can be imported into the video-editing program?

Finally, completing mini-projects will help teachers identify where documentation or instruction will be needed for students. Teachers can create this documentation themselves or have students create it as a part of the assignment. Such homemade documentation is valuable because it is tailored precisely to *local* digital resources, written with the *specific* needs of students in mind, and pitched at a *level of expertise* that class members can appreciate. Some teachers will want to make such documentation an option for students—both to create and to use. In the course of an assignment, if students are getting by without specific instructions for downloading and transferring audio and video, teachers can hold back on tutorials; but if students are having difficulty, step-by-step instructional sets can be produced. Sometimes, students will learn better if they're allowed to *discover* how to use technology themselves. In Appendix 7, teachers will find a sample of homemade documentation—itself an example of a multimodal composition built around both words and images. *This documentation is only a sample, however*—it will not suffice for other classrooms with different digital equipment, software, students, and needs. Readers are encouraged to compose—or work with students to compose—documentation that will meet their own local needs.

✔ **Put explicit value on creativity, and open the door for experimentation.** Creativity is difficult to teach and easy to stifle, but multimodal assignments provide a rich opportunity to focus on creative possibilities. Because the genres of (and expectations for) multimodal works have yet to be fully or rigidly established, teachers can encourage students to experiment with new audiences and approaches, modalities and media, purposes and strategies. To make explicit a value on creative problem solving in composing tasks, teachers should make sure to discuss with students the close relationship between creativity and purpose, audience, and form—and specify creativity as a key component in the multimodal assignments they design. In addition, they should make sure that creativity is identified as one of the factors for which multimodal projects will be assessed (see Chapters 8 and 9).

To encourage students to take creative approaches to multimodal composing, teachers should plan to start multimodal projects by bringing in a wide range of projects to show students—and encouraging students to bring in their own examples. From these, students can identify strategies, techniques, genres, and creative approaches that they can borrow and adapt. Appendix 27 provides some ideas about where to look for such projects.

Because many students will enjoy the experience of multimodal projects that challenge both their creativity and problem-solving skills, they may also invest unusual amounts of time and effort in their composing efforts. Teachers should be prepared to be flexible in terms of assignments and their constraints (see *Chapter 3: Designing Multimodal Assignments*). Teachers should also make sure to leave room for experimentation—both for themselves and for students. Because multimodal assignments always present teachers and students with new challenges, teachers should be as flexible as possible with assignment due dates, and plenty of room should be scheduled for class discussions and reflection on the learning that students have done. More formal studio days should also be scheduled for peer-reviews so that students can display their work without being concerned about being graded and to get detailed feedback about making their projects better. For specific guidelines and suggestions about studio sessions, see Chapters 8 and 9. For all assignments, teachers should be sure to discuss how creativity relates to audience, purpose, content, and modalities, and be explicit about the rhetorical criteria that will count in the final assessment of the project.

To encourage their own creative problem solving, teachers can make a habit of setting goals for their assignments that seem slightly out of reach at the beginning of the semester—making sure that they have to stretch as far as do students. Teachers can learn new software applications, find new examples of student-authored work, create their own multimodal essays, improve assignments, or try new digital tools that students may find useful.

✓ **Remain cool in the face of technology difficulties, and ask students to help solve problems. This approach will lower everyone's anxiety.** There are sure to be times in the multimodal classroom when digital technologies do not work as planned. On these days, teachers can model good problem-solving strategies: When the class reaches an impasse in using a particular technology or software, teachers can admit they are stumped and ask the class as a whole to identify some collective problem-solving approaches. The set of instructions in Figure 7.2, for instance, illustrates the problem-solving strategy protocol one class created for occasions when a digital data projector didn't seem to be working with a computer. This protocol prevented a great deal of anxiety when students were showing their projects to the class in formal peer-review studio sessions. Students can also share successful approaches online, using a class listserv to suggest solutions to classmates' difficulties.

Teachers can make these systems work by modeling the right habits of mind for approaching problems—how to think critically, productively, and often collaboratively; how to retain a value on experimentation; and exercise a sense of humor—even when the solution to a problem is not readily available.

WHEN THE DATA PROJECTOR DOESN'T WORK . . .

Step #1: Check all plugs, adapters, and cables that go from the wall to the computer. Make sure all plugs, adapters, and cables are securely seated in their sockets.

Step #2: Check all plugs, adapters, and cables from computer to projector. Make sure plugs and adapters are securely seated in their sockets.

Step #3: Check all plugs, adapters, and cables from the projector to the cart to the wall—or from the projector to the wall. Make sure plugs and adapters are securely seated in their sockets.

Step #4: Check all plugs, adapters, and cables from the speakers to the projector or to the computer. Make sure plugs and adapters are securely seated in their sockets.

Step #5: Turn off the computer.

Step #6: Turn off the projector.

Step #7: Check to make sure that all power lights are off.

Step #8: Turn the computer back on.

Step #9: Make sure the monitor settings are correctly set for display with a projector.

Step #10: Turn on the projector. Find the correct input channel for the computer.

Step #11: Check the sound controls on the computer (the main volume control), within the application (the sound control slider in the window of the application you are using), on the projector (which often has a separate dial on the cord leading to or from the speakers), and on the speakers themselves.

FIGURE 7.2 Class troubleshooting protocol for a projector

Teachers can also model for students how to maintain good relationships with information technology specialists within a department or in a central campus office. These colleagues should be consulted before the term begins with a description of assignments and some idea of the hardware and software that will be needed to complete multimodal projects. Teachers may also want to ask if technical staff members are available during class time. Although resources may not allow for this arrangement, it never hurts to ask. During the term, if staff members cannot be present, it is wise to call on these specialists only when the class has exhausted its own expertise and problem-solving abilities. Communicating respectfully with these colleagues and expressing gratitude for a job well done is also always in order (R. Selfe, 2004).

Finally, teachers should encourage and test their own creativity by experimenting with the assignments they give. Teachers can keep a focus on the value of experimentation by changing and improving on multimodal assignments, each semester. They can add new components and tasks so that multimodal assignments grow with new technologies that become available. Teachers can encourage their own creative problem solving by setting goals that seem slightly out of reach at the beginning of the semester.

CHALLENGES TO STAYING FLEXIBLE AND EXPERIMENTAL

Staying flexible and experimental with multimodal assignments isn't always easy. Changing technologies, limited time, few resources, and other factors may affect both teachers' and students' success. Perhaps the best advice is to have high expectations and let students know when they are succeeding.

Following is a list of challenges that work against flexibility and experimentation, and some additional strategies for overcoming those challenges.

Students and teachers come to multimodal composing with different levels of expertise. Reward personal initiative and discovery. Many teachers are surprised to find out how radically individuals within a class differ in terms of their digital literacies, experiences, learning styles and expertise. The best teachers help students learn how to do something (e.g., frame a video scene, record an interview, add a special effect in iMovie) and then ask them to teach what they have discovered to others in the class—using small workshops or evening lab sessions for this purpose. If at all possible, teachers should adjust course requirements and course credit for students who expend a significant amount of time doing such work.

Teachers might also want to consider giving knowledgeable and helpful students an extra hour of course credit for their services as technology assistants—identifying these assistants with the help of a technology survey given early in the semester (Appendix 8). Other teachers regularly advertise for student technology assistants—recruiting them from outside the classes they are taking. Students who plan careers in education, management information systems (MIS), computer science, and other disciplines often enjoy the opportunity to practice their teaching skills (R. Selfe, 2004).

Compatibility problems may make it difficult to work on projects outside of the classroom. Although software today is much more likely to be compatible with different hardware and cameras than in the past, universal compatibility is a myth. Identifying compatibility issues before the term begins may help prevent some frustration, but compatibility problems will arise throughout the term when students try to work on their projects at home and at school—using entirely different computers and software, Compatibility problems can also make collaboration within a group difficult—especially if students are trying to work with different software packages and hardware.

Students who do want to work in different environments might benefit from trying out a mini-project early in the term. Depending on the assignment, these students can

1. create a trial mini-version of an audio or video project—downloading a few readily available pictures, video clips, or audio files from the web;
2. download recorded audio, photographs, and video from the recorders and cameras they will be using;
3. briefly practice editing video or audio for this mini-project, using the appropriate software.
4. export a compressed version of a mini project on a CD.

Students who do *not* want to deal with compatibility problems—or who have less experience in doing so—can be encouraged to work in a lab context where compatibility has already been tested and where they can meet other students from the class. Teachers will want to work with information technology specialists to identify a lab or computer classroom that has established compatibilities among cameras, audio recorders, computers, and software.

 **Creative and rhetorically thoughtful approaches to multimodal composing take time to explore and develop. Such approaches demand assignments with minimal constraints, flexible due dates, and plenty of encouragement.** Creativity takes time. Similarly, effective rhetorical approaches to composing with new modalities cannot be developed overnight. Teachers should not expect to pack assignments into a course when they and students are just beginning to experiment with multimodal composing.

The best approaches to assignments allow enough time for students and teachers to learn how to use digital equipment, view and discuss a range of multimodal projects that might encourage creative responses, collaborate on solving problems, and practice and experiment with video- and audio-editing techniques. Forward-thinking teachers will build flex time into their syllabi (see Chapter 3) that can be profitably used in showing and analyzing examples of multimodal projects students identify as interesting, scheduling multiple peer-response studio sessions (see Chapters 8 and 9), reflecting—individually (Appendix 14) and in groups (Appendices 15 and 16)—on the learning that students are doing, and sharing new strategies for composing. Many teachers will find it beneficial to be flexible about project due dates as long as students demonstrate a consistent commitment to composing efforts.

Creativity also demands flexible, open-ended assignments that give students room to explore and experiment with a variety of approaches. Teachers can encourage creative responses by recognizing that students bring differing abilities, interests, and literacies to the classroom and building a minimal number of constraints into their assignments (see Chapter 3). Teachers will also want to recognize that students in most composition classes have a range of different experiences with and exposure to digital composing tools—especially audio- and video-editing programs, which are not always widely accessible in high schools. For this reason, multimodal composition classes will succeed best when students are encouraged to share their knowledge and their problem-solving strategies with others—in person, on a class listserv, in email, or via project logs (Appendix 10)—helping the class to form a collaborative group of the whole.

In Table 7.2, we summarize some of the strategies previously mentioned for staying experimental and flexible, focusing on creativity and effective problem solving.

TABLE 7.2
THE BENEFITS OF STAYING FLEXIBLE AND EXPERIMENTAL

STRATEGIES FOR STAYING FLEXIBLE AND EXPERIMENTAL	
Build confidence.	**Focus on rhetoric:** Use principles of rhetorical analysis (audience, purpose, organization, arrangement, form) to structure discussions of sample multimodal texts and studio reviews of students' projects.
	Admit your limitations: You don't have to pretend to know everything. Be honest with yourself and students. Ask students for problem-solving help and involve them in creating problem-solving protocols or homemade documentation (Appendix 7). Model effective approaches to collaboration and critical thinking.
Solve compatibility issues early.	**Make a student expertise grid:** Survey students on their experiences with and knowledge about digital technologies (Appendix 8). Also, survey students to find out what resources they have available. Have students make an Expertise Grid (Appendix 9).
	Take a dry run: Complete a mini-version of your own multimodal assignment to troubleshoot tasks and document processes of downloading, uploading, and transferring; saving and archiving; publishing and sharing.
Invite and value creativity.	**Design assignments that encourage creativity and rhetorical effectiveness, and that are characterized by flexibility:** Identify specific requirements for creativity in assignments and in the assessment rubrics for multimodal projects. Design projects that have minimal constraints and flexible due dates—but always focus on rhetorical effectiveness.
	Schedule peer-response studio sessions: Allow students the opportunity to see what others are doing, rehearse the use of specialized terminology, ask questions, and make suggestions for improvement.
	Share creative texts: Use class time to show examples of multimodal texts and discuss how the author achieved rhetorical success,
Maintain cool in the face of technological problems.	**Take a deep breath:** It's amazing how often taking a deep breath will allow people to work through technology problems.
	Identify problem-solving protocols: Have students identify problem-solving protocols for approaching common problems that they encounter as a group.
	Work respectfully with the IT Department: Consult the IT departments *before* the term begins to let people know what kinds of assignments you are going to try. Ask for specific support.
	Create homemade documentation: Work with students to create homemade documentation (Appendix 7) that meets their specific needs. Incorporate these mini-research projects into the class as composition practice.
	Reboot: Sometimes it is simple to fix a technology problem. Turn the computer off, and turn it on again.

TRYING OUT MULTIMODAL COMPOSING AS A CLASS

Teachers who think about introducing multimodal assignments like those outlined in Chapter 2 often imagine students bent studiously over keyboards—physically and mentally cut off from other people, discussion, social exchange. But that is, of course, playing into the myth of technology as inherently alienating and isolationist. In reality, the optimum learning environment for experimenting with multimodal assignments is one in which students and teachers collaborate in analyzing sample multimodal texts, try out multimodal technologies, discover effective rhetorical strategies, and work together in active social environments. In these classrooms, students exchange ideas, supportive strategies, and peer-responses even when working on separate projects. Such collaboration can take a number of forms. (For a more detailed examination of collaboration, see Chapter 4.) In the next sections, we identify a few of the strategies that can work well in keeping multimodal classrooms experimental and creative, while keeping a focus on rhetorical effectiveness and social interaction. Individual teachers, of course, will want to pick and choose from among the strategies according to the needs of students and the local conditions, as well as their own pedagogical style.

My Turn, Your Turn: Learning and Teaching

One of the first lessons that teachers learn in the multimodal composition classroom has to do with the benefits of test-driving hardware, software, and digital equipment themselves before asking students to use them.

By working with new technologies in advance of students, teachers not only gain a bit of first-hand experience with new composing modalities, vocabulary, software and hardware, and infrastructural challenges, but—if they open their minds to learning—they can also acquire some empathy with students and, importantly, a sense of humility that will allow them to approach students as fellow-learners, much as Paulo Friere suggests. This approach can help shift the dynamic of power in some classrooms, refocusing attention on the task of learning not only in a theoretical manner but in a nuts-and-bolts practical way. Teaching multimodal composition doesn't require teachers to give up their disciplinary expertise—rather it encourages them to use the opportunity of learning about composing with new modalities to become a student again—and, in doing so, to rediscover a sense of experimentation and creative thinking about the task of making meaning.

Many teachers who take the opportunity to teach multimodal composition also come away from it with an increasing respect for what students know about these new literacies and their willingness to share this knowledge. Students bring a host of new literacies to contemporary classrooms—along with some semiotic sensibilities that help them make effective use of these literacies. And teachers who manage to tap into this knowledge—instead of dismissing it or ignoring it—often gain new appreciation for what students know about videos and video games, music and lyrics, computers and digital tools.

Successful multimodal classrooms also manage to expand students' feelings of investment and involvement. This is not to suggest that all students will already have the skills and knowledge necessary for the multimodal projects teachers might have in mind. However, when students see instructors who are willing to learn about new digital literacies and new modalities of composing, try new media, acknowledge student literacies in respectful ways, and reflect honestly on their successes and failures, they are often encouraged and even surprised. In multimodal classes taught by such teachers, students often become comfortable enough to take chances themselves, experiment with new composing modalities, and try their hand at helping others learn.

Teachers can help make their own test-driving experiences visible and ensure that they work for the entire class by making a technology learning record—or a technology learning log—of their experiences (see Fig. 7.3) and sharing parts of this record with students.

TECHNOLOGY LEARNING LOG

Keep a technology learning record of your experience with a new piece of technology (e.g., a digital camera, a new software program, a minidisc recorder). Answer such questions as:

✔ For what purpose did you use this technology?

✔ What are the particular affordances (the special capabilities) of this technology?

✔ How did you learn to use this technology (e.g., relied on the manual, had a friend help me, figured it out myself, used the help files online, went to a demonstration)?

✔ With what aspects did you have problems?

✔ What characteristics/functions do you like?

✔ What characteristics/functions do you dislike?

✔ Were there any tasks that you needlessly complicated? What tricks did you discover?

✔ What project did you complete?

✔ Is there any advice you can offer new users?

Share your learning record with students and learn something about their own encounters with new media or composing styles.

FIGURE 7.3 Making a technology learning record

One Is the Loneliest Number

Human beings are social creatures. In composition classes, working with collaborative partners is invaluable when students are exploring new modalities or trying out new digital tools. At the most basic level, being a member of a group means individual students multiply their own mental resources. One student will notice one thing, but her partners will notice others. In collaborative situations, students have at their disposal the cognitive synergy that results from small group conversations. In such circumstances, both teachers and students can be proud when a group solves a technical problem, discovers an effective rhetorical approach, or helps an author compose a better project.

In a multimodal classroom, small groups are ideal environments for helping students become familiar with the basic characteristics of relevant equipment and software applications—from the placement of the zoom and record buttons on a video camera to the screen layout of an audio-editing program.

In fact, a terrific way for teachers to begin a multimodal composition assignment is to give students one or two class periods to play around with relevant media and technology in small groups (see Fig. 7.4, as well as Appendices 21 and 22). Although at first glance, this approach might seem to divert valuable class time from composing and rhetoric, such sessions can actually create rich opportunities to discuss rhetorical possibilities of digital media and allow teachers to become familiar with students' relative level of comfort and proficiency with digital media. If teachers prefer that students get more experience in writing, they can have students participate in authoring homemade documentation (Appendix 7) for each of the digital tools that the class will be using.

SHOWING IT OFF

Have small groups choose a piece of technology, such as a minidisc player, a digital video camera, or a digital still camera (equipment used in the Chapter 2 case studies), and under the guidance of someone familiar with that technology (an instructor, teaching assistant, or technologically gifted student), explore how it is put together and how it works.

After students have done this, have them verbally describe the relevant piece of equipment to the group that will next work with the equipment. We often learn as much in the role of teacher as we do in the role of student.

FIGURE 7.4 Showing It Off

Keeping Track of Equipment

One of the major challenges associated with multimodal composition classrooms is to keep track of the digital equipment that students use. Although some institutions have a central office in Instructional Technology or a library where students can check out digital equipment, many teachers of multimodal composition start by borrowing a few cameras and recorders from various places around campus for a semester. In such cases, teachers are often obliged to set up their own system for checking equipment out and back in again. To help keep track of equipment—and to avoid the headaches of losing expensive and hard-to-replace parts—teachers may want to try the some of the following approaches:

 Put each camera and digital audio recorder in its own padded equipment bag along with all the small accessories (e.g., cables, mics, discs, batteries). Within every bag, label every accessory with tape and a permanent marking pen.

 Number and label each equipment bag and make a specific **equipment check-out sheet** for it. Include pictures of unfamiliar components to teach students specialized vocabulary and keep important parts from getting lost. When students check in equipment, use the sheet to make sure each piece is present and accounted for (see Appendix 23).

 Find a locked location for the equipment, one accessible to the teacher and to any staff members or students who might help check out equipment.

 Create a **class equipment schedule** that will allow students to see when various pieces of technology are available and reserve them for check out. Post it wherever equipment is stored (see Appendix 24).

 Create a written set of **check-in and check-out procedures** so that all students know how to deal with equipment (see Appendix 25).

 Create a set of **equipment check-in file folders** numbered from 1 to 31, one folder for each day of the month. Students can use these to file their **equipment check-out sheets**—filing them under the day they will return the equipment. When equipment is checked in, go to the appropriate folder, locate the student's equipment check-out sheet, and make sure all components have been returned.

Creating Homegrown Multimodal Specialists and Digital Coaches

Multimodal projects often involve teachers and students working in a computer lab or some analogous, technology-rich space. (See Chapter 12 for more information about forming robust communities of practitioners in such spaces.) These spaces provide another place where teachers can experiment with combining their understanding of rhetoric, digital technologies, and multiple modalities for composing meaning in productive ways. Such spaces also provide environments within which teachers can cultivate a class of homegrown student experts—small groups and individuals who can help each other and work together in pursuit of class projects.

To create an environment within which such homegrown specialists and coaches can develop, teachers need to schedule ample studio time for working on multimodal projects during class—much as they might schedule workshop sessions in more conventional writing courses. During these sessions, teachers can assign students strategic project-based activities that involve class members in talking to one another, sharing both problems and discoveries, and teaching each other.

One systematic way to cultivate specialists in multimodal composition classrooms is to ask each team to compose homemade documentation for one process that they can share with the rest of the class (see, e.g., Appendix 7). Teachers need not, however, make unnecessary work for students. There are also many free user manuals and sources of documentation available on the web for most of the software packages and equipment mentioned in this book. Most of these resources are quite good, and students can use them productively in many cases. In Appendix 26: Sources of Documentation on the Web, we indicate where teachers and students can find such resources.

Another method for cultivating homegrown specialists for multimodal classrooms is to assign each team—or every student—the responsibility for conducting a mini-research project on one major technical concept: **framing**, **compression**, **length of shot**, **clipping**, and so on. After they conduct their mini-research efforts, students can compose a multimodal explanation of the term they have been assigned—using words, but also including still images, embedded video clips, or embedded audio clips that explain, illustrate, or help unpack the technical term. These new local experts can also be made responsible for answering class members' subsequent questions on this topic throughout the semester.

Through these kinds of assignments and activities, students quickly become troubleshooters, technology specialists, and motivational coaches as indicated in Figure 7.5—in short, invaluable resources for teachers who are themselves learning about multimodal composing.

COMMON STUDENT SPECIALISTS

- students who are especially good at brainstorming ideas, mapping out projects, writing scripts, editing alphabetic elements

- students who are especially proficient at editing sound

- students who are especially good at collaborating and sharing group strategies that work well

- students who are especially proficient at applying special effects in audio or video environments

- students who are especially proficient at using the web to find video and sound clips in the public domain

- students who provide emotional support and encouragement to others

- students who are especially proficient at operating various pieces of equipment (i.e., minidisc recorder, video camera, etc.)

- students who are especially proficient at downloading, saving, and calling up files

FIGURE 7.5 Common student specialties developed in multimodal classrooms

Saving, Cloning, and Other Preventative Measures

Flexibility, creativity, and experimentation are fine goals, but anyone who works with multiple modalities in digital environments can tell stories about computers that have frozen at the wrong moment, CDs that have failed, or programs that have shut down in the middle of an editing session. With memory-intensive software applications like video and audio editing, *prevention* becomes a key concept. Students should save their files often and back up their work after every major session at the computer. Making a regular practice of copying files can also allow students to experiment more boldly with compositions.

Teachers working in environments with adequate mass-storage availability may want to encourage students to *clone* their projects at various stages of the composing process—to make *strategically* chosen copies of their composition to preserve or to try out a particular organization, effect, or arrangement. Not only does this cloning remind composers of the possibilities of the media in which they are working, but it can remind them of the possibilities of revision. These archived, cloned copies can be invaluable in the case of catastrophic power failures, editing mistakes, or computer problems. If students are taught to save their work on a regular basis and clone back up copies for safekeeping, teachers can safely encourage a sense of open-endedness and experimentation in digital composing environments. Teachers will want to remind students, however, that such cloned files take up valuable memory and, thus, should be organized and discarded when they are no longer of use.

Look What I Found!

One of the most effective strategies for encouraging creative and rhetorically effective texts in the multimodal classroom is to provide students with plenty of opportunities to hear and see other authors' multimodal projects—not only the projects of classmates, but also projects originating outside the class. Students who have had little exposure to audio composition, for instance, will need time to develop the ability to listen closely and articulate their understandings of the affordances that audio offers as a composing modality. They will also benefit from listening to examples of different genres: soundscapes, audio documentaries, sound portraits, and audio narratives, among others. Airing a range of audio essays will also allow students time to assemble an effective set of rhetorical techniques that they can later apply within their own projects.

Teachers can locate these examples in a number of ways: by asking colleagues, surfing the web, contacting faculty who teach multimodal composition at other institutions, and by talking to students. Because increasing numbers of faculty are working with multimodal compositions in their classrooms, many teachers will know colleagues who can pass along their favorite examples of student work or suggest audio- and video-essays that should be aired in class. Some teachers will want to check with colleagues in departments of digital arts, communication, cultural studies, design, video production, radio production, or education.

Teachers can also use a search engine like www.yahoo.com or www.google.com to search for sites containing audio and video essays. Appendix 27 lists web sites that provide teachers and students with a range of video and audio compositions to view and listen to.

For a homework assignment, teachers might want to ask students to search the Internet for multimodal compositions. Students can choose a project that they particularly like and bring a copy of this project to the next class session. During this session, as a whole class or in small groups, teachers will want to direct the class in discussing the rhetorical effectiveness of such compositions and the appeals they use, as well as analyzing their purpose, audience, and organization. (See Chapter 5 and Appendices 18, 19, and 20 for more information about the rhetorical analysis of such compositions.)

Beginner's Mind, Expert's Mind

In the best multimodal composition classes, flexibility extends far beyond the design of projects and the incorporation of student choice into assignments. In these classes, experimentation is encouraged as a general attitude. The American Zen teacher, Shunryu Suzuki, was fond of saying, "In the beginner's mind there are many possibilities, but in the expert's mind there are few." The best possible motto for a multimodal composition class is "try it and see what happens." If teachers can get students to internalize this dictum and overcome their initial fear, if they can model experimentation and creative approaches to rhetorical problem solving *themselves*, most students will follow suit. In fact, sometimes the *less a teacher confesses to knowing* about multimodal composing and digital composing tools, the *more completely students feel able to invest* their own time. If teachers don't make all the rules, if they are not in possession of all the understanding, then students can claim increasing amounts of intellectual and creative space for their own efforts.

In any case, we advise teachers to develop their own genuine curiosity about new forms of literacy and different modalities of expression and to talk to students about what they know of these topics. We also suggest asking students to take on some of the instructional burden in multimodal composition classes—drawing on their understandings and perspectives to help teach and insuring the investment of their own energies in the class.

IN CONCLUSION

Few of the suggestions in this chapter are novel as pedagogical approaches. Teachers do not need to invent completely new teaching practices to integrate multimodal composition assignments into their classes. Their own comfortable approaches and practices may, however, need to be altered slightly to make room for the kinds of open-ended exploration that multimodal composing can involve.

Experimentation should not be a process restricted to the initial stages of learning about multimodal possibilities. Rather, it is—and should be—an attitude that teachers continually foster and reward in students and in themselves.

REFERENCES

Selfe, R. J. (2004). *Sustainable computer environments: Cultures of support in English studies and language arts*. Cresskill, NJ: Hampton Press.

From *Crafting a Family Tradition*, Sonya Borton

CHAPTER 8
Responding and Assessing

Sonya C. Borton
Brian Huot

In this chapter, we focus on assessment—maintaining that the instructional process associated with *all* composing tasks, including multimodal projects, should be informed both broadly and deeply by a *rhetorical understanding of composition*. Within this context, all multimodal assignments, all instruction in the use of digital and nondigital composing tools, and all assessment of multimodal compositions, should be tailored to teaching students how to use rhetorical principles appropriately and effectively.

We use the term *composing* self-consciously—as suggested by Geoff Sirc's (2002) *Composition as a Happening*—to focus on the rhetorically informed process of producing texts appropriate for a specific purpose and audience. Although the multimodality of texts does *not* depend on their digitality, and multimodal texts can take many nondigital forms (see nondigital assignment ideas in Chapter 3 and Chapter 10), we believe, as Pamela Takayoshi says, that teachers should pay particular attention to the alternative text-generating capabilities of computers because these tools can be used to help teach writers "that there are no correct or easy answers for writing. Instead, there are rhetorically informed decisions writers make about text" (1996, p. 249).

Especially important to our argument is the important relationship between instruction and assessment: Rhetorically based understandings of composition should *drive and inform* teachers' approach to assessment in multimodal composition classrooms. As Brian Huot (2002) and others have argued, assessment is an important component of learning to compose with rhetorical effectiveness. When we help students learn to *assess* their own compositions and the compositions—the texts—that others create, we are teaching them valuable decision-making skills they can use when *producing* their own texts.

Using assessment to teach about the design and production—the composition—of texts seems especially relevant in a multimodal classroom because it is entirely possible that the processes of creating texts that go beyond the alphabetic will be less familiar to many students than the processes involved in creating more conventional word-based texts. In such contexts, we need to teach students not only how to compose in multiple modalities, but also how to connect their understandings with the rhetorical principles that guide all language use. In this way, we also heed Cindy Selfe's (1999) call for students to be *critical users of technology*, people who understand a wide range of constraints, demands, and principles of effective communication in both digital and nondigital environments.

Our chapter, then, has two purposes. First, we want to outline assessment strategies that help students compose increasingly appropriate—and rhetorically effective—multimodal texts. Second, we want to provide teachers with some effective strategies for assessing texts that are very different from those traditionally associated with composition classrooms, and make sure that such strategies are soundly based in the rhetorical tradition we share as a profession.

ASSESSING AND TEACHING

All writing teachers incorporating digital media and the production of multimodal texts into the classroom face important challenges. These challenges are especially crucial if teachers believe (as we do) that assessment is an integral part of rhetorical instruction. The kind of assessment we recommend for teachers assigning, responding to, and assessing multimodal texts can probably best be understood as **instructive evaluation** or **instructive assessment**. Both terms denote techniques that help students learn to assess texts rhetorically—their own texts and the texts of others, *as they* compose and *after* they do so. In this way, assessments of student work become part of instruction.

> Instructive evaluation requires that we involve students in all phases of the assessment of their work. We must help them set the rhetorical and linguistic [and multimodal] targets that will best suit their purposes in writing and then help them evaluate how well they have met such targets, using this evaluation to help them reach additional targets and set new ones. . . . Instructive evaluation requires that students and teachers connect the ability to assess with the necessity to revise, creating a motivation for revision that is often difficult for students to feel. (Huot, 2002, pp. 170-171)

In an educational context, assessment is often divided into *formative assessments* that provide feedback to students while they are still working on assignments or projects, and *summative evaluations* such as final assignment grades or final course grades that are given only after an assignment or project has been completed. Although summative assessment is a necessary part of the composition course, understanding and incorporating formative assessment in the composition process can remind students of the rhetorical constraints and possibilities involved in any composing task, and give them the tools to create rhetorically effective compositions in any medium.

In contemporary composition classrooms, it is not unusual to find both formative and summative assessment practices being used by teachers, and to find that such assessments are shaped within rhetorically informed instructional contexts. It is now a relatively common practice, for example, for composition teachers to work with students to compile a list of criteria for use in composing (Fig. 8.1). Teachers then use these criteria to create a related grading rubric for a particular writing assignment—one that takes into account purpose, audience, the forms that rhetorically effective texts might take, as well as possible contexts for circulation.

In the context of *formative assessment*, this kind of approach helps to focus students' attention on a rhetorical understanding of a text as they are in the process of composing it. Such collaboratively composed rubrics can also serve a *summative function*—providing teachers and students with a strategy for evaluating the rhetorical effectiveness of the final composition product after they have completed texts.

- The composition conveys a specific purpose.

- The composition identifies a specific audience—either explicitly or implicitly.

- The composition employs a tone consistent with the designated purpose and audience.

- The composition is organized around an appropriate controlling idea. This idea is clear to readers/viewers/listeners.

- The composition uses transitions to guide the audience effectively from one set of ideas to another.

- The composition synthesizes relevant information from research efforts with composer's own ideas and arguments—in a way that increases the rhetorical effectiveness of the whole.

- The composition uses detailed description, examples, sound, music, color, and/or word choice to convey ideas in an effective and appropriate way to the audience.

- The composition accounts for anticipated contexts of circulation and the systems of distribution within which the text will be read and used by others.

Note: The list will vary depending on the context of each assignment.

FIGURE 8.1 Possible criteria for formative assessment

Because such an approach to instructive assessment offers an effective way to make sure that students understand the role of rhetoric in a conventional composition classroom, it is probably an even more important strategy to use in a course that includes multimodal texts. In these classes, students are likely to have less experience authoring, designing, and thinking rhetorically about multimodal texts. Creating a collaboratively constructed rubric—or using other similar instructive–assessment strategies—helps to make classroom expectations, including the newer elements of multimodal texts, more apparent for both teachers and students. Such activities also harness the opportunity to use assessment to *teach* composition. Collaboratively constructed rubrics and/or lists of evaluative criteria can be used in various productive ways. As Brian Huot (2002) explains,

> In one classroom, students evaluate samples of writing, ranking them and providing criteria for each ranking. The discussion is synthesized on a handout given to students. In another classroom, students create wall charts of features of good writing, revising them throughout the year as their ideas about writing evolve. And finally, students and teachers generate lists of statements about what makes good writing, and this list is used by students selecting pieces for their portfolios. In each of these scenarios, students learn to write by learning to assess. (p. 171)

Making rhetorically based, instructive assessment a more visible and conscious part of teaching—*a formative feature as well as a summative feature of instruction*—helps students produce multimodal essays that are rhetorically effective, while harnessing the instructive power of assessment for both students and teachers. Such an approach also keeps teachers and students appropriately focused on rhetorical matters, whether they are composing multimodal essays or essays that are primarily alphabetic-only. In Figure 8.2, we provide some key questions that should help shape assignments within an instructive-assessment context. These questions are broadly applicable to both conventional and unconventional composition assignments.

- What is the teacher's rhetorical purpose for this assignment?

- Does the assignment allow students to choose a purpose authentic to their own interests? Experiences? Can students effectively articulate and address the purpose?

- How will the media and the composing modalities specified for this assignment help students identify and address the needs of an authentic purpose for their compositions?

- What is the teacher's understanding of the possible audiences for this assignment?

- What options does the assignment allow students for identifying an authentic audience within the context of their lives and experiences?

- How will the media and the composing modalities specified for this assignment help students identify and address the needs of an authentic audience for their compositions?

- How do the assessment criteria for this assignment—both formative and summative—address the composition's purpose and audience in rhetorically informed ways? Have students been involved in identifying these assessment criteria? Do they have opportunities for using such criteria in both formative and summative contexts?

- How do the assessment criteria for this assignment—both formative and summative—address the composition's organization in rhetorically informed ways? Its tone? Its focus? Its use of sound, color, and image—both still and moving? Have students been involved in identifying the assessment criteria? Do they have opportunities for using such criteria in both formative and summative contexts?

- How does the assignment recognize the contexts of circulation and distribution within which student texts will be used and read?

Note: Questions will vary depending on the context of each assignment.

FIGURE 8.2 Shaping assignments in the context of instructive assessment

LEARNING TO RESPOND TO AND ASSESS MULTIMODAL TEXTS

Charles Moran and Anne Herrington (2003) write about evaluating academic hypertexts, noting that electronic hypermedia and their multimodal cousins provide new challenges for teachers who have had to make evaluative decisions primarily about alphabetic documents (although all alphabetic texts, of course, also incorporate a visual modality). Importantly, Moran and Harrington also recommend assessment approaches that involve many of the same characteristics we have already identified—assessment that is formative as well as summative, assessment that is rhetorically based, and assessment that is used for instructional as well as evaluative purposes. We believe this situation highlights how instructive assessment of multimodal texts can become an important way to teach rhetorical principles of both composing and producing these texts. As Moran and Herrington read digital texts, they begin to develop criteria inductively for assessment.

> Therefore the criteria that we ordinarily use in judging academic essays of this genre seem to apply across the media: Focus and Central Claim, "Evidence of Constructive Thinking, Organization/Coherence . . ." "Documentation was also a criterion for us . . . " "Syntax/Style" and "Grammar/Proofreading" became criteria for us as well . . . "Graphic Design" . . . included the visual elements of the hypertexts: choice of fonts, page layout, choice of colors. (p. 249)

It's important to note that Moran and Herrington are developing criteria to make judgments about both hypertext and traditional academic essays. In all cases, however, assessment criteria should be developed with an eye toward *both instruction and evaluation.* Ideally, instructive evaluation in composition classrooms *always* reflects not only the media with which students work and the semiotic modalities (words, images, sound, color) that they employ to make meaning, but also a course's specific instructional goals and a contextual understanding of other rhetorical constraints and possibilities having to do with purpose, audience, content, genre, circulation, and organization, as well.

What does this mean in practical terms and in a multimodal classroom? In addition to more conventional concerns such as making sure that students understand and effectively address a composition's audience, purpose, organization, circulation, and tone, for instance, teachers might want to identify criteria that have to do with students' success in identifying appropriate sound levels for specific audiences or the authors' ability to relate multiple modalities in ways that communicate more than the sum of their parts within a particular rhetorical context. Similarly, an important assessment criteria for a multimodal text might be whether a student has taken advantage of the specific affordances, or capabilities, of each modality in a way that helps to achieve the text's purpose or increase its overall effectiveness with a specific audience.

Ultimately, Moran and Herrington see themselves as learners of new forms of composing and expression at the same time they are learning to evaluate students' efforts. This feeling of being a learner *and* a teacher—of learning to teach a multimodal class *while recognizing that we lack* the same certitude and sense of expertise that we bring to more conventional courses—not only helps us bridge the gaps between teachers and students (see Chapter 7), it also helps us to contextualize assessment. As we struggle to articulate rhetorical assessment criteria for multimodal compositions along with students—for instance, the principles for assessing the effective organization of an audio essay aimed at an NPR audience, the grammatical rules operative in music videos, the extent to which still images are rhetorically sensitive to the needs of a particular reader—we also develop a much clearer idea of the challenges students face as the authors, composers, and designers of multimodal texts.

Developing this intimate sense of the challenges involved in composing essays is an essential part of any successful composition course. We do not want to suggest that every composition teacher will want to—or need to—develop extensive expertise in creating multimodal texts. However, we *do* feel strongly that *teachers who want to assign and evaluate multimodal texts need to develop some understanding of the challenges involved in composing such texts.* This insight is not limited, of course, to a particular kind of text. We have observed, for instance, that the most effective teachers of alphabetic composition have some personal experience in struggling with the complex tasks involved in writing such texts—and that these experiences help teachers design instructional and assessment strategies that work for practicing writers. Similarly, we have observed that teachers who have learned to design and produce at least one web site are more effective in structuring assignments that help students create and evaluate web texts.

But how do teachers know when they have acquired *sufficient experience composing and understandings of* multimodal texts to help students? And how do they develop additional understandings and experience without keeping students from experimenting themselves with these new kinds of texts? We think that working within the context of instructive assessment—which encourages teachers to work carefully and thoughtfully with students in identifying and articulating the challenges that authors encounter when composing multimodal texts—may help teachers close the gap between their alphabetic and multimodal composing experiences.

Using Studio Sessions for Formative Assessment

Given our own experience, we can predict that some students in multimodal classrooms will complete assignments with ease, enjoying the opportunity to use their creativity and to incorporate media that they often use for "fun" in a more formal academic setting. It is also true, however, that other students may well be overwhelmed by the number of choices associated with this new type of composition. For these students, getting started or working within particular modalities of composition may be difficult. Teachers can help both kinds of students through informal responses to projects—making sure that their responses are both rhetorically based and formative. This practice can be particularly important for multimodal assignments because students can be afraid to admit that they are overwhelmed by the new demands of composing in multiple media and modalities. Responding and assessing formatively as students are in the process of composing provides teachers with an invaluable source of information about how and where students are struggling, and when they most need additional instruction.

Within this context, teachers should plan a regular series of **studio review sessions**, during which students bring their projects to class so that both teachers and classmates can informally review and respond to these texts. In these sessions, teachers should model how to focus on rhetorically based questions about a text's purpose and audience, a student's sense of the rhetorical situation, and the effects of various organizational approaches and production techniques. Even students who feel comfortable with the new approaches to composing digital video or audio essays can use these more frequent formative assessment opportunities to make sure they are staying focused— in terms of their rhetorical goals—and that the projects are developing effectively as communicative texts.

Using Progress Journals for Formative Assessment

As students compose complex multimodal texts (and, indeed, complex texts of any sort) they often forget that an audience may lack the same experiences and understandings that they, themselves, have developed. When this situation does occur, and students create author-centered texts that ignore the needs of readers, revision can become a tedious and time-consuming process. The use of formative assessment activities—particularly when they are consistently informed by an awareness of rhetorical possibilities and constraints—helps give student authors frequent and focused feedback about where they need to develop their ideas in order to communicate effectively with a particular audience for a particular purpose.

As faculty engage in these frequent informal assessments of the multimodal essays, they may want to keep a **progress-assessment journal** in which they jot down notes about the progress individual students are making, as well as information from conferences and project observations. A systematic record with dated entries of encounters and thoughts on individual students' projects (see Fig. 8.3) can help teachers make more succinct and helpful comments based on past encounters. In Appendix 28, we provide one possible template for a teacher's progress-assessment journal.

Some teachers may also find it useful to assign students a **progress journal** (Fig. 8.4) in which they, too, can record their developing assessments of their own composing processes and products. In Appendix 29, we provide readers with one possible template for a student's progress log.

In the classroom contexts we have described, instructive assessment can become an even more important tool for students learning to compose multimodally—such approaches can help students become more aware of both their progress and limitations. This awareness has historical antecedents. In part, the power of the process movement in composition studies during the 1970s and 1980s, for example, was that it allowed writing to become a more visible activity. Having both instructors and students keep track of their ongoing assessments of multimodal projects can increase the visibility of rhetorical concerns and our appreciation for rhetorical theory in general— not only in connection to the processes of multimodal composing but to assessment processes as well. In other words, highlighting rhetorical concerns and possibilities as students compose *multimodal* texts can increase their understanding of rhetoric's explanatory power for *alphabetic* texts.

TEACHER'S PROGRESS-ASSESSMENT JOURNAL

STUDENT: Sarah Parker

Project: Video essay on dogs and the people who love them.

Purpose: To tell case-study stories of dog owners who have formed a special relation-ship with their pets.

In telling these stories, to provide people insights about how and why such relationships are important to humans.

Video will be used as fundraiser by the local animal shelter.

Audience: Donors to the animal shelter, potential pet owners, kids.

PROGRESS-ASSESSMENT NOTES:

1/18/04

Needs to complete video interviews with three human-pet pairs and download raw footage onto the computer.

Working on opening sequence of shots (people interacting with their dogs)—needs music that helps convey the tone of the interactions to the audience.

1/23/04

Interviews too long to keep audience's attention in a video. Focus editing on concise scenes in which owners identify what they get from their relationships with their dogs.

Show more of the dogs' responses to the humans—audience needs to see why the humans feel as they do.

Use voice over narration to set up the basics of each story.
Use owners' words to describe their relationships with pets.

FIGURE 8.3 Sample of informal notes from a teacher's progress-assessment journal

STUDENT'S PROGRESS JOURNAL

STUDENT: Sarah Parker

Project (purpose, audience, media, modalities):

Video for the animal Shelter. They want to use it to raise money and educate people about healthy relationships between people and dogs. Audiences are donors and school kids.

PROGRESS JOURNAL (focus on progress and rhetorical rationale for changes. Include date, hours spent on project):

1/16/04   1.15 hrs.

For first draft, downloaded first three video interviews. Second one is best. Use #3, but toss #1—won't work for kids. Folder/file name; <Dog Town/Cl Drive/Lab/Sarah>.

On Thurs. take some shots of kids at the shelter playing with dogs, show how crowed kennels are. Use this footage at the end.

1/18/04   2.35 hrs.

Changed scanned snapshots of Charlie and Fetch from color to black and white, used the aged-film effect to indicate snaps are history not now. Used cloned file to test—folder/file name <Dog Town2/Cl Drive/Lab/Sarah.2>. Need to get at least two more like these to use in segment.

Second draft—for Zeke's story about Sarah dying, found sad music to fade in and help indicate sadness/loss.

Reorganized the Sarah-Zeke sequence to clarify storyline for audience. At the end, inserted fade-out on picture of Sarah in her bed to show she died.

1/20/04   .40 hrs.

After studio critique in class, hanged ending to include shelter's address.

FIGURE 8.4 Sample page from a student's assessment journal

ONE EXAMPLE

Although we have outlined in general terms how important assessment can be in teaching multi-modal composition, we include an example here from a multimodal assignment that Sonya Borton uses for a first-year composition course focused on research and analysis of sources. This assignment is designed to be completed in groups, and each group is allowed to choose a topic from a list of approximately 30 topics, which changes on a frequent basis. Topics deal with subjects such as America's foster-care system, the future of agriculture in the United States, cyberwarfare, the depletion of oceanic species, wearable technology, and so on. Each group in the class is asked to present to the class some brief background on the topic and one possible solution to the problem or direction for the future. The audience for these presentations is identified as an interested community group: for example, Rotary Club, a City Council, or a funding foundation board. Research is a necessity, and a Works Cited page is required for each presentation. Groups choose the most effective medium for their presentations, and past presentations have included posters, scrapbooks, PowerPoint, and video essays, among other forms of communication. The goals of this assignment are to encourage students to think creatively in a collaborative environment, help them develop their research and documentation skills, and provide them with the opportunity to present their analysis of research in a group presentation that is rhetorically effective for their classmates.

When the assignment is announced, the class looks carefully at the teacher's goals for the assignment, discusses the rhetorical purpose of the group presentation, and thinks in practical ways about the needs of the audience. The class then uses their understanding of this rhetorical situation to develop a rhetorically informed rubric for the assignment (see Fig. 8.5).

Because these group projects require a great deal of work outside the classroom, formal class meetings are suspended until the assignments are due. During this time, groups are free to decide on the medium and the modalities they will use for their final presentation. Often these choices depend on the digital literacies and understandings that group members already possess and the access they have (or the teacher can help them have) to video- and audio-recording equipment.

Each group meets with the instructor on a weekly or twice weekly basis—depending on need—to discuss the group's progress, problems, and plans for the time remaining. During these meetings, the instructor and the group members provide an informal, instructive assessment of the group's progress using the first rubric developed as a guide, and someone in the group is required to take minutes of each meeting, which are turned in with the Works Cited page. The summative assessment of all projects is based on the amended rubric. The weekly meetings are also used to conduct formative reviews of the presentations themselves, focusing on a similar set of rhetorical concerns and questions—about the purpose, audience, organization, and tone of the composition, and the effective use of color, words, image, or sound—all of which we have mentioned in this chapter.

Right before the group projects are finished and presented, the class discusses the rubric again and revises it if needed (see Fig. 8.6). The summative assessment of all projects is based on the amended rubric.

This assignment usually proves to be the students' favorite of the semester. Although the rhetorically informed assessment process is fundamentally the same as it is for more conventional compositions, students enjoy choosing the media and modalities that make their presentations most effective, reviewing, the ongoing process of the presentations, and the collaborative atmosphere that is enhanced through the weekly assessment meetings.

SAMPLE GROUP-PRESENTATION RUBRIC

1-POOR	2-WEAK	3-AVERAGE	4-GOOD	5-EXCELLENT

Content & Organization of Presentation—50%

I. Critical Thinking Skills

    A. Analysis of topic assigned is effective for the audience and rhetorical purpose.

    B. Summary of relevant details is clear for the audience and rhetorical purpose.

    C. Composition demonstrates a synthesis of relevant details with composers' ideas and arguments in a way that makes the text an effective, rhetorical document.

    D. Composition shows a rhetorically informed understanding of topic, purpose, contexts of circulation, and audience.

Rating 1-5 ____ x5=____

II. Organization and Coherence

    A. Overall organization supports a controlling idea that is communicated clearly, appropriately, and in a rhetorically effective way for the audience.

    B. Coherence

        1. The authors use transitions to guide the audience through the composition. These transitions work effectively with the media and the modalities that are used, and the audience's expectations for/understandings of these media and modalities.

        2. The authors achieve overall unity for the presentation—given the media and the modalities that are used, and the audience's expectations for/understandings of these media and modalities.

Rating 1-5 ____ x5=____

Documentation Style and Source Materials—30%

I. Source Materials

    A. Researched sources are appropriate for achieving the rhetorical purpose of the presentation and help make the presentation credible for an audience.

    B. Synthesis of researched sources with composers' ideas and arguments help achieve the rhetorical purpose of the presentation and make the presentation credible for an audience.

Rating 1-5 ____ x3=____

II. Works Cited page produced is in the current MLA style.

Rating 1-5 ____ x3=____

Difficulty—20%

I. Level of difficulty represented by the medium and the modalities of composition

II. Level of difficulty associated with the issue

Rating 1-5 ____ x4=____

Total Grade: _____

FIGURE 8.5 Sample group-presentation rubric with rhetorically based criteria

REVISED GROUP-PRESENTATION RUBRIC

| 1-POOR | 2-WEAK | 3-AVERAGE | 4-GOOD | 5-EXCELLENT |

Content & Organization of Presentation—50%

I. Critical Thinking Skills

   A. Analysis of topic assigned is effective for the audience and rhetorical purpose.

   B. Summary of relevant details is clear for the audience and rhetorical purpose.

   C. Composition demonstrates a synthesis of relevant details with composers' ideas and arguments in a way that makes the text an effective, rhetorical document.

   D. Composition shows a rhetorically informed understanding of topic, purpose, and audience

Rating 1-5 ____x5=____

II. Organization and Coherence

   A. Overall organization supports a controlling idea that is communicated clearly, appropriately, and in a rhetorically effective way for the audience.

   B. Coherence

      1. The authors use transitions to guide the audience through the composition. These transitions work effectively with the media and the modalities that are used, and the audience's expectations for/understandings of these media and modalities.

      2. The authors achieve overall unity for the presentation—given the media and the modalities that are used, and the audience's expectations for/understandings of these media and modalities.

Rating 1-5 ____x5=____

Documentation Style and Source Materials—25%

I. Source Materials

   A. Researched sources are appropriate for achieving the rhetorical purpose of the presentation and help make the presentation credible for an audience.

   B. Synthesis of researched sources with composers' ideas and arguments help achieve the rhetorical purpose of the presentation and make the presentation credible for an audience.

   C. Works Cited page is produced in the current MLA style.

Rating 1-5 ____x5=____

Mode of Presentation—25%

I. Level of difficulty represented by the medium and the modalities of composition

II. Authors' choice of medium and the modalities as means of exploring the issue

III. Effectiveness of medium and modality in achieving audience engagement

Rating 1-5 ____x5=____

Total Grade: _____

FIGURE 8.6 Sample revised group-presentation rubric with rhetorically based criteria

WHEN IS THE COMPOSITION "COMPLETE"?

Because students become so invested in multimodal compositions, it may be difficult for them to find a stopping point for their efforts. From our experience, there is always one more thing that can be changed or added or moved. Although some version of this problem exists with alphabetic essays, the expanded range of choices that multimodal essays present can exacerbate the tendency toward perpetual revision. In addition, students' and teachers' limited understanding of the genre can also makes closure difficult. Finally, the learning curve for some multimodal software can make it more difficult to decide that a composition is, indeed, finished. By the time some students learn an audio- or video-editing program, for example, they have invested a great deal of time on their composition.

In such circumstances, revising a composition, trying to perfect it, may become even more important to students. Hence, the most important elements of a rhetorically informed, instructive assessment can be the flexible set of in-progress deadlines a teacher sets for the composing process and the final due date identified for a project. Both teachers and students need to remember that effective learning goes on even when every project may not be as perfect as they would like it to be.

CONCLUSION

Throughout this book we have tried to convey the sense of enjoyment and engagement that teachers can get from working with students on multimodal texts. To make these projects as successful as possible, we have made a series of recommendations for teachers. Among these, we recommend that teachers understand their own rationale for wanting to use multimodal texts in the classroom. We also recommend that teachers make rhetorically based, instructive assessment a visible part of every class (see Fig. 8.7), and that they remind themselves of the importance of assessing their own decisions and practices associated within every composition class. Multimodal texts can offer important sites in which students learn rhetorically based composing processes and a rhetorical understanding of the design principles inherent in all effective communications.

In assessing multimodal texts, teachers need not find themselves at a loss, nor should they resign themselves to starting from scratch. Smart teachers will use what they already know about rhetorical theory and practice to assess multimodal texts effectively They will use what they already know about both formative and summative evaluation to help students assess their own work and the work of others. Common pedagogical practices, such as compiling and using assessment criteria or creating rubrics for evaluating compositions, can work as well or better in a multimodal classroom as they do in a more conventional classroom—especially if they are informed by rhetorical theory. In the end, however, we believe that those teachers who have struggled with composing multimodal texts themselves will be the most effective in assessing the challenges presented by such projects, designing assignments and classroom activities that address these challenges, and understanding students' efforts to compose rhetorically successful texts.

TEACHERS' TIPS FOR RHETORICALLY BASED
INSTRUCTIVE ASSESSMENT OF MULTIMODAL PROJECTS

- Determine your rhetorical purpose for this assignment.

- Get experience creating your own multimodal project.

- Focus all assessment efforts—both formative and summative—around criteria that are rhetorically informed.

- Make both formative and summative assessment efforts instructive for students and base them on rhetorical criteria.

- Involve students in identifying and assessing these rhetorically based assessment criteria for multimodal compositions.

- Make yourself available for informal consultations during the composing process.

- Have students bring their multimodal compositions to class on a regular basis during the composing process.

- Spend class time reviewing each project and responding to them with rhetorically informed questions.

- Help students practice assessing their own and others' texts by asking rhetorically based questions about multimodal compositions during class reviews of projects.

- Keep a journal or log of your ongoing formative assessments of students' compositions. Encourage students to keep a similar journal in which they assess their own progress on an ongoing basis.

- Set a series of deadlines for specific parts of each multimodal composing project and a firm due date for finished compositions.

FIGURE 8.7 Rhetorically based instructive assessment in the multimodal classroom

REFERENCES

Huot, B. (2002). Toward a new discourse of assessment for the college writing classroom. *College English, 65*(2), 163-180.

Moran, C., & Herrington, A. (2003). Evaluating academic hypertexts. In P. Takayoshi & B. Huot (Eds.), *Teaching writing with computers: An introduction* (pp. 247-257). Boston: Houghton Mifflin.

Selfe, C. (1999). *Technology and literacy in the twenty-first century: The importance of paying attention.* Carbondale: Southern Illinois University Press.

Sirc, G. (2002). *English composition as a happening.* Logan: Utah State University Press.

Takayoshi, P. (1996). The shape of electronic writing: Evaluating and assessing computer-assisted writing processes and products. *Computers and Composition, 13,* 245-258.

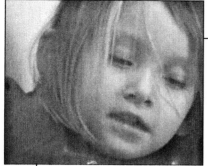

Literacy Practices and Literacy Events, Kara Poe Alexander

CHAPTER 9
More about Reading, Responding, and Revising: The Three Rs of Peer Review and Revision

Kara Poe Alexander

The media, contexts, and purposes of multimodal compositions can range greatly and need not be limited to digital audio or video assignments like those outlined in Chapter 2. Indeed, multimodal work can take the form of comic strips or web pages, children's books or video essays, PowerPoint presentations or posters. In this chapter, we offer teachers another sample assignment (Fig. 9.1) that leaves open not only author's choice of medium (e.g., paper, computer, human voice), but also modality (e.g., words, images, sound, color), and genre of texts (e.g., pamphlet, advertisement, political speech, web site).

In fact, the great range of projects that can take advantage of multiple modalities presents a unique set of challenges when students bring in their projects to be reviewed by peers, as well as when they revise their projects based on the comments from studio reviews. This chapter sheds some additional light on the complex issues of *peer-review studio sessions* (formal review sessions in which student authors present their work to the class and receive feedback from their peers, as well as from the teacher) and *revision* (which entails students considering the feedback they received during peer-review studio sessions and revising their projects accordingly) within the context of a multimodal composition course.

Although both of these processes—peer review and revision—figure into the composing of conventional alphabetic texts, they may look and feel very different for multimodal essays. Partly because of the complex material nature of such texts, peer review may present new challenges to teachers, challenges that differ from those associated with more conventional essays. In addition, students may find that revising such texts—including the essays we describe in this chapter—may not be as quick or, in some ways, as simple as making changes to an alphabetic essay that requires only the use of a word-processing package. For example, the work involved in composing a *draft* of a photo essay, a collage, or a scrapbook essay, and in *revising* such a text in response to peer-review and revision suggestions, may require changes to words, still photographs, images, and color schemes; several software packages (e.g., photo-manipulation, word-processing, page-layout); and several composing tools or pieces of equipment (e.g., a camera, computer, stamps, scrapbook). With multimodal texts, then, peer review and revision may be complicated by both the range of genres available to student authors and the materiality of texts. Because of this additional complexity, teachers and students will need to plan ahead about how both to present texts to others and then revise texts after studio review sessions.

TECHNOLOGY AND LITERACY IN YOUR FUTURE

Literacy activities occur in more places than English class and the school environment, and these practices assume an increasing variety of forms. Although literacy and learning might be the focus in these environments, reading, writing, and communication activities occur in the majority of work environments, no matter where you are or what you're doing. From reading emails, memos, reports, and technical documents to writing prescriptions, screenplays, and journal articles; from composing music, designing web sites, and building a home, to writing an editorial, a sermon, or a dissenting opinion, literacy abounds in all walks of life. Because I want you to realize and learn what to expect when you are confronted with these activities in the future, I want you to learn now, as a first-year student, the predominant literacy activities that you will face as a future employee in your job of choice. I also want you to inform an audience of interested high school students about these literacy practices.

GOALS:

- To make you and your audience—a group of interested high school students who are considering various careers—aware of the different literacies you will face in your career

- To expose you to different modalities of reading and composing

CONTENT:

You are to compose an original essay that informs your audience of the reading, writing, and technological activities that you will participate in once you leave college and join the workforce. Consider all forms of communication that happens in the progression you choose: words, images, video, audio, art, etc.

RESEARCH COMPONENTS:

- **Personal Interview/primary research** (required)—you will need to interview a person who is working in your major field. He or she needs to be in a position that you would like to hold.

- **Secondary research** (required)—you may conduct secondary research to learn more about this career.

- **Field research** (optional)—you may also observe this person "at work." In other words, you can watch how he/she operates on the job to gain additional insight into the profession.

Using some of the interview and profile strategies we have discussed in class, as well as our discussions on literacy and technology, you should thoroughly and convincingly describe:

1. What type of reading, writing, and technological activities occur?

2. How often do they occur?

3. In what context do they occur?

4. What are the purposes of these activities?

5. How much you still need to learn before you can be an active participant in these literate activities?

FIGURE 9.1 Sample multimodal assignment that does not require digital tools or environments

This composition can take any shape or form—the only requirement is that it must be a *multi-modal* essay, which is (in this assignment) one that combines two or more modalities of composing, such as audio texts, video texts, still photography, printed text, images, line art, web documents, animations, and so on.

Your essay should have the following characteristics:

- The essay should employ the affordances (capabilities) of the modalities you are using in effective rhetorical ways.

- The essay should help high school students think in informed ways about their choice of careers.

- The essay/project should be appropriate for an audience of high school students.

- The essay should add information value to our discussion of literacy issues/themes.

- The essay should be instructive, that is, inventive/creative/insightful.

- The essay should do more than simply inform us about the literacy demands of your career; it should also help readers/viewers reflect on/gain insight into the subject/career.

IDEAS FOR FINDING A PERSON TO INTERVIEW:

You could visit businesses, schools, hospitals, courthouses, and so on, where you would like to work in the future. You could use connections provided by family and friends to set up an appointment and interviews. You could also talk to a professor in your major field and get some ideas from him/her about whom you can contact and who might be willing to help you. (Though professors have experience in fields related to their scholarly work, you should not use them as your interview resource, unless you want to be a college professor.) You need to interview someone who is *currently* working in a certain field. *If you have questions or concerns about finding a person/place on which to focus, please see me and we can brainstorm possibilities together.*

NOTE FOR UNDECIDED MAJORS:

Some of you have not yet selected a major field of study. In this case, I would advise you to think of a few different fields that interest you and then narrow that down to one. Even if you decide not to enter the particular field that you study here, your essay will still inform you and your readers about the options and literacy activities required.

REQUIREMENTS:

- The main requirement is that you *compose* some sort of multimodal essay that profiles literacy practices and values in your future career.

- Because of the freedom you have in this assignment, I'm not setting a required length. If you have questions about whether or not you think your project is sufficient lengthwise, ask me, and we can work something out together.

PEER REVIEW: Peer Review date: April 12.

After peer review, you will have one week to revise this essay. Because you are working in various modes, revising will take much longer than a traditional essay. Be prepared to work most

FIGURE 9.1 Sample multimodal assignment that does not require digital tools or environments
(continued)

of the week revising this essay in accordance with the guidelines of this assignment and the suggestions you were given during the peer review.

DEADLINES:

Teacher Draft due date: <u>April 19</u>

EVALUATION:

I will be evaluating your project based on the following criteria:

- Evidence of carefully planning and completing all assignment requirements
- Value of the information
- Reflective focus
- Use of the affordances of the appropriate medium
- Creative/Insightful project

FIGURE 9.1 Sample multimodal assignment that does not require digital tools or environments
(*continued*)

ENCOURAGING EFFECTIVE PEER-REVIEW STUDIO SESSIONS AND REVISION FOR MULTIMODAL COMPOSING

In the following section, teachers will find eleven tips for shaping peer-review studio sessions in multimodal composition classes. The goal is to provide some practical advice for teachers who are thinking about incorporating these sessions into their courses. The suggestions overlap and are recursive. They are not meant to be followed in a linear, step-by-step manner.

Because teachers and students in various situations may lack access to digital audio recorders and digital video cameras, this chapter also assumes that teachers might want to encourage and incorporate additional kinds of multimodal essays into their classrooms—essays that may be composed with the *help of computers* (e.g., word-processing packages, photo-manipulation programs, the web), *but are not necessarily composed entirely within digital environments*. Therefore, the assignment outlined in this chapter extends beyond the sample assignments provided in Chapter 2 of this text to include multimodal compositions in the form of collages, comic strips, scrapbooks, brochures, charts and graphs, PowerPoint presentations, and web pages, to name just a few alternative genres.

 Tip #1: Provide students with examples of the kinds of projects called for by the assignment; discuss genre characteristics, modalities and affordances; purposes and audiences, strengths and shortcomings

As students begin work on their multimodal projects, teachers will need to spend time showing them sample projects in class. Teachers can present several projects on one day, or devote a smaller amount of class time on different days to displaying individual projects. If possible, these projects should include compositions authored by students and those that employ the modalities in which class members will be asked to compose. For instance, if an assignment offers students the chance to compose a comic strip as an option, several examples of comic strips with a range of purposes and audiences should be shown to students; the rhetorical genre of comic strips and its social/cultural characteristics should be discussed; and reader expectations for comic strips should be analyzed. Although the sample projects may not follow the parameters of the upcoming assignment *exactly*, teachers can use these discussions to help students identify how the author has used the *affordances*, or special capabilities, of the text's modalities in effective or less effective ways. If an assignment leaves modality open, teachers will want to show a range of projects that feature those from which students will be choosing.

After each project is shown, teachers will want to model the elements of a productive peer review—focusing on how, where, and why each project succeeds and falls short; how and where each author uses the affordances of modalities effectively or misses doing so; and making productive and concrete suggestions for a possible revision. Importantly, this process of showing examples of completed projects and reviewing their successes and shortcomings not only provides students with new ideas for their own essays and suggests a range of possibilities for multimodal composing, but also acquaints students with the basic components and structures of formal studio-review sessions. During these early sessions, students become familiar with the vocabulary of multimodality and get a sense of how to respond to the efforts of their peers' compositions. Many students will lack experience composing in modalities other than words and will need to know what to look for and how to respond to their peer's work in constructive ways. This preliminary review of projects will also help alleviate some of students' apprehensions about multimodal assignments.

If teachers are showing sample projects by student authors in these preliminary sessions, they should be sure to have written release/consent forms on file, giving permission to use the essays in this manner and to clear this activity with their institutional review board (IRB).

 Tip #2: Conduct both formal and informal peer-review studio sessions throughout the term to provide students with formative feedback

Informed feedback from both teachers and fellow students is essential in classrooms that ask students to produce multimodal compositions—especially because students may not have had extensive experience in authoring such pieces.

Conducting several peer-review studio sessions during the course of an assignment—especially sessions focused on rhetorically based feedback (Chapter 8) is one useful way to help students shape their multimodal essays. These sessions also help ensure that potential problems are identified as early as possible and that students are following the assignment's guidelines. Several rounds of peer-review feedback can also help provide students with a clear idea of what is expected in their final products.

We can provide three suggestions for integrating peer review into the multimodal classroom:

- Teachers should schedule class time for both informal peer reviews of projects and more formal peer-review sessions.

- Students should take the responsibility of seeking ongoing formative responses to works-in-progress throughout the course of an assignment, rather than limiting their responses solely to formal studio review sessions.

- For formal peer-review studio sessions, students should sign up to bring their projects into class. In these more formal sessions, the entire class focuses on one project at a time and provides rhetorically based responses both verbally and in writing to the student author. The teacher also participates in such sessions—modeling how to focus responses on rhetorically based criteria (Chapter 8). Students should take notes during these sessions and, from them, make plans for revising.

Tip #3: Explain peer-review expectations and project expectations to students.

In this chapter, we provide advice about how to focus formative responses (both from peers and from teachers) on rhetorically based criteria: what works and what fails to work *for a particular audience*, what elements of a multimodal project helps or hinders it from achieving *its specific purpose*, and how the author uses the affordances (the capabilities) of various modalities and media effectively or ineffectively *to achieve a purpose* within a specific rhetorical context.

To help students focus on such rhetorically based feedback, teachers need to make clear the goals of peer-review sessions, their structure and procedures, and the ways in which students are expected to use feedback in revising their projects.

One way to help students understand their responsibilities during peer-review sessions—in which they learn to provide formative feedback to others and consider such feedback in connection with their own texts—is to involve them in creating **assessment criteria sheets** for assignments. To assure that feedback is instructive—in terms of focusing on rhetorically informed criteria—we suggest that teachers encourage a focus on such topics as *the purpose of the project* and how that is addressed in both modality and medium; the *audience for the composition*, their expectations and experiences with various modalities, and their needs; the information the composition is meant to convey; and *the effectiveness of arrangement, organization, and affordances in light of the rhetorical context* and the rhetorical demands of the systems of circulation within which multimodal texts will be distributed. Ideally, the criteria on these feedback sheets will be used in a revised form to serve the purposes of summative assessment when the assignment is completed.

Students will find such feedback sheets helpful both as they compose and revise their own texts, and as they participate in peer-review sessions focused on others' work. Figure 9.2 provides one example of a rhetorically focused feedback sheet for the sample assignment featured earlier in the chapter.

To prepare students for participating in productive peer-review studio sessions, teachers will want to emphasize the need to be prepared, professional, and constructive in terms of feedback. As extensions of these three behaviors, students should be encouraged to identify both those elements that are working well within the rhetorical context of the multimodal composition and those that are working less effectively.

It is also useful to remind students of how much time, energy, and creativity goes into multimodal projects. If audio- or video-recording and editing are involved, for instance, the ratio of finished product to work time is 1:200. That is, for every 1 minute of a finished audio or video essay, an author puts in 200 minutes of authoring and production time. And this is a conservative estimate. Given this context, teachers and peers alike must be sure to point out the wonderful, creative, and insightful parts of the texts that authors share in peer-review studio sessions.

Of course, the very best gift to authors is constructive feedback. In peer-review studio sessions, the students should be encouraged to

- Start with what works well in the essay (before going on to talk about what doesn't work so well).

- Focus feedback on *rhetorical* criteria (criteria based on a clear understanding of the audience, purpose, content, and form of the essay under consideration).

- Talk about personal understandings and responses to a piece, your response as an individual reader of—or listener to—a text (rather than making claims about how all audience members will respond to a piece).

PEER FEEDBACK ON RHETORICAL CRITERIA FOR MULTIMODAL ASSIGNMENT

1. **Evidence of careful planning for the rhetorical task and context. Project meets the audience's needs. Modality and medium fits well with audience's expectations and experiences. Student has shaped the project for a specific circulation/distribution context.**

   | 1 | 2 | 3 | 4 | 5 |

   Minimally Successful   Of Average Success   Successful in a Major Way

   Comments about what works well and what does not:

2. **Completion of all assignment requirements: two or more genres, interview, literacy activities, contexts, purposes, diagnosis.**

   | 1 | 2 | 3 | 4 | 5 |

   Minimally Successful   Of Average Success   Successful in a Major Way

   Comments about what works and what does not:

3. **Value of the information (about reading, writing, technology and chosen job) for the intended audience.**

   | 1 | 2 | 3 | 4 | 5 |

   Minimally Successful   Of Average Success   Successful in a Major Way

   Comments about what works and what does not:

4. **Author achieves the assignment's purpose of creating a reflective focus that adds in significant and informed ways to classmates' conversation about literacy.**

   | 1 | 2 | 3 | 4 | 5 |

   Minimally Successful   Of Average Success   Successful in a Major Way

   Comments about what works and what does not:

5. **Attention to needs of audience/readers.**

   | 1 | 2 | 3 | 4 | 5 |

   Minimally Successful   Of Average Success   Successful in a Major Way

   Comments about what works and what does not:

FIGURE 9.2 Sample feedback sheet

6. **Purposeful and careful composition (arrangement, organization, style), thematic selection, and aesthetic coherence within the rhetorical context.**

| 1 | 2 | 3 | 4 | 5 |

Minimally Successful   Of Average Success   Successful in a Major Way

Comments about what works and what does not:

7. **Appropriate attention to affordances of modalities and media within a rhetorical context.**

| 1 | 2 | 3 | 4 | 5 |

Minimally Successful   Of Average Success   Successful in a Major Way

Comments about what works and what does not:

8. **Appropriate documentation of images, audio, video, and other source material.**

| 1 | 2 | 3 | 4 | 5 |

Minimally Successful   Of Average Success   Successful in a Major Way

Comments about what works well and what does not:

9. **Creativity of project within constraints of the rhetorical context**

| 1 | 2 | 3 | 4 | 5 |

Minimally Successful   Of Average Success   Successful in a Major Way

Comments about what works and what does not:

10. **Appropriate attention to issues of clarity (style, grammar, and punctuation) for rhetorical context.**

| 1 | 2 | 3 | 4 | 5 |

Minimally Successful   Of Average Success   Successful in a Major Way

Comments about what works and what does not:

Total Number of Points: _____ **Project Grade:** _____

FIGURE 9.2 Sample feedback sheet (*continued*)

- Focus on the project itself (rather than on the author/composer of the text).

- Offer help (contributing a piece of music that may be more appropriate, identifying a source of photographic images, pointing out a useful web site, offer to help teach someone an application).

Teachers might want to remind students of these points before beginning a peer-review studio session. These guidelines are outlined, along with other suggestions, in Table 9.1.

A key difficulty students can have during studio sessions is not knowing how to respond to drafts. Students have no difficulty *watching* a video, *viewing* a photography exhibit and *reading* curatorial comments, *browsing through* a creative scrapbook, or *hearing* a new audio project, but *they may not know what to say* in response to these multimodal texts—or how to help their peers make them better. One tip teachers can give students is to pretend they are the specified audience for that text, and then *read* the text from that perspective. From this position, students can talk about how the text works, or fails to work, for them personally. Teachers will also want to play most audio or video projects twice to ensure that class members get plenty of time to focus on the elements they contain. Of course, for some teachers time does not permit multiple studio reviews of every project by the whole class. In such cases, teachers can consider splitting students into smaller groups and having them conduct peer-review studio sessions of projects in their own groups. We talk more about this option later in the chapter.

TABLE 9.1
GUIDELINES FOR CONDUCT DURING STUDIO SESSIONS

BEHAVIOR	ACTIONS
Preparedness	• Talk to students about the processes of drafting—>review—>redrafting. • Work with students to identify rhetorically based criteria for peer-review. • Schedule enough time to show/air audio/video projects twice. • Help students think about ways to prepare drafts for peer reviews. • Help students become familiar with the affordances (Appendix 31) of various modalities so that they can offer more informed responses. • Remind students to have their assignment sheet with them as they review each other's essays, and take written notes, so that they can continually refer back to the rhetorical context (goals, purposes, content, genre, etc.) and guidelines for the assignment. • Help students use rhetorically based criteria to guide their responses to texts.
Professionalism	• Praise first; critique second. • Focus responses on the project, not the individual author. • Focus on personal response to the project and avoid generalizing to others.
Constructive Responses	• Offer concrete, specific suggestions. • Suggestions should be keyed to rhetorically based criteria. • Focus on concrete strategies for improving the project. • Respond from a *reader's* point of view. • Offer to help (contribute more appropriate music, suggest a source for still photographs, offer to teach an application).

During a peer-review studio session, it is useful to follow a few basic procedures. First, all students—except the authors—should take notes on some kind of feedback sheet (see Fig. 9.3), so that their important feedback will not be lost to the author. Authors should be encouraged to give a very short introduction to their project and then remain mostly silent while the rest of the class holds an oral discussion about the project's strengths and where it can be revised to make it even better. At the end of the session, authors should be encouraged to ask questions about how their projects are read by the audience and which elements seem to be working well. This approach keeps student authors from responding immediately and defensively to constructive observations made by others about their work.

Most teachers will also find it beneficial to give students a peer-response form that they can use as they review each project and write notes to the author. Such feedback sheets guide peer-response for students and provide authors with tangible suggestions for revising their multimodal composition. If a whole class participates in a peer-review studio session, authors will have a range of valuable responses. These forms will vary, of course, depending on the context and specific goals and purposes of an assignment. Figure 9.3 provides a second sample of a peer-response form. This form is simple and uses very broad, open-ended prompts for peer feedback: Strengths/What I Liked, Suggestions for Improvement, and Other Comments or Ideas. If the class can remain focused on the rhetorical context of individual assignments (e.g., their purpose, audience, content, and form), such open-ended peer-response forms can be effective for a wide range of different kinds of compositions. Such forms provide students the freedom to focus on the areas of individual compositions they find most interesting and provide feedback on whatever features of the project they consider most important. Some teachers find that the more complex peer-review sheets are, the less feedback students will give. In such cases, students have a tendency to focus on answering the questions identified on the sheet even when these are not immediately applicable rather than providing meaningful and constructive suggestions to the author. In contrast, broad, open-ended prompts can allow students freedom to respond to numerous and diverse areas of the project.

Providing students with a peer-review form also allows them to respond both *during* and *after* a presentation rather than having to remember all their comments until after a project has been fully read/shown/aired. Some projects can be quite lengthy, and although summary comments can be valuable to authors as a reflection of the piece's overall impact, more local and immediate comments that address a small element or part of a project can also be useful.

Explaining the expectations for peer-review studio sessions also means that teachers should reveal how much revision they expect to occur based on the feedback authors receive. Some teachers, for instance, expect students to incorporate most of the comments from peer-review studio sessions into their revised drafts. Other teachers may encourage students to be more selective about the suggestions to which they respond. In any case, faculty need to let students know their expectations so that authors can plan accordingly.

  Tip #4: Help students think about how to present their projects in peer-review studio sessions.

Assignments that allow students a wide range of options sometimes present them with unusual challenges during peer-review studio sessions. In particular, students often have difficulties figuring out how best to present drafts of their projects to the class—particularly projects that might involve complexly constructed documents with many parts (e.g., scrapbooks, comic strips, and collages). In many cases, these difficulties have to do with three primary factors: *how finished* such a project can be in a draft stage, *what elements to fix permanently in place* before a studio review, and how best to present and circulate a multimodal project so that students and the teacher can provide useful and productive feedback.

Author: _____

Type of Project (audio, video, collage, etc.): _____

Date: _____

Strengths/What I Liked:

Suggestions for Improvement:

Other Comments or Ideas:

Your Name (responder): _____

FIGURE 9.3 Open-ended peer-review form

A comic strip, for example, might need to be fairly detailed and complete before readers can see and understand it as a draft text. Revisions of such a text can entail extensive work. Thus, teachers will need to help students prepare for the feedback and revision process: suggesting that the strip be completed in pencil, for instance, and that individual panels be rendered, photocopied, and circulated on separate pages so that the revision of one panel won't affect work already completed on others.

Scrapbooks and collages can present similar challenges. The individual pieces of ephemera and materials used within such projects—once they are affixed on a page—are difficult to move, change, or alter without making much larger changes. Students composing such texts face a difficult situation: they want to get the most accurate and complete feedback possible during peer review; however, knowing that changes will need to be made, they must keep their project in a semi-fluid state until the peer-review has been completed. Teachers can help in such situations by emphasizing the recursive processes of drafting—>review—>redrafting that characterizes all projects, and reminding students early in the assignment cycle to remain flexible when creating drafts of their texts: for example, mounting photographs temporarily on draft-quality paper (so that these images can be removed and resequenced) and storing annotations in a word-processing program (so these can be revised). However, students should also be encouraged to produce a draft that is as close as they can come, at that point in time, to a final text: for instance, using the same color scheme in the draft of a scrapbook as they will for the final text (in order to gauge the audience's response to color as a modality) or, for a collage, circulating color photocopies of all images that will be included in the final draft (so that readers can see details of each image's composition).

In some cases, teachers do not have the time or resources to teach their students how to use certain technologies, such as audio, video, or web pages. In such situations, teachers should consider being somewhat more open about the revision requirements due to the extensive time required—inside and outside of class—to revise in various modes. If a classroom does not provide access to software that students are using in their projects, it is important to think about how much revision we should really expect from our students.

 Tip #5: Teachers should schedule peer-review studio sessions well ahead of time and participate actively in both formal and informal reviews of compositions.

To provide students with a strong sense of expectations for their final projects—and their revision efforts—teachers should participate in the peer-review process, both during formal and informal sessions. When teachers can provide students with shorter informal reviews, for instance, they help reassure authors that that they are on the right track with a particular project. When teachers participate in more formal peer-review studio sessions, they help the whole class to understand expectations for final projects.

Although many composition teachers now downplay final grades of assignments by foregrounding the learning that goes on at various points of the composing process, students still understand that, ultimately, teachers will assign a grade to their projects or their portfolio, and that these grades may figure significantly in an assessment of their performance within a course. The usual concerns that accrue to such an understanding may be exacerbated, moreover, by the fact that students may have little experience with teachers' expectations for projects involving audio, video, and other modalities beyond the alphabetic.

To address such concerns, teachers will want to offer students as many informal and formal occasions for reviews of their projects as possible within the constraints of a course schedule. To make peer-review sessions—formal or informal—as productive and successful as possible, teachers should schedule these sessions well ahead of time and let students know when they are coming.

Teachers will also want to take some of the considerations listed in Table 9.2 under advisement when planning more formal peer-review studio sessions.

 Tip #6: The range of media and modalities used for an assignment may shape the structure of peer-review studio sessions.

As we compose this book, we know well that readers will vary widely in the media and support resources they have available at their institution, within their program or department, and for their particular classes. Some teachers may have access to enough computers, digital video cameras and audio recorders, software packages, and technical staff to support an entire class. Other teachers, with access to less equipment, may need to design assignments that allow students to work in small groups or in multiple media and modalities so that the demands on any one kind of equipment are minimized. In Table 9.3, we identify some of the advantages and disadvantages of both approaches.

TABLE 9.2
THINGS TO CONSIDER BEFORE SCHEDULING A PEER-REVIEW STUDIO SESSION

❖ Determine the primary purposes for each peer-review studio session.

- Do students need feedback early on in the process to help direct their projects from the beginning and help them glean ideas from the projects of their peers?
- Do students need a review of almost-completed projects? What expectations for revision should shape such peer-review sessions?
- Do students need feedback throughout their composing processes? What kind of review is most productive? When?

❖ How will whole-class peer-review studio sessions be structured?

- Will every peer reviewer be able to respond both verbally and in writing? Is there time? If so, how long does the class have to discuss each project?
- Is there time to air audio/video projects twice so that the class can attend to the important elements?
- Will every peer reviewer be able to respond both verbally and in writing? Is there time?
- What special equipment/rooms are needed to display/project/air projects? Can they be scheduled?
- Should students be scheduled by the teacher for a studio session, or should they be allowed to volunteer for a particular session themselves?
- What peer-feedback criteria will be used? Have students participated in identifying criteria?
- What comments should authors make? Should they be limited?
- Should additional audience members be invited for projects that have identified an audience outside of the teachers and/or the class? Should these audience members participate in writing feedback? Should students invite these people? Or should the teacher?
- How will the teacher participate in the peer-review studio sessions?
- How much time will students have to revise after they are provided with peer-review suggestions?
- What are the expectations for revision of projects after peer reviews?

❖ How will small-group studio sessions for peer reviews be structured?

- Which students are working in the same media and modalities? Are there natural groupings of students who can respond to each other's projects?
- Should peer-review studio sessions for small groups involve additional audience members who provide feedback?
- Should small-group studio sessions be held in class? Should class be cancelled so that studio sessions can be conducted in the teacher's office?
- Does it matter if small groups are evenly balanced in number? With regard to students' abilities? Personalities?
- How will the teacher participate in the peer-review studio sessions?
- How much time will students have to revise after they are provided with peer-review suggestions?
- What are the expectations for revision of projects *after* peer reviews are completed?

Teachers can also decide to combine small- and large-group approaches, scheduling several, less formal small-group feedback sessions before scheduling one, whole-class session in which students get to see each other's projects.

If students are working in a wide range of modalities, teachers may want to use small groups for peer-review studio sessions. Small groups often work best when students who are working on similar projects or in similar modalities can work together. Teachers may encounter a situation, for instance, in which two students want to create a video for a public service announcement, three want to compose a scrapbook of a famous alumnus, four others want to design comic strips that teach key concepts in a field of study, and several others want to create a photography exhibit with curatorial comments for a campus display space. In such a class, small group peer-review studio sessions may work best for providing formal and informal feedback on projects. In this situation, it is best to group all of those working on the video together in one group, those creating the scrapbook in another, and so on.

Small groups are particularly valuable if students are working on projects that are difficult to circulate and show to a large audience—for example, a comic strip, a children's book, or a scrapbook. In addition, smaller groups that are working within one medium and with similar modalities can be useful because students become increasingly familiar with the affordances of the modalities and the media with which they are working. Once they have thought about the issues of affordances, students can give increasingly constructive feedback to their peers. Smaller groups may also help some students gain confidence before they present their projects to a larger group of people. Teachers who use small groups for peer-feedback sessions may want to schedule work days for the rest of the class and, if possible, meet with small groups to review projects.

Small groups—especially when they are working on a wide range of projects—can be difficult for teachers to schedule, manage, and track, however. So teachers should schedule carefully and plan ahead. When forming smaller groups for peer-based collaborative work, some teachers may want to identify students who have more experience with specific technologies so that these individuals can help the members of their small group learn to make use of certain pieces of equipment.

Some teachers who read this book may have access to enough resources to allow all the students in a class to work on the same kind of project or assignment—and enough time to allow whole-class studio reviews of projects in various stages of being drafted. This arrangement is ideal, for example, when everyone in the class can work on an audio or video assignment such as the one we offer in Chapter 2 of this book. Studio sessions that involve the whole class in providing peer-review feedback provide authors with a wider range of feedback from more people. Large-group peer-review sessions also allow the entire class to hear the teacher's feedback and, thus, adjust their own expectations and responses to classmates' projects. Although these larger sessions take more time, they may also be easier for teachers to schedule.

For some students, however, whole-class studio sessions can be intimidating and frightening. In such sessions, feedback seems increasingly public. As a result, students who are shy or lack confidence may view them with an increased level of anxiety for which teachers can plan. To help ameliorate such feelings, teachers can prepare the class—providing examples of how to phrase and deliver feedback constructively, focus on suggestions that will improve a project, understand feedback within the context of a specific rhetorical situation, and select the comments that will provide a focus for productive revision efforts.

 Tip #7: Take every opportunity to remind students of the assignment and encourage them to think in rhetorical ways.

This point is especially important when students are composing in media and modalities that are new to them as authors. In such situations, when students must learn new technologies as they

TABLE 9.3
GROUP SIZE FOR PEER-REVIEW STUDIO SESSIONS

SMALL GROUP PEER REVIEW	WHOLE CLASS PEER REVIEW
Use when resources are scare and must be carefully managed, when students are working in a wide range of media and modalities, or when projects cannot be shown to the whole class at once. Group students with similar projects together.	Use when sufficient resources are available for the entire class and when all students are working on similar kinds of projects.
Advantages: • Students are familiar with the media and modalities being used—and their affordances. • Projects that are hard to show/share can be seen by a small group. • On a smaller scale, students can get ideas from one another and from the teacher for use in revising. • Students can gain confidence in composing by receiving feedback in a small-group setting. • Teachers can focus on one group at a time and schedule work sessions for students who are not participating in a peer review.	*Advantages:* • All students are familiar with the media and modalities being used—and their affordances. • Projects can be seen by the entire class using presentation or projection devices. • Students can get ideas from every member of the class and from the teacher for use in revising. • Students receive a broader range of feedback from all members of the class. • The teacher can schedule one series of peer-review studio sessions. • Students can observe as the teacher models studio feedback procedures and uses specialized vocabulary.
Disadvantages: • Peer reviews for smaller groups can be more difficult to schedule, manage, and track.	*Disadvantages:* • Some students may find it difficult to show their work to so many people and to receive public feedback.

compose, it is easy to forget about the rhetorical situation that gives a text shape and substance—the purpose, audience, information, and genre of a composition. In addition, both teachers and students can get caught up in grappling with the new formats available to them within a multimodal composing assignment while forgetting about the project's purpose, audience, format, or context of circulation.

For teachers, the best remedy for such a situation is to give students *an authentic rhetorical context for composing that extends beyond the classroom.* This can be accomplished by designing assignments that ask students to compose for audiences other than the teacher, for purposes that are important outside the classroom (as well as inside), and in genres that convey information effectively within specified contexts of circulation.

Teachers will also want to think reflectively about the rhetorical issues that inform multimodal assignments—early and often—and encourage students to do so as they compose. Table 9.4 illustrates some questions that both teachers and students can consider to help maintain a focus on the rhetorical context of multimodal assignments.

 Tip #8 During peer-review studio sessions, focus teacher feedback on three to five issues of primary rhetorical concern.

As students can attest, revising compositions after peer-review studio sessions can be challenging. This can be especially true with multimodal compositions, given the range of elements with which students are working. In revising a photographic exhibit with curatorial comments, for instance, students may have to retake some pictures with a camera to frame shots differently or to change their focus; use a photo-manipulation program to alter some of the pictures in the exhibit; use a web browser to conduct additional research; and use a word-processing program to rewrite some of the curatorial comments.

Although composing technologies will continue to change and revising multimodal compositions will become increasingly easy in some technical senses, some of the challenges of authoring effective compositions to achieve a given rhetorical purpose will, doubtless, remain. For this reason, the very best approach that both teachers and students can take to multimodal composing is to engage in rhetorically focused decision making so that all composing and revision efforts are undertaken with a specific goal in mind.

Within this framework, teachers can work to create assignments that open up authentic purposes for students to compose and realistic audiences for them to address, providing students the choice of interesting information to convey and contemporary genres to use. And students can be charged with paying attention to the purpose and audience for their text; the larger rhetorical context which shapes this purpose and audience; the genres best suited to this context; the organization, arrangement, and conventions that make a composition most effective within the context; and the systems within which their text will be circulated.

In Table 9.4, we identify some of the rhetorical considerations that teachers and students will want to think about.

 Tip #9: During peer-review studio sessions, encourage *both* written and verbal feedback.

Students benefit a great deal from getting written feedback on their projects from peers and the teacher during studio-review sessions, These written comments—especially when they are grounded in the rhetorical context informing the composition, come from a range of class members with different perspectives, and provide multiple suggestions for revising a composition in specific ways—can be invaluable to an author.

A class will also benefit, however, from an *oral* discussion of each project. Authors, for example, often respond very differently to oral feedback than they do written suggestions because such feedback is both cumulative and public. And oral discussions of a project, given their public nature, often prove useful to teachers, as well, because they provide a sense of how different readers respond to a single project. Finally, such discussions are helpful to peer responders. A large group of students can often collaboratively *discover* a metadiscursive consensus about the strengths and shortcomings of a project—even when individual members of the class remain unsure of the audience's expectations for a specific genre, the conventions associated with a particular medium, or all the affordances of a modality. By listening to the comments of peers, student responders can learn

TABLE 9.4
QUESTIONS FOR RHETORICAL CONSIDERATION

PAYING ATTENTION TO RHETORICAL ISSUES

Teachers

- Does my assignment allow students to identify an authentic *purpose* for composing—one that extends beyond the classroom and is meaningful in students' lives?

- Does my assignment help students identify an authentic *audience*—one that they know and can predict in terms of expectations and responses?

- Does my assignment allow students to select a *topic* (*information*) about which they have some interest or expertise? Or one in which they can develop expertise in a relatively short period.

- Does my assignment allow students to choose—or to learn about—a format and genre they know from some perspective?

- Does my assignment provide sufficient guidance for students in terms of helping them identify the conventions of organization, arrangement, and grammar that characterize the medium in which they are working? The affordances of the modalities with which they are working?

- Do the methods of formative and summative feedback I use for this assignment recognize students' efforts to shape compositions according to rhetorical criteria?

Students

- What is the *purpose* of this composition? What do I want it to accomplish? What difference do I hope it will make?

- What is the *audience* for my composition? How much do I really know about their needs? What can I predict about their expectations and responses? In what circumstances/contexts will the audience read/view this project? How can I find out more?

- Have I selected a composing task that allows me to communicate about a particular *topic* (*information*) with which I have some interest, understanding, or expertise? If not, can I develop this interest/understanding/expertise in a relatively short period?

- What do I know about the format and genre for this composition? As an audience? As an author? Do I have latitude in selecting the format and genre to meet my own areas of expertise/ understanding? The needs and expectations of the audience I have identified?

- What guidance does the teacher provide me—and what understandings can I contribute—in identifying the conventions of organization, arrangement, and grammar that characterize the medium in which I am working? The affordances of the modalities with which I am working?

- Does my composition accomplish the purpose I have identified, meet the needs and expectations of the audience, focus on my selected topic, and make effective use of the genre? Where does it succeed in these takes? Where does it fall short? How do I know? How can I communicate the rhetorical decisions I have made to the teacher? To classmates?

where their own personal assessment of a project is congruent with the opinions of others and where it differs. Students also benefit from such discussions because they hear how teachers respond to projects—how their feedback is phrased, how responses are linked to the rhetorical context of a project, how critique is framed in terms of specific suggestions for revision.

Finally, the oral exchange of feedback, under the best of circumstances, becomes a productive two-way conversation, a dialogue, between authors and readers—one in which authors have the unusual opportunity to ask for clarification, seek the audience's response to a particular approach, ask for help with a technological problem, or test their thinking. Written comments, although they provide many of the same benefits for the author, do not provide for this same two-way exchange of information or for broad-based instruction.

 Tip #10: After studio sessions, encourage students to complete a follow-up reflection on the revision suggestions they have been given.

One of the most valuable aspects of peer review is the opportunity it provides for reflection. For students who have little experience composing multimodal essays, reflecting on peer reviews after studio sessions can result in significant learning. Taking the time to reflect on their compositions in draft form allows students the time and focus they need to synthesize the suggestions they have received from others, formulate some effective plans for revising, and connect their experiences as readers of such compositions with their experiences as authors.

Such reflections can also serve teachers well. Some faculty ask that reflections be included in the logs that students keep during a project so that they can gauge the effectiveness of students' peer-review suggestions and authors' revision efforts. Still other teachers read reflections to identify what should be changed in future classes. Reflections also allow teachers a rare glimpse into students' thoughts about multimodal composition—what individuals are trying to accomplish, what components of the composition authors consider effective, what aspects they think continue to need work, and how authors interpreted the peer-review suggestions of others. In Figure 9.4, we provide some questions that students and teachers might find useful as prompts for a reflection on multimodal projects.

 Tip #11: Leave sufficient time between peer reviews and project deadlines for effective revision

As we have discussed, multimodal assignments can be challenging both to design and undertake. Teachers may need to organize and manage new sets of resources, students may need to learn new genres, classes may need to practice with unfamiliar equipment or software, and both teachers and students may need to develop rhetorically sound strategies for articulating revision suggestions.

REFLECTING ON MULTIMODAL ESSAYS

Reflect on the feedback you received in your recent studio session, and answer the following questions in your Progress Journal:

- What parts of your essay work well within a rhetorical context? Which need the most work?
- What are the three most important suggestions you heard during the peer-review studio session on your composition?
- What are your plans for revision? Sketch a timeline for your revision efforts.

FIGURE 9.4 Example of a reflection prompt

Given these circumstances, teachers should be conservative in the time they schedule between peer-review studio sessions and subsequent project deadlines—allowing enough time for authors to respond to the feedback they receive and undertake thoughtful revision.

CONCLUSION

Multimodal compositions may be different than conventional essays in the media and the modalities they employ, but the authors of such texts—like any authors—can benefit from well-structured peer-reviews provided in carefully designed studio sessions that focus on rhetorical issues.

Both teachers and students, however, must prepare for such sessions—scheduling the time for multiple readings, preparing and responding to the feedback, articulating productive suggestions, focusing on rhetorical responses, reflecting on others' readings of a project, and synthesizing contradictory responses. In Figure 9.5, we provide readers a summary of our suggestions for peer-review studio sessions.

- Provide examples of multimodal projects—preferably those composed by students. Practice analyzing, reading, and responding to them with productive suggestions for revision.
- Schedule and conduct both formal and informal peer-review sessions during an assignment sequence.
- Structure peer-review studio sessions carefully. Articulate expectations and procedures.
- Help students think about effective ways to present their projects in draft form.
- Schedule studio sessions well in advance and participate actively in both formal and informal review sessions.
- Understand that the range of media and modalities used for an assignment will shape peer-review studio sessions.
- Continually remind students of assignments and their requirements.
- Focus teacher feedback on rhetorically informed issues.
- Encourage both written and verbal feedback during peer-review studio sessions.
- Leave sufficient time between peer-review studio sessions and subsequent due dates for a project.
- Encourage students to complete a follow-up reflection after a peer review and revision process.

FIGURE 9.5 Summary of tips for conducting peer-review studio sessions in multimodal classrooms

CHAPTER 10
When Things
Go Wrong

Sylvia Church
Elizabeth Powell

A FEW WORDS ABOUT FAILURE

Nobody likes to experience failure. It's painful, frustrating, and humbling. However, in tandem with success, failure can be a powerful teacher. To minimize the sting and reduce the discouragement that may come with excessive frustration, teachers do need to provide trouble-shooting support for students working with unfamiliar technology and multimodal compositions. Using audio and video as composing modalities, for example, will be new and uncharted territory for many writing teachers, and for some composition students as well. In this territory, it is likely that no one individual in the classroom will be able to address all the challenges that arise. Most teachers find, however, that when the students pool their understandings and information, a class, collectively, can identify a solution that will work.

When things go wrong in the multimodal composition classroom, there are three areas where the trouble generally begins: **with teachers**, when they cannot or do not communicate some vital piece of information (perhaps because this information is new or not available to them); **with students**, who may be struggling to learn new concepts and address the constellation of challenges associated with learning to use new media and modalities to make meaning; and **with the technology**: system crashes and hardware failures, difficulties with software and the limitations of specific applications, and lost/damaged/misplaced files.

It is difficult to discuss the specifics of trouble-shooting technological problems when the hardware, the networked environments, and the software applications used to create multimodal compositions vary so widely from classroom to classroom and institution to institution. However, there are some common problems and solutions that teachers and students can try when projects fail. The rest of this chapter describes the kinds of things that might go wrong and offers suggestions for both avoiding such failures and recovering from them when they occur.

TROUBLESHOOTING IN THE FACE OF FAILURE: TRANSFERABILITY OF STRATEGIES

For teachers new to multimodal composition—and especially the use of audio and video as composing modalities—there is nothing more daunting than anticipating all the things that can go wrong with new technologies. Teachers and students have always had to deal with unexpected problems that crop up in composition classrooms—whether or not they work within digital contexts. In the recent past, for instance, we have learned that there are many things that can go wrong within word processing programs—with revising and saving documents in those programs, printing and sending such documents to other people, posting papers on a network, dealing with incompatible formats (saving a paper in one word-processing package and then being unable to open it in another), working with spelling and grammar checkers, recovering files and repairing broken printers. All these situations require patient trouble-shooting and sometimes even reconstructing a project. Because word processing has become increasingly prevalent as a component of composition classes, however, both teachers and students have developed a repertoire of effective strategies for solving problems that arise and cause projects to fail. Many teachers, for instance, know to refer students to an application's Help function when they need guidance with formatting; many remind students against relying too heavily on spelling and grammar checkers; many advise students to make regular backup files; and many now accept papers via email or posting to a web site if printing becomes a problem.

Our point here is that composition teachers and students adapt well to technological environments when they have the motivation to do so—and when they share information with each other about which strategies work well and which do not. Working with audio and video modalities will present similar challenges. And because these modalities may be less familiar to teachers and students than the modality of words, the task of dealing with human and technological error may *seem* even more difficult at first.

The trouble-shooting strategies we suggest teachers and students use when composing in different modalities build on the skills they already practice when creating and revising alphabetic texts: predicting when and where things might go wrong, trouble-shooting when things do happen unexpectedly, and problem solving when all else fails. We focus specifically on the modalities of audio and video in these strategies because we believe they will be less familiar territory for most readers.

WHEN THINGS FAIL WITH AUDIO

When composing with audio, students go through a series of processes:

- **recording** (e.g., interviews, background sounds, live performances)

- **downloading sound** (e.g., music from a CD, sound files from the web, sound files from a digital audio recorder)

- **editing sound** (using Audacity or some other sound-editing software program to delete and change parts of a sound file, alter the volume of a file, or layer sounds on top of one another)

- **publishing audio files** (by compressing files into a format—QuickTime, .WAV, .MP3, etc.—that can be put on a CD or DVD, or on the web).

To avoid problems with these various processes, teachers and students will want to think about when and where things can go wrong *before* the start of any project. Many common problems in audio have to do with sound quality or lost or damaged files.

Recording Audio

 Have students practice recording audio by pairing up and interviewing each other in class. (See Appendix 21 for a sample in-class activity).

 Before students go out to record sound, make sure they have a good plan that identifies the audio segments they will need for their multimodal composition. (See Appendices 11 and 12 for examples of a heuristic for audio essays and a planning diagram.)

 Make sure that the assignment timeline allows for rerecording material if there is an equipment failure. (See Appendix 5 for hints on preparing for interviews.)

 Develop a checklist for students to carry with them. This way, they can make sure that they have completed all necessary steps for optimal recording. (See Appendix 32.)

 Make sure that students get signed release forms from all individuals they interview or record. (See Appendix 6 for a sample Interview Release/Consent Form.)

Downloading Audio Files onto a Computer

 When students are downloading audio from a digital recorder into an audio-editing program such as *Audacity*, create a test file or listen on isolating headphones to make sure that the volume is at an appropriate level. If the volume is too high, then digital clipping of the sound waves can occur (Fig. 10.1)—that is, the tops and bottoms of sound waves can be cut off,

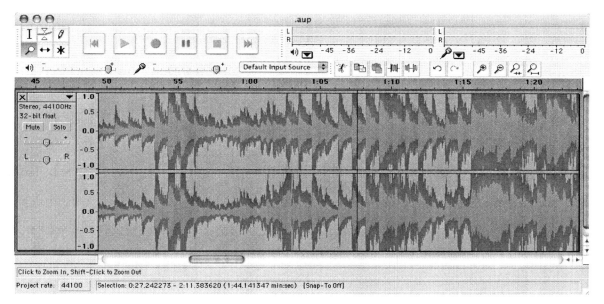

FIGURE 10.1 A example of digital clipping. (Note how the sound waves are flattened at the top and the bottom—in both tracks of this stereo file. This flattening means that part of the signal has been digitally clipped, and the sound is distorted.)

producing distortion. To avoid digital clipping, make sure the tops of the sound waves are not touching the top of the audio track.

Similarly, if the volume is too low, students may not be able to hear background noises or static, which may render their recording unusable. When this occurs, students may waste time downloading a problematic sound file and fail to discover that their audio is unusable until they try to increase the volume (or gain) for their project.

Save, save, save. Students should *always* label and save the raw files that they have recorded. With this approach, if disaster happens when digitized files are being edited on a computer, the original files will provide a backup.

In classrooms that do not have access to digital audio recorders, students and teachers may find it easier to record sound directly into a sound-editing program such as *Audacity*, using the computer's built-in microphone or a plug-in microphone. Given the quality of built-in microphones and the ambient noise levels in most computer classrooms, this approach generally yields only low- to medium-quality sound files. For students' first attempts at composing with audio, however, such solutions may prove sufficient. Students can also construct audio essays out of sounds (music or oratory) downloaded from the web. In all cases, however, they should pay close attention to clearing permissions, adhering to the constraints of licensed content, and citing all sources fully.

Editing Audio Files

Read the instructions. Although software documentation can be difficult to read, it can also be a life-saver if students are faced with an immediate problem they have to solve. Make sure you have program documentation available—in print or online. If the documentation is available in print, make sure there are plenty of copies available for students to use.

Practice before editing valuable files. Have students create several short audio files that they can practice editing for the purpose of learning. Have them use these files to work through tutorials for the audio-editing package that will be used in the class.

Save, save, save. The most important lesson for students working with audio is to save often and backup their work. Especially when working with freeware programs such as *Audacity*, students should save early and often. Large audio files—especially when they are stored on older computers with limited memory—are unstable.

Make two copies of all original audio files (alpha and beta) and edit only the beta copy. Reserve the alpha copy in case of an unexpected disaster.

Break larger audio files into smaller files. In planning diagrams, have students identify the major audio segments in their multimodal compositions. Then, divide larger audio files into smaller files, using a file for each segment in the project. With this segmented approach, problems affect only a limited amount of audio material.

Consult program documentation for cautions about storing and handling large audio files. Different programs may, for instance, have constraints about naming or storing files. Large audio files may also cause problems when they are sent across a network until they have been exported in their final form. This means that students may need to work on the same computer for the entire duration of an assignment and not move from computer to computer. If students work with segments and export each segment as an mp3, pieces of their projects can be transferred to a flash drive or burned to a CD for greater portability.

Encourage students to help each other. Increasing numbers of students are becoming familiar with audio-editing software as they edit, manage, and store files for their personal music collection. These young people can provide valuable help when a whole class is working on audio essays. To identify the expertise in a class, use the Student Expertise Grid included in Appendix 9.

Encourage students to keep a detailed log of their audio work so that problems can be traced back to their source whenever possible. We have included a sample page from a collaborative project log in Appendix 10, and sample pages from an audio-editing log in Figure 10.2 and Appendix 34.

Remain flexible. Students should anticipate challenges when editing audio and be ready to re-record segments if needed.

TRACKS	ACTION [what you do]	TIMELINE [note minutes, seconds, duration]
Track One	Inserted the sounds of a busy restaurant	00:00-00:20 (seconds); fade in first 5 seconds, fade out last 5 seconds
Track Two	Inserted Excerpt #1 of interview	00:20-1:30
Track Three	Music: Pachelbel's Canon CD	Play low during the D from Interview Excerpt, 00:20-1:30; increase volume at 1:30-2:00.

FIGURE 10.2 Audio editing log

Publishing audio in digital formats

Compress and export completed audio projects in a commonly available format (e.g., QuickTime, .WAV, .MP3) that can be easily accessed or imported into a video file. (See Chapter 6 for explanations of *compression* and common *audio formats*.)

Save, save, save. Students should save exported files onto a CD and file CD in a safe place.

 When using audio clips recorded by others, students should be sure to cite the source of these clips correctly and follow licensing/copyright guidelines for obtaining permission. (See Chapter 6 for advice on citing digital materials.)

Table 10.1 identifies some of the more common problems in working with audio files and offers strategies for solving and preventing them.

TABLE 10.1 COMMON PROBLEMS IN WORKING WITH AUDIO FILES			
PUTTING AUDIO INTO DIGITAL FORMAT	**WHAT CAN FAIL (symptoms)**	**PREVENTION**	**SOLUTIONS**
Recording sound directly into a a computer (using a built-in microphone and recording program)	Mediocre sound quality	• Use higher quality microphones (See Chapter 2 for suggestions.)	• If the audio-editing program has a noise filter, use it to eliminate excess noise from files.
	Unwanted noise (air conditioning hum, fan noises, people talking)	• Have students complete a preliminary sound check to identify and eliminate excessive noise before recording the bulk of the project. • Have students plan where and when they will record so that they can avoid unwanted noise. • Have students use isolating headphones so that they can hear unwanted background sounds and eliminate them. • Hang a "Do not enter— studio recording in progress" sign on the door. • Have students record several seconds of silence or background sound.	• Students may need to re-record or live with poor sound quality if time is critical. (Note that students need to allow plenty of time for the learning curve —perhaps even triple or quadruple the amount they might spend in a more familiar medium.)

		Some audio programs have filters for eliminating excess noise, but they need a sample reading of background silence for comparison.	
Recording sound with a microphone and digital sound recorder	Mechanical or human failure—forgetting to press the record button, neglecting to plug in microphone securely, forgetting to use new batteries.	• Provide students with a checklist for audio recording. • Have students practice recording with audio recorders in class.	• Reschedule recording session.
	Quality of sound is compromised, background noise.	• Consider a higher quality external microphone. • Have students do a sound check before beginning a recording session and periodically check their recorder during the session. • Have students record interviews in soundproofed rooms, and hang a "Do not enter—studio recording in progress" sign on the door. If quiet rooms are not available, record interviews in a car with the engine turned off and windows closed. • Have students wear isolating head phones so that they can hear background noise and eliminate it if possible. • Have students record several seconds of silence or background sound so that excess noise can be filtered.	• Reschedule recording session. • Students may need to re-record or live with poor sound quality if time is critical. (Note that students need to allow plenty of time for the learning curve—perhaps even triple or quadruple the amount they might spend in a more familiar medium.)
Downloading digital audio files from a digital recorder	Problems transferring audio files from a recorder to audio-editing program on computer.	• Have students practice downloading short test files in class. • Have students practice with software tutorials using a test file to learn controls and menu options.	• Check power/batteries on the recorder. • Check the cables and connections from the recorder to the computer (see Chapter 7). Make sure they are firmly plugged in.

		TABLE 10.1 COMMON PROBLEMS IN WORKING WITH AUDIO FILES (continued)	
PUTTING AUDIO INTO DIGITAL FORMAT	**WHAT CAN FAIL (symptoms)**	**PREVENTION**	**SOLUTIONS**
		• Review manuals for help with software and equipment. • Create a set of of step-by-step instructions or mini-tutorial for the software the class is using (see Appendix 7).	• Check manuals and online help files for software, recorder, and computer. • Ask technical support staff or a knowledgeable student to check that cables are plugged into the correct sockets and computer's audio settings are correct. • Turn the volume up on the computer and on the digital recorder.
Downloading audio files from the Internet	Finding appropriate files, dealing with different file formats	• Google for audio files with specific formats such as ".MP3" or ".WAV". • Listen to files with isolating headphones before downloading. Some sound quality may be poor.	• Use audio-encoding (audio-ripping) software that transforms files from one format into another—from .wav to .mp3 (e.g., Audiograbber, Cdex, RazorLame).
	Respecting intellectual property.	• Find Web sites that contain open-source audio materials. (See Chapter 7 for a list of these sites.) • Have students review intellectual property guidelines and appropriate citation formats for digital materials (see Chapter 6). • Read the "permissions" section of potential resources before using any files (see Chapter 6).	• Use music from commercial CDs, but cite copyrighted material in a bibliography and do not circulate multimodal projects outside the classroom or post them on the web where others could misuse the intellectual property in ways that would violate the author's/artist's rights.

Using a digital audio editing program to revise—shorten, lengthen, change—audio files.	Losing files	• Save, Save, Save early and frequently. • Have students use descriptive file names (e.g., dog, interview, cheering). • Have student create folders, label with their names, and place all audio files there. • Have students keep a production log in which they note the names and locations of files (See Appendices 10 and 34). • Have students back up files after every working session on portable hard drive.	• Have students use the Find function on their computer to locate the file; replace it in the correct folder. • Re-record the missing bit.
	Varying sound quality among audio segments	• Record all segments with the same equipment. • Try to keep volume settings consistent and eliminate unwanted noise.	• Adjust volume (gain) for individual segments to even out variation. • Re-record problematic segments.
	Corrupted files and loss of audio data	• Divide longer audio files into smaller segments—edit and save these smaller files separately so that damage will be limited. • Simplify naming and storage, minimize file movement—do not change the name of files or move them; store them in one folder. • Have students keep production log with information about where files are stored and what they are named (See Appendices 10 and 34). • Have students back up audio files on a removable hard drive or jump drives.	• Download raw audio files again and re-edit.

WHEN THINGS FAIL WITH VIDEO

When composing with video, students go through essentially the same series of processes as they do with audio:

- **recording or shooting** (e.g., interviews, live performances, documentaries)

- **downloading** (e.g., video from a digital video camera, video clips from the web, still photographs from a digital camera or from the web, audio files from the web, CDs, or digital audio recorders)

- **editing video** (using a video-editing software program such as *Movie Maker*, *iMovie*, *VideoStudio* to delete, add, change video segments; add transitions and title screens; layer audio and video tracks on top of one another)

- **publishing video** (by compressing files into a format that can be shared— QuickTime, .MOV, .WMP, etc.)

To avoid problems during each of these stages, teachers and students will want to think about what can go wrong before the start of any project and identify productive and transferable strategies for dealing with challenges that arise.

Recording Video

Have students practice recording video by pairing up and interviewing each other with digital video cameras in class so that they will understand the various functions of a video camera (zoom, focus, night lighting) and the differences between hand held and tripod shots. (See Appendix 22 for a sample in-class activity.)

Before students go out to record video, make sure they have a good plan that identifies each of the video segments they will shoot. (See Appendix 13 for an example of a video planning diagram.)

Make sure that the assignment timeline allows for re-recording video material if there is an equipment failure. (See Appendix 5 for hints on preparing for interviews.)

Develop a video recording checklist for students to carry with them. This way, they can make sure that they have completed all necessary steps for optimal recording (see Appendix 33).

Make sure that students get signed release forms from all individuals they interview or record. (See Appendix 6 for a sample Interview Release/Consent Form.)

Downloading Video

When transferring video from a digital video camera to the computer, students can transfer all of the video they have shot or some of the video. Because video takes so much memory to store on a computer, encourage students to review what they have shot using the VCR playback function on the digital video camera *before* they transfer all their raw video to the computer. During this process students can identify those shots they will need by logging the minutes and seconds in their production logs (Appendices 10 and 35).

 Have students choose small segments of video to download to a computer for editing, and label these segments with descriptive titles. Have students backup these smaller video segments on DVDs that they can store in a safe place.

 If recorded video is problematic in places, encourage students to use still images downloaded from a digital still camera or images downloaded from the web. Cut away to these still images during problematic video sequences.

Editing Video

 Have program documentation on hand or online. Although documentation of computer programs can be difficult to read, it can also be a life-saver if students are faced with an immediate problem they have to solve. Make sure there are plenty of copies of program documentation available for students.

 Have students practice with the video program they are going to use before they begin editing their projects. Have students create several short video files, import some audio, still photographs, and video clips so they can experiment with the program. Have them use these files to work through tutorials for the video-editing software available in the classroom.

 Save, save, save. As with audio, the most important lesson for a student working with video is to save backup files at various major points of their composing process. Large video files may be unstable, especially on older machines or machines with limited memory.

 Encourage students to keep a detailed log of their work, noting file and folder names and when work was backed up.

 Editing video can be challenging, especially if authors use still images of different sizes and qualities. Mixing still images and moving images creates more complications. For example, Elizabeth Powell's video, *Literacy and Public Transportation* (see DVD), contains a mixture of photographs downloaded from the web, moving video captured by the author, and still images also taken by the composer.

 When combining video, still images, and sound files, students need to make sure that audio and visual elements work with each other, and that each semiotic system contributes additional meaning to the entire composition and exists in a productive conversation with other modalities.

 Students should edit audio segments within an audio-editing program before importing them into the video composition.

When using images from the web, students should be sure to download the largest possible images rather than smaller, thumbnail images. Smaller images, when expanded in video formats, become pixilated and distorted.

 Break larger video files into smaller files. Using a video-planning diagram (Appendix 13), have students identify the major video segments in their multimodal compositions. Then, divide larger video and audio files into smaller files containing each segment. Be sure to store every file in the same project folder. With this segmented approach, any problems encountered in editing will affect only a limited amount of material.

 Encourage students to help each other. An increasing number of students are becoming familiar with video-editing software. These young people can provide valuable help when students are working with video. To identify the expertise in a class, use the Student Expertise Grid in Appendix 9.

 Encourage students to keep a detailed log of their video work so that problems can be traced back to their source. We have included sample pages from such a log in Figure 10.3 and Appendix 35.

 Remain flexible. Students should anticipate challenges when editing video and be ready to re-record segments if needed.

Publishing Video in Digital Formats

 Compress and export completed video projects in a commonly available format (e.g., QuickTime, .MOV, .MP3). Teachers may want to identify a standard compression format for the entire class. (See Chapter 6 for explanations of *compression* and common *video formats*.)

 Save, save, save. Students should save exported video files onto a DVD and file it in a safe place.

 When using video clips recorded by others, students should be sure to cite the source of these clips correctly and follow licensing/copyright guidelines for obtaining permission. (See Chapter 6 for advice on citing digital materials.)

 When using images created by others, students should be sure to cite images correctly, following licensing/copyright guidelines for obtaining permission. (See Chapter 6 for advice on citing digital images.)

Putting Video into Digital Format

Table 10.2 identifies some of the more common problems in working with video files and offers strategies for solving and preventing them.

TRACKS	ACTION [what you do]	TIMELINE [note minutes, seconds, duration]
Segment One	1. Moving image of bus 2. fade-out 3. title screen 4. fade-out 5. three still images of bus 6. fade-out 7. final title screen Audio: "On the Road Again," fade out after final title.	1. 20 seconds 2. 5 seconds 3. 10 seconds 4. 5 seconds 5. 5 seconds each 6. 5 seconds each 7. 10 seconds Duration: 00:00–00:55
Segment Two	Visual: explanation screen; civil rights images (three); fade out between each. Audio: Fade in/fade out clip from Buffalo Springfield.	Each screen is 10 seconds in duration with a five second fade-out in-between. Audio fades in for 3 seconds, fades out for 3 seconds. Duration: 00:55–01:15
Segment Three	Visual: 1. screen introducing interviewee; 2. Image of moving bus in daylight; 3. image of moving bus at night; 4. still image of interviewee with name at bottom of screen. Audio: 1. Interview segment #1 2. Clip from CD "I Get Around"	Visual: 1. 01:15-1:25; fade out to 1:30 2. 1:30-140; fade out to 1:45 3. 145-1:55; fade out to 2:00 4. 2:00-2:10; fade out to 2:15 Audio: 1. 1:30-2:10 2. (Played very softly) 1:15-2:15

FIGURE 10.3 Video editing log

SUMMARY

This chapter is designed to help teachers anticipate some of the more common problems they might encounter when working with audio and video compositions, and to identify some strategies for avoiding and addressing these problems. Many of these problems can be avoided with a few common sense strategies:

 Plan ahead and help students to do so as well (e.g., make assignment timelines longer, plan for peer-review studio workshops, create video- or audio-planning diagrams, make copies of documentation available, identify online tutorials for video- and audio-editing software)

Learn together (e.g., practice with equipment in class, look at sample video compositions—or listen to sample audio compositions—to analyze elements that work well and those that do not, put together your own audio or video composition, share problem-solving strategies as a class)

 Practice and experiment (e.g., have students create short experimental audio and video compositions for practice, hold peer-review studio workshops in which students can compare composing strategies)

 Find and provide expertise (e.g., identify students with video or audio skills, find staff members or other teachers who can help) ·

TABLE 10.2
COMMON PROBLEMS WITH VIDEO COMPOSITIONS
AND SOME TROUBLESHOOTING STRATEGIES

PUTTING VIDEO INTO DIGITAL FORMAT	WHAT CAN FAIL (symptoms)	PREVENTION	SOLUTIONS
Recording digital video with a video camera	Dark video	• Check night light setting on camera to make sure it is on. • Shoot in a lighter, brighter place. • Make sure that the light source is *behind* the videographer. • Read the manual for the camera or a beginning book of hints for making successful videos.	• Re-record video segments. • Use downloaded images from a camera or the web.
	Excessively shaky, jumpy video	• Use a tripod to hold the camera while filming to eliminate shaking. • Use the camera's steady shot function if available. • Read the manual for the camera or a beginning book of hints for making successful videos.	• Re-record video segments. • Use downloaded images from a camera or the web.

	Image is unclear or too small to see clearly	• Use the focus controls and the tight-wide zoom control. • Read the manual for the camera or a beginning book of hints for making successful videos.	• Re-record video segments. • Use downloaded images from a camera or the web.
	Poor quality audio in video	• Make sure the camera volume control is turned to high. • Ask subjects to speak louder. • Consider buying a better outboard microphone for the video camera—one that will pick up more sound, isolate sound from one direction, and result in higher quality sound. • Read the manual for the camera or a beginning book of hints for making successful videos	• Re-record video segments. • Use downloaded images from a camera or the web.
	Camera won't come on	• Make sure camera is plugged in. • Make sure batteries are charged.	• Re-record video segments. • Use downloaded images from a camera or the web.
	No image on camera screen	• Make sure the lens cap is off.	• Re-record video segments. • Use downloaded images from a camera or the web.
Downloading digital video from the web	The link for a video clip downloads, but not the entire clip	• Read documentation for downloading video in Chapter 6, Appendix E. • Make sure video clip is in the public domain.	• Consider using a series of still images.

TABLE 10.2
COMMON PROBLEMS WITH VIDEO COMPOSITIONS
AND SOME TROUBLESHOOTING STRATEGIES (continued)

PUTTING VIDEO INTO DIGITAL FORMAT	WHAT CAN FAIL (symptoms)	PREVENTION	SOLUTIONS
	Quality of downloaded video clip is poor	• Download the video clip in a different format.	• Shoot your own video or still photographs to use as a substitute. • Consider using a series of still images.
Downloading still images from the web to use in a video	Images are not in the public domain	• Look at web sites with more liberal policies for use of images. Try web sites that provide images licensed for use by others, such as the Creative Commons collection <http://creativecommons.org/>.	• Shoot your own digital photographs.
	Images can't be found	• Use Google and search the Images library.	• Shoot your own digital photographs.
	Quality of still images is poor	• Preview images within the context of the video. • Check the size of images —small images will become pixilated or distorted when imported into video contexts. Search for larger images with a better resolution (more pixels per inch).	• Shoot your own digital photographs. • Manipulate the images in photo-editing software before placing them in the video—change the resolution.
	Images are in an incompatible format	• Download the images in another format. • Test images out in the video-editing software.	• Shoot your own digital photographs. • Manipulate the images in photo-editing software before placing them in the video—change the resolution.

Editing digital video	Learning the software	• Have students complete smaller practice videos that involve experimenting with different effects and making editing changes. • Make copies of software documentation available to students. • Identify online tutorials for the packages students will be using. • Experiment with different effects and make changes.	• Have students complete online tutorials. • Have students read the documentation. • Find a third party book on the software package that covers its use at a level—or in a way—that is more appropriate for students. • Choose an easier software package to use—one without as many choices, but with a reasonable learning curve.
	Choosing which video to include in a project	• Have students complete a video-planning diagram or revise their original video-planning diagram. • Have students identify, tell, rehearse the story they want to tell with their video topic. • Have students do some writing about their video and what they want it to accomplish with viewers.	• Have students complete a video-planning diagram or revise their original video-planning diagram. • Have students decide what story they want to tell with their video topic. • Have students do some writing about their video and what they want it to accomplish with viewers.
	Loosing data from large files	• Start simple. • For longer projects, work in short segments.	• Encourage students to scale down their projects and focus on a smaller, more reasonable project.
	Audio doesn't match video or still images	• Show students samples of videos in which audio matches closely with video and still images, and in which audio contributes a large portion of the overall meaning.	• Edit audio segments in an audio-editing program to provide a better match with visual images. • Have students choose different audio elements. • Have peers suggest and/or help find different audio elements.

TABLE 10.2
COMMON PROBLEMS WITH VIDEO COMPOSITIONS
AND SOME TROUBLESHOOTING STRATEGIES(continued)

PUTTING VIDEO INTO DIGITAL FORMAT	WHAT CAN FAIL (symptoms)	PREVENTION	SOLUTIONS
	Audio doesn't enhance video	• Show students samples of video in which audio matches video very poorly and adds very little to video	• Have student consider using voice-over narration to clarify train of thought or story line.
	Audience can't follow author's train of thought or story line in video.	• Conduct peer-review studio sessions in which students focus on audio portions of video compositions.	• Have student consider using alphabetic text on title screens to carry some of the semiotic burden for the video.
		• Conduct peer-review studio sessions in which students tell the author what story they are seeing in the video.	• Have students revise multimodal composition.
	Video seems boring or one dimensional	• Show students multiple samples of videos in which authors use a variety of techniques and strategies to make meaning: close-ups, medium shots, and far shots; panning and zooming; framing; still shots and video clips; music and voice over; title screens. Have class identify and analyze how the elements contribute meaning effectively and ineffectively.	
		• Conduct peer-review studio session in which students suggest to the author different video techniques and other multimodal composition strategies to make meaning more effectively.	
Publishing video	Finished video is too large	• Hold class discussion on the tradeoffs between video quality and file size.	• Compress video into a smaller file size (see Chapter 6).

		• Have students read documentation for the video-editing program and review the section on compression and/or sharing videos. • Have students compress an experimental video into several different sizes. Discuss how video compression affects video quality.	
	Finished and compressed video is low quality	• Hold a class discussion on the tradeoffs between video quality and file size. • Have students read documentation for the video-editing program and review the section on compression and/or sharing videos. • Have students do a mini-research project on common compression problems and solutions. • Have students compress an experimental video into several different sizes. Discuss how compression affects final video quality. • Discuss tradeoffs between quality of video and size of video.	• Compress video into a larger file size (see Chapter 6).
	Video can't be opened by audience.	• Have students read documentation for the video-editing program and review the section on publishing or sharing videos. • Determine what viewing programs the audience will be using and determine what video formats are compatible.	• Recompress and re-export video to a more commonly compatible format (e.g., .WMP, .MOV)

Before leaving this chapter, teachers may want to consider one important point. Although working with multimodal compositions can be challenging, it can also create a classroom environment within which teachers and students explore exciting new modalities for composing and work together as learners on a common project of inquiry. In such situations, teachers give up a some of the expertise and prestige that accrues to them by virtue of what they know about conventional composing strategies—about alphabetic texts. They give up some of their extensive knowledge of genre, their finely tuned understanding of composing processes, and their familiarity with composing tasks and outcomes.

What teachers gain, however, is an exciting opportunity to join students as fellow learners. They gain the opportunity to collaborate with students in learning new composing strategies and experiencing new genres of composition. They can also gain additional insights, we believe, about students' literacies and a renewed appreciation of students' many abilities.

In this kind of classroom, we believe that students can learn to appreciate teachers from a new and productive perspective—not as masters of the classroom who wield the power of grades without understanding, first hand, the challenges associated with making meaning through composing, but rather as co-learners and role models in the challenging process of learning.

CHAPTER 11
Making Connections
with Writing Centers

Jo Ann Griffin

This chapter is designed to speak to instructors new to multimodal composition and, through these readers, the writing centers at their institutions. As John Branscum and Aaron Toscano point out in Chapter 7 of this book, introducing multimodal composition into the classroom can be daunting. Teachers blazing the trail for multimodal composition in their departments or institutions can feel lonely as they attempt to meet those challenges. As Anne-Marie Pedersen and Carolyn Skinner, in Chapter 4, and Richard Selfe, in Chapter 12, point out, collaboration with colleagues can help ease the burden on teachers who are wrestling with new and unfamiliar composing processes and environments. Writing centers can also help support teachers and students if faculty are willing to lay the groundwork for collaboration.

One important step in that process is appreciating the capabilities and understanding the concerns of writing center directors and staff members—especially in connection with multimodal composition.

Multimodal composition and reading differ in important ways from the alphabetic composing and reading most familiar to readers and writing center staff. But, because readers will approach this chapter as a resource for exploring multimodal composition, the focus here is on correspondences and opportunities rather than differences.

BUILDING BRIDGES

In most institutions, writing center resources are stretched thin, and many writing center directors, when faced with the prospect of helping teachers and students on multimodal composition assignments, will express concerns about time, attention, and material resources.

> Directors fear that in embracing too many literacies, "we may not be able to address any set of literate practices particularly well."
>
> Pemberton (2003, p. 21)

To build a stable and enduring bridge with writing centers, teachers who want to experiment with multimodal composing can begin by reassuring writing center directors about the ways in which *existing* resources and rhetorical approaches can serve multimodal needs. Multimodal composition need not, in other words, stretch resources beyond the breaking point if both teachers and writing center staff focus on approaches that work across the boundaries of different communicative forms.

> Significant elements of rhetoric and composition apply "across forms."
>
> Pemberton (2003, p. 17)

Of course, the resources available within specific writing centers vary widely according to local situations and the conditions of individual institutions, departments, and writing programs. Some writing centers may already be thinking far ahead about the suggestions we provide in this chapter and in this book. Teachers in programs and departments just beginning to experiment with multimodality, however, may be working with writing centers that do not yet have experience supporting such assignments. The sections that follow may help generate some connective tissue between the old and the new, between alphabetic writing and multimodal composition.

Discovering Rhetorical Correspondences

Writing center directors and staff members may be most comfortable connecting with multimodal assignments when they can see the task in familiar terms, for instance, when they can identify correspondences between rhetorical concepts and the demands of multimodal composition and expression. For most writing centers, in most institutions, this means that student texts are likely to present composition issues that writing centers and consultants can help address with their existing knowledge of composition. When writing center staff members think of video or audio essays as rhetorical documents, they bring to bear on these essays considerable prior knowledge about how to support both teachers and students. And, talking to writing center directors and staff about the rhetorical dimensions of such assignments will provide a sound and shared basis for understanding.

Considering issues of audience should suffice as an example for most readers. In any type of composition—alphabetic, audio, or video—a major challenge confronting authors and composers of any text is audience. Composition teachers work hard to identify authentic audiences for writing assignments—audiences beyond the classroom teacher and even the academy—so that students have some motivation for thinking about a wide range of audience concerns, issues, and interests. In classes that focus on audience concerns, students pay a great deal of attention to understanding readers' needs, expectations, previous experiences with genre, motivation, and cultural and social context. Writing center staff members have a great deal of experience in helping students think about audience. They can serve as an informed and interested audience for students' essays—one that exists outside the formal boundaries of a class and provides additional perspective on the potential impact of a multimodal essay.

Focusing on a concern for audience, clearly, is only the beginning of the help that a writing center staff can provide students. Staff members can also help students think about additional rhetorical issues that apply across forms and modalities—as Pemberton (2003) notes, those rhetorical "aspects of textual production and reception" that are common to all sorts of texts shared between people (p. 17).

In Table 11.1, we list just a few of the rhetorical issues that provide a bridge for teachers who want to talk to writing center staff members about multimodal essays. Readers will want to consult Chapter 5 for additional information on using rhetorical theory to think about multimodal compositions.

TABLE 11.1
SOME RHETORICAL ISSUES THAT CROSS FORMS

	ALPHABETIC ESSAYS	AUDIO ESSAYS	VIDEO ESSAYS
Audience	• To whom is the essay written? • What is their stake in this topic? • What are the audience's expectations for this written essay?	• Who will listen to the audio essay? • What is their stake in this topic? • What are the audience's expectations for this audio essay?	• Who will watch the video essay? • What is their stake in this topic? • What are the audience's expectations for this video essay?
Purpose	• Why is the student writing this essay? • What does the author hope to accomplish in composing this essay?	• Why is the student composing this audio essay? • What does the author hope to accomplish in composing this audio essay?	• Why is the student composing this video essay? • What does the author hope to accomplish in composing this video essay?
Form	• What genre or written form best suits the purpose and audience of this written essay?	• What genre or audio-based form best suits the purpose and audience of this audio essay?	• What genre or video-based form best suits the purpose and audience of this video essay?
Context	• To what contextual issues is this written essay responding? Why?	• To what contextual issues is this audio essay responding? Why?	• To what contextual issues is this audio essay responding? Why?

Organization	• How is this written essay organized for readers?	• How is this audio essay organized for listeners?	• How is this essay organized for viewers?
	• Of what constituent parts is this written essay composed? How do sentences, paragraphs, transitions work together? Separately?	• Of what constituent parts is this audio essay composed? How do audio tracks, sequences, transitions work together? Separately?	• Of what constituent parts is this video essay composed? How do shots, scenes, framing, transitions work together? Separately?
	• What organizational signposts—topic sentences, headings, conceptual maps— are provided readers?	• What organizational signposts—voice-over narration, music, audio fade-ins and fade-outs— are provided listeners?	• What organizational signposts—establishing shots, title screens, fade-ins, fade-outs, duration of shots, credit screen—are provided viewers?
Unity/ Focus	• What unifying elements —thesis statement, consistent use of sentence subjects, consistent language—make the parts of this written essay cohere?	• What unifying elements —keynote sounds, signal sounds, speakers, voice-over narration, music—make the parts of this audio essay cohere?	• What unifying elements —related images, camera angles, music, voices track, transitions, framing, visual effects— make the parts of this video essay cohere?
Detail/ Support	• What written details, support, evidence does the author provide readers for the essay's thesis?	• What audio sequences, examples, support, evidence does the author provide listeners for the essay's thesis?	• What video sequences, shots, documentary footage, vocal elements provide supporting detail, evidence to viewers for the essay's thesis?
Style	• How does word choice, syntax, diction, and voice contribute to a recognizable style in this written essay?	• How does the use of voice, accent, keynote sounds, background noise, sound effects, music contribute to a recognizable style in this audio essay?	• How does the use and duration of camera images, sound tracks, shots, special effects, framing, credits, titles, and transitions contribute to a recognizable style in this video essay?
Correctness	• Are the grammar and mechanical aspects of the written essay appropriate for the purpose and audience?	• Is the editing of elements cleanly done? Are there distracting variations in volume, sound quality, ambient noises, distortion, problematic transitions, layered sounds that keep listeners from hearing and understanding the audio essay?	• Is the editing of elements cleanly done? Are there distracting variations in focus, lighting, image quality, visual transitions, audio elements? Are title screens and shots sufficiently long in duration for audience to read?

Connecting through WAC, WID, CAC Principles

Some readers of this book will, doubtless, be working at institutions with writing-across-the-curriculum (WAC), writing-in-the-disciplines (WID), or communication-across-the-curriculum (CAC) programs. These programs, too, can provide ways for teachers to build important bridges with writing center staff in connection with multimodal essays. If, for example, the writing center also supports an institution's WAC, WID, or CAC program, the consultants and staff will already be skilled at thinking about different audiences, purposes, forms, and contexts for written communication. In such cases, the principles that inform WAC, WID, or CAC programs can also inform and shape a writing center staff's understanding of multimodal assignments. In Table 11.2, for example, we identify a few important WAC principles that apply across forms.

Readers who want to build bridges to the writing center through WAC, WID, or CAC may want to visit Southern Illinois University–Carbondale's web site, *Communicating Across the Curriculum* <http://www.siu.edu/departments/cac/guide.htm>, to see how one institution has expanded the original understanding of WAC in ways that can encompass multiple modes and multiple disciplines. Readers who want some practice in understanding how writing centers support WAC, WID, and CAC efforts can browse the "WAC Clearinghouse Links Page" edited by Stephen Bernhardt and Kevin Brooks at <http://wac.colostate.edu/links/index.cfm?category=WritingCenters>.

Readers may also want to refer to Barb Blakely Dufflemeyer's and Anthony Ellerston's excellent article "Critical Visual Literacy: Multimodal Communication Across the Curriculum" at <http://wac.colostate.edu/atd/visual/dufflemeyer_ellerston.cfm>.

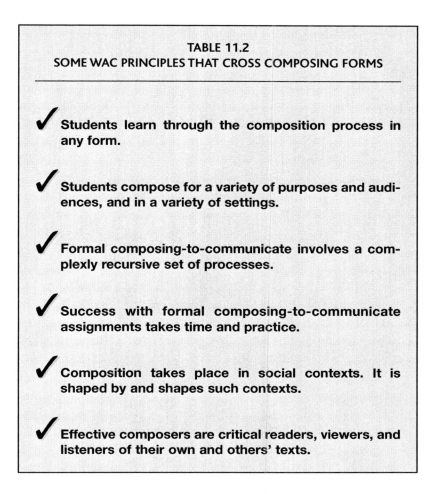

TABLE 11.2
SOME WAC PRINCIPLES THAT CROSS COMPOSING FORMS

✔ **Students learn through the composition process in any form.**

✔ **Students compose for a variety of purposes and audiences, and in a variety of settings.**

✔ **Formal composing-to-communicate involves a complexly recursive set of processes.**

✔ **Success with formal composing-to-communicate assignments takes time and practice.**

✔ **Composition takes place in social contexts. It is shaped by and shapes such contexts.**

✔ **Effective composers are critical readers, viewers, and listeners of their own and others' texts.**

Focusing on Visual Issues

Working from another familiar base, instructors may want to open their conversations about multi-modal assignments by talking to writing center staff about the increasing role of visual elements in communicative exchanges. For example, the standards of the American Psychological Association (APA) are already familiar tools in the writing center tool kit, and the fifth edition of the *Publication Manual of the APA* recommends a number of techniques to help writers present arguments in graphic or photographic formats. Currently, the *Publication Manual* devotes 33 pages to the fine points of presenting information in tables, and 25 pages to presenting information in figures. The *Publication Manual* explicitly recognizes that some material is more readily accessible to readers in formats other than alphabetic text. Tables, for instance, enable readers to perceive some arguments as less dense than do paragraphs.

Given this background, writing center staff members familiar with the *Publication Manual* already have a conceptual foundation for thinking about the visual presentation of information that can benefit students working on multimodal assignments that include video. In Table 11.3, we identify a few of the issues associated with visual elements in alphabetic texts that can also be used to discuss visual issues in video compositions.

TABLE 11.3
SOME VISUAL ISSUES THAT CROSS ALPHABETIC AND VIDEO TEXTS

VISUAL ISSUES FOR ALPHABETIC COMPOSITIONS (APA PUBLICATION MANUAL)	VISUAL ISSUES FOR VIDEO COMPOSITIONS
• Crop images to focus on the desired area of an image and exclude extraneous detail. • Give attention to size and proportion: equal size implies equal importance.	• Use camera shots, angles, framings that focus on the desired subject.
• Make sure that contrast of images allows good reproduction.	• Make sure that the contrast in images and the lighting in video sequences allows ease of viewing.
• Provide figures and tables with titles, and photographs with captions that provide the necessary contextual information for readers.	• Use title screens as needed in video compositions to provide the necessary contextual information for viewers.
• Make sure that figures augment rather than duplicate text.	• Make sure that title screens augment rather than duplicate images and video clips.
• Make sure that figures have a consistent style: design, type font, labeling, etc. to avoid visual clutter.	• Make sure that title screens have a consistent rhetorically appropriate style: design, type font, size. • Make sure that images and video clips have a consistent rhetorically appropriate style: black-and-white or color, transitions, lighting, etc.

Teachers seeking additional tools for bridge-building with writing center staff members with visuals may want to try Cheryl Ball and Kristin Arola's CD-ROM, *ix visual exercises*. *ix* can help writing center staff think about familiar composing concepts such as audience, framing, purpose, organization, emphasis, and context in the vocabulary of visual composition.

Using Listening as a Bridge

Audio compositions may feel like more of a stretch to many writing centers, given the prevailing disciplinary distinctions maintained between most composition programs and communications departments. Nonetheless, listening and speaking skills also provide a conceptual bridge for teachers who want to talk to writing center staff about the rhetorical nature of speaking and listening as communicative acts. After all, much of the work in writing centers involves active listening and careful, thoughtful speaking. Much of the research in writing center scholarship explores the consultant-client conference as a multimodal exchange encompassing speaking, listening, and gesturing, as well as tone, facial expression, and body language. Writing center staff members are familiar with the kinds of speaking-listening exchanges that characterize classes, teacher-student conferences, oral presentations, and writing center conferences. Working from this experience, many writing center staff members can provide students valuable feedback on audio essays. They will also be able to provide individual audience responses to these essays from a perspective that may differ from those of classmates and teachers.

The rhetorical power of audio composition

Audio and audiovisual modes of argument appear to enhance the effectiveness of a speaker's message. These modes encourage listeners to use "speaker-related heuristics" when forming opinions. Reception of alphabetic text, on the other hand, is dominated by "systematic [or listener dominated] information processing."

Sparks, Areni, and Cox (1993, p. 108)

In Table 11.4, we identify some of the common concerns about speaking and listening in writing center conferences and apply these concepts to audio essays. Readers interested in exploring further can look to Paula Gillespie and Neal Lerner's (2004) *Peer Tutoring* and Laurel Black's (1998) *Between Talk and Teaching* for a full exploration of these conferencing concepts. Readers will also want to experiment with the "Connecting Sound and Writing" exercise in Appendix 36.

TABLE 11.4
SOME LISTENING AND SPEAKING ADVICE THAT APPLIES
TO CONFERENCING AND AUDIO COMPOSING

ADVICE FOR LISTENING AND SPEAKING IN CONFERENCES	ADVICE FOR AUDIO COMPOSITIONS
• Critical and active listening is important to comprehension; ask open-ended questions.	• Critical and active listening is important to comprehension in audio essays. Open-ended questions help compare author intention with listener perceptions.
• Taking notes promotes active listening.	• Taking notes during an audio essay can result in feedback that authors can use for revision, especially as there is no text to annotate.
• In conference, voice, gesture, and sequence emphasize key points. Higher order concerns usually come before lower order concerns.	• In audio essays, voice, music, organization, gain (volume), and silence all serve as tools of emphasis.
• Personal anecdotes and humor can help connect with nervous writers.	• In audio essays, humor and personal narratives enliven the presentation for listeners and sometimes forge connections between the author and listener.
• Always consider issues of gender and cultural difference between consultant and client.	• Consider carefully the associations that are to be conveyed with culture-specific sounds, music, voices, and expressions.

GOING A STEP FURTHER: WORKSHOPS AND COLLABORATIVE LEARNING

In many institutions, multimodal assignments are beginning to appear in science, math, engineering, and English courses of various kinds. Faculty can most effectively enlist the support and help of writing centers in such efforts if they lay a careful conceptual groundwork that focuses on the expertise that already exists in such centers, and if they recognize the realistic constraints on writing center resources. Readers will also want to refer to Chapter 12 in which Richard Selfe discusses the importance of forming communities of practitioners interested in multimodal assignments.

Collaborative learning works best when groups of interested learners share what they know without concern for the authority of definitive expertise. Writing centers can create a focal point for communities of practitioners through workshops on multimodal composition, especially if those workshops are supported by interested instructors.

Faculty members who understand the importance of such work can keep in mind the following suggestions that will help writing centers foster communities of practitioners:

 Share student work with other instructors and classes and invite writing center staff members. Ask students to introduce their compositions at writing center workshops; use these opportunities to provide real audiences for students and introduce new instructors to the possibilities of multimodal compositions.

One of the challenges to faculty who have not yet considered multimodal composition is envisioning the end product and what to do with it. Interested faculty can help new practitioners understand what student products might look like. Sonya Borton and Brian Huot provide valuable assessment guidelines in Chapter 8 of this book, as does Kara Alexander in Chapter 9.

 Ask students to reflect (in traditional essay form) about the differences between what and how they communicate in their multimodal assignments and in traditional assignments. Help them (and others) identify the special affordances of multimodal compositions. Share these reflections with other faculty and writing center staff members.

PowerPoint slides excerpted from student reflections and accompanied by student projects can provide vivid illustrations of the affordances specific to audio and visual composing practices and the rhetorical lessons students learn from practicing with those affordances.

 Demonstrate assignment conversions to interested faculty and writing center staff. Writing centers often maintain files of writing assignments from across the curriculum. Teachers or writing center staff can convert those assignments to multimodal formats and offer a library of examples to members of the collaborative community. Table 11.5 presents a series of sample conversions created by Carolyn Skinner.

 Both teachers and students experimenting with multimodal composition need **hands-on experience** in order to overcome natural apprehension and begin to appreciate the affordances of multimodal composition; help the writing center at your institution plan workshops that allow participants to create a finished or nearly finished product, however modest.

Gather images and bits of music that can be assembled into very short (less than 1 minute) multimodal mini-essays. Content should vary with the workshop audience and the software and hardware available.

- Images are available from many sources. Check the Resources List at the end of this book, make use of Google's images search, or scan images to digital files, being sure, of course, to explain the limits of fair use.

- Even if the available hardware will not accommodate elaborate audio or video files, PowerPoint is available on a great many campuses. This program allows the combination of still and moving images with music clips.

- In the workshops that writing centers offer to faculty, time will be at a premium because the workshop often must fit within the institution's class schedule. Free and low cost software such as Audiograbber, Audacity, and PowerPoint allows workshop planners to preselect and trim music clips to suit the limits of the workshop's timeframe.

TABLE 11.5
TRADITIONAL ASSIGNMENTS CONVERTED TO MULTIMODAL ASSIGNMENTS

TRADITIONAL ASSIGNMENT	MULTIMODAL ASSIGNMENT
200-LEVEL ECONOMICS **Read a newspaper article and produce a critical analysis.**	

• Analyze in 2–4 pages, double-spaced.
• Use graphs or diagrams.
 	
• Style and organization count.
• Have someone respond to your text.
• Be creative and try to enjoy.
	• Analyze in 2–minute video.
	• Capitalize on affordances of video
	  ➢ Use graphs or diagrams to illustrate difference
	  ➢ Use voice-overs or text to define theory
	• Structure counts: intro, focus, thesis, conclusion.
	• Have someone view and respond to your text.
	• Be creative and enjoy.

500-LEVEL WOMEN'S STUDIES **Explain and demonstrate how a significant institution, idea or power relationship affected sexual meanings or behaviors for the time period.**	

• An essay of 4–6 pages
• Use class readings and discussions
 	
• Evaluation
  ➢ Clarity, organization
  ➢ Accuracy, coverage
  ➢ Freshness, originality
  ➢ Readability
	• A video of 3–4 minutes
	• Use class readings and discussion <www.archive.org> for images
	• Evaluation
	  ➢ Clarity, organization
	  ➢ Accuracy, coverage
	  ➢ Freshness, originality
	  ➢ Ease of viewing
	  ➢ Affordances of video

HUMANITIES – HISTORICAL PERSON ESSAY **Assess the political, cultural, economic and social milieu that influenced the individual. How did the individual affect the society and its institutions?**	

• Individual assignment
• Unspecified length
• Give examples from the person's life experience
	• With a partner
	• 5–minute video or audio essay
	• Give examples from the person's life experience
	  ➢ Use one consistent voice for character
	  ➢ Examine autobiography or diary
	  ➢ Use music and photographs appropriate to an historical time and place

Groups from within one department might work well in pairs, each pair developing a short video essay from the images and music relevant to a discipline-specific topic. Even 30-second projects composed from the same materials can produce remarkable variety.

More diverse workshop groups may prefer working individually with materials that are less obviously focused. Table 11.6 displays a selection from a set of materials themed around "transportation." Table 11.7 shows the selections made by a workshop participant in forming a brief but coherent and thought-provoking mini-essay.

TABLE 11.6
A SAMPLE MODULE'S COMPONENTS

TRANSPORTATION MODULE – MULTIMODAL WORKSHOP

Images	Music
• Apollo launch • Ocean liner • Conestoga wagon • Bullet trains and steam locomotives • Children's pedal cars • Helicopters • Hot air balloons • Automobiles from many eras • Oceans • Highways	• 30-second clip from "Movin' On" from the *Chicago* soundtrack. • 47-second clip from Dixie Chicks' "Wide Open Spaces."

TABLE 11.7
CONSTRUCTION OF A SAMPLE MINI-ESSAY

ANNA MARIE JOHNSON'S MINI-ESSAY

Images	Music lyric	Titles Added

• Hot air balloon
• Long passenger train
• Vast dark blue ocean
• Road map
• Child on pedal tractor
• Fade to black
	• She needed wide open
	• spa- . . . . . .
	• ces . . . . ces
	• Room to make her big
	• mistakes.
	• She needs new faces.
	  She knows the high stakes.
	  She knows the high stakes . . .
	• Music fades.
		• How long?
		• How far?
		• How deep?
		• Will you go?
		• The decision is yours alone

Participants in any group will enjoy their composing experience in proportion to the time available to experiment and play with the possibilities.

 Serve as a resource for faculty and writing staff members who want to read about multimodal composing. As always, peers and colleagues often provide the most relevant resources. Share the following resource list (see Fig. 11.1), as well as materials from the Resources List at the end of this book.

TOOLS FOR BUILDING BRIDGES

TARGETED TOOLS

- Americanrhetoric.com at <http://www.tsg.xnc.edu.cn/others/old/others/dzfw/address/index.htm> offers examples of 37 traditional rhetorical principles such as Epistrophe, Alliteration, and Hyperbole in brief excerpts from modern popular culture texts (including films and song lyrics), as well as familiar orations.

- *Kentucky Works* <http://www.wfpl.org/KY_works/default.htm> offers multimodal essays well within the reach of undergraduate students with basic tools.

- *This American Life: Lies, Sissies & Fiascoes.* Rhino Records, 1999, featuring Ira Glass, Jack Hitt, Dishwasher Pete, Sarah Vowell, Scott Carrier, Sandra Tsing Loh and David Sedaris: for sharing audio compositions in classrooms not equipped with internet access.

- Ira Glass. "Mo' Better Radio." *Current.org.* May 25, 1998 at <http://www.current.org/people/p809i1.html> offers a transcript (edited by Glass) of a lecture he gave at Macalester College in St. Paul, Minnesota. Glass describes how to tell stories with sound.

FINDING MORE TOOLS

- David Sheridan, Associate Director of the MSU Writing Center at Michigan State University, offers a series of ethical puzzles highlighting dilemmas for visual composers; the same ethical quandaries plague alphabetic and visual composers as well:

  ➢ Slanted arguments

  ➢ Overuse of pathos

  ➢ Author ethos

  ➢ Nuances of presentation

- Sheridan also offers links to the following websites—free, accessible, and packed with useful bridge-building materials for consultants based in traditional rhetorical principles:

  ➢ Andrew Mundi's *Principles of Graphic Design* at <http://www.mundidesign.com>.

  ➢ Peggie Stark Adam's *Color, Contrast & Dimension in News Design* at <http://poynterextra.org/cp/colorproject/color.html>.

  ➢ sreenath sreenivasan's fascinating exploration of photo ethics at <http://www.sree.net/teaching/photoethics.html>.

  ➢ Greg Apodaca's *Digital Retouching Portfolio* at <http://homepage.mac.com/gapodaca/digital/digital.html> provides students with visual rhetoric opportunities to study real-world examples of photo "correction."

FIGURE 11.1 Resource list

REFERENCES

Ball, C. E., & Arola, K. L. (2004). *ix visual exercises* (CD-ROM). Boston: Bedford/St. Martins.

Black, L. J. (1998). *Between talk and teaching: Reconsidering the writing conference.* Logan: Utah State University Press.

Carbone, N. (2004, July 2). Visual rhetoric in tutor training. Online posting. Wcenter Listserv. <wcenter@lyris.ttu.edu>.

Dixie Chicks. (1998). Wide open spaces (S. Gibson). *Wide open spaces.* New York.

Gillespie, P., & Lerner, N. (2004). *The Allyn and Bacon guide to peer tutoring* (2nd ed.). New York: Pearson.

Johnson, A. M. (2005). Mini-essay (CD-ROM). University Writing Center Workshop, University of Louisville, Louisville, KY.

Pemberton, M. (2004). Planning for hypertexts in the writing center . . . or not. *Writing Center Journal, 24,* 9-24.

Sheridan, D. (2004, July 2). Visual rhetoric in tutor training. Online posting. Wcenter Listserv. <wcenter@lyris.ttu.edu>.

Skinner, C. (2005, March). *Preparing students and faculty for success in the multi-modal world.* Paper presented at the CCCC Convention, San Francisco.

Sparks, J. R., Areni, J. R., & Cox, K. C. (1998). An investigation of the effects of language style and communication modality on persuasion. *Communication Monographs, 65,* 108-125.

Zellweger, R., & Zeta-Jones, C. (2003). Movin' on. *Chicago Soundtrack.* New York.

CHAPTER 12
Sustaining Multimodal Composition

Richard J. Selfe

Increasingly, English studies teachers—kindergarten through college—are coming to realize that literacy and digital technologies (i.e., computers, digital audio recording, and digital video) are inextricably linked in the practices of individuals and groups who exchange information in online environments in the 21st century (C. Selfe, 1999). As a result, teachers, their programs, and their institutions are also realizing that they must learn to manage the integration of digital technology in their courses and curricula in ways that are professionally meaningful (Hull, 2003; Kist, 2003; R. Selfe, 2004; Wills, 2004; Williams, 2002), and *sustainable*.

Sustainability is a key concern for English studies professionals because the rapid pace of technology innovation means that computer-supported instruction continues to be exploratory. If teachers don't have *ongoing* opportunities to learn, explore, evaluate, and re-try new digitally based pedagogies, they will not only have a difficult time developing the expertise, pacing, and management skills needed to make multimodal composing meaningful in terms of instruction, but, perhaps more importantly, in *maintaining* such efforts. Even those teachers who seem to be "naturals" when it comes to incorporating new technologies into their teaching need a chance to engage in this interactive cycle of development. This kind of sustainable practice over time is essential to the enterprise outlined in this collection.

What kind of sustainability are we talking about here? We hope that readers of this book will think about sustainability on at least two important levels: creating a sustainable system of relationships with other people to support multimodal composing, and identifying a sustainable system of technological support for such projects.

Perhaps the most challenging part of these efforts—for many teachers—is the task of identifying sustainable communities of people interested in multimodal composition. In the end, we believe that it is friendly and supportive *social* environments that make multimodal composing so enjoyable—and even possible—for teachers and students to experiment with on a sustainable basis. Without such environments it is difficult, moreover, to motivate programs, departments, or institutions to integrate these new kinds of composing efforts into the fabric of curricula.

For that reason, we begin this chapter with a discussion of communities and their importance.

FORMING SUSTAINABLE COMMUNITIES OF PRACTITIONERS

When teachers think beyond the immediate boundaries of their first multimodal composition assignment, they begin to understand the benefits of forming sustainable communities of practitioners interested in undertaking similar efforts. These communities are effective in multiplying efforts and make all the difference in the world during both good and difficult moments as teachers work with multimodal composition.

The Big Picture

The rapid pace of technological change, as most teachers know, can be both frightening and wearing—even as it seduces us with communicative possibilities. One of the best ways to cope with this continuous parade of change is to form communities of practice whose members—students, technical staff members, administrators, and fellow teacher/scholars—can share expertise, support, and strategies. Scholars such as Lave and Wegner (1991), Brown and Duguid (2000), and Nardi and O'Day (1999) offer extensive explanations about how such groups form and why they are so valuable. Teachers who have been members of such groups find that their interactions with others helps them deal with the constant pace of technological change.

For teachers of multimodal composition, such communities of practice can be exceedingly helpful (Selfe, 2004). Working in a team-based environment provides composition teachers a space within which to share stories of what works and what does not, learn more about effective strategies for instruction, and expand their understandings of technology. Because these groups provide such useful support, communities of practice are important if teachers want to sustain a multimodal composition program over time, work in environments where others are working on media-rich projects, and explore the expanded possibilities of multimodality.

In this context, communities of practice work best when they involve stakeholders who have some investment in making multimodal composition work well within an institution. These participants recognize and act on their interest in digitally based composition projects. They get to know why others care about these projects and the systems and spaces (i.e., classrooms, labs, networks) needed to support this kind of digital work. A community of practice that includes teachers, students, staff members, administrators, and community members, for instance, might talk not only about why multimodal composition may be important for teachers of composition and English studies, but also about how students respond to such efforts; how curricula may need to be altered to accommodate such efforts; how access to technology affects multimodal assignments; what kinds of technological expertise might be needed to support such efforts; how multimodal compositions influence the software, hardware, and lab fees; how computer-based work spaces need to be altered in support of this kind of work; who controls computer access and purchasing in an institution; and what kinds of jobs require skills in multimodal composing. These are all important and perfectly reasonable topics of concern for those interested in sustainable multimodal instruction. And this list represents only a few of issues at stake (Selfe, 2004). The important point here is this: communities of practice multiply and enhance instructional efforts. Members of these communities have a rare opportunity to participate in educational culture, get to know people with different perspectives, and share approaches that work and fail to work. In the long run, what sustains programs of multimodal composition is the collective expertise of a team-based enterprise and the opportunity to have a stake in these exciting educational endeavors.

Microcommunities

If larger communities of practice are valuable, however, they almost always start with one teacher, and they take time to build, foster, and sustain. Thus, teachers who are only beginning to experiment with multimodal composition in their class may need to start slow and think small as they grow comfortable with such practices. Teachers in this situation, for instance, may find it sufficient to form a relationship with one technician, one knowledgeable student, or one other colleague.

How can teachers go about developing these microcommunities? Our best advice is to rely on approaches that most composition teachers already have at their disposal. Begin with observing students as they are responding to multimodal assignments. Recruit those students who work well with audio and video recorders or editing software, and then identify those individuals who possess the personality traits of patience, a willingness to share knowledge, and dependability. Often, students who have these traits are quite willing to help other students learn to use a digital audio recorder, demonstrate how to download video clips in class, or explain how they achieved a particularly effective video effect in their multimodal composition. In exchange for their help, offer these students extra credit, an independent study opportunity as a teaching assistant, or a letter of reference that focuses on their technical or teaching skills. Within your department or college, explore the opportunity of work-study jobs for such students. Students are rarely afforded an opportunity to lead, help teach, and engage in projects that are ongoing and substantial. As a result, good students are often hungry for such experiences, and teachers of multimodal composition have the opportunity each term to offer them exceptionally rich leadership opportunities.

Teachers might also want to talk to other colleagues about the multimodal assignments they are trying—within their home department, the writing center, and within other departments as well. A teacher can open such conversations by telling colleagues why audio and video compositions are interesting in his or her discipline, and continue conversations with those faculty who express interest. As more teachers learn the new technologies, plan assignments, implement those assignments in the classroom, and assess the outcomes of those explorations—they will be able to offer additional insights into assignments, approaches, and strategies. They can also form a critical mass of colleagues willing to argue for sustainable funding for the equipment, software, and hardware needed for multimodal composition efforts. If there are no obvious colleagues in a teacher's home department, he or she might want to talk to people in engineering, the sciences, history, communication, arts, education, or medicine. Each of these areas is experimenting with multiple semiotic systems for making and communicating meaning, and colleagues can often be helpful in locating resources—fiscal, human, and technical—of which composition teachers can take advantage.

Technical support staff—those people who help manage digital spaces, equipment, and software—can also make valuable members of a community of practitioners. Many technical staffs relish the idea of working with faculty and students on computer-supported projects. In meeting and working with these people, teachers will want to take the time to explain why assignments or projects are important for students and to understand why these staff members think the way they do. Teachers often find that technical support staff are never given the opportunity to talk about why their work is important to students. They normally hear only complaints about bottlenecks, breakdowns, and brown outs. A little respect for the constraints within which these individuals work will accomplish wonders. In many cases, they will go far beyond the call of duty just to see teachers succeed.

Administrators, too, can be valuable stakeholders in multimodal composition efforts. Writing program administrators and English Department chairs, for example, have a clear stake in thinking about literacy, texts, and composition—and exploring an expanded understanding of digitally based semiotic systems. In addition, these individuals understand the importance of educating students for the worlds outside the university as well as inside it—and, thus, they often have an interest in computer-supported communication. These administrators may also have a stake in the digital scholarship of various faculty members, the effective and innovative uses of computer-supported classrooms, and the leadership profile of a department and a university with larger professional or public communities.

Finally, teachers might want to make connections with stakeholders outside the university: community members interested—or experienced—in working with audio and video, businesses that might be able to contribute the cost of a camera or a digital audio recorder, senior citizens or public school teachers who might be willing to serve as resources for student authors, or local community center leaders and theater managers who might be willing to showcase student projects.

Forming small communities of practice that involve one or more of the people just listed can provide English composition teachers the opportunity to understand how other people perceive digital communication, teaching and learning experiences, and the role of institutions in preparing literate citizens. These microcommunities can help make multimodal composition efforts sustainable in the long run by extending teachers' efforts beyond a single classroom and expanding their understanding of what it means to compose meaning in digital environments.

SUSTAINING TECHNOLOGICALLY BASED EFFORTS

Planning for multimodal composition usually starts with a good assignment. Smart teachers, however, will quickly progress to questions about the technological resources needed to support and sustain such assignments. Certainly, the assignments we discuss in this book should prompt questions like the following:

- What types of projects are reasonable?

- What kind of computers (hardware) and software are needed to support video and audio recording?

- Who has the expertise in digital audio and video production to help?

- How many digital cameras are needed? How many digital audio recorders?

In addition to these questions about hardware and software, cameras and audio recorders, teachers will have questions about people:

- What do I need to know/learn about computer hardware/software, audio and video recording and editing, to make this project work smoothly for students? Who can help me learn what I need to learn?

- What do students need to know about audio- and video-recording equipment, about audio- and video-editing software, and about computer hardware for this assignment?

- What do staff members and technical support staff need to know about my assignment? About my plans for hardware, software, equipment?

- How will I need to shift my teacherly expectations to sustain this type of technology-rich instruction? Can I expect students to work individually or in groups? What can I expect students to learn themselves? What will I have to teach them?

In the sections that follow, we provide some thinking about each of these questions.

 What types of projects are reasonable?

Start short, start simple. When teachers first begin assigning multimodal compositions in their classes, we suggest that they focus on projects that are 5 minutes or less in length. There are at least two important reasons for this suggestion.

First, although students may be used to hearing or seeing compositions that use audio and video, they may not be experienced in *producing* such compositions. If this is the case, even short multimodal compositions will take a great deal of time to put together. Teachers and students will have to learn how to operate video and audio recorders, download sound and video to computers, edit audio and video in digital contexts, and compress and publish audio and video for audiences to see or hear. If teachers need help from technical support staff, short projects will also be helpful.

Second, although video and audio work is becoming easier as new software products are developed, the ratio of composing and production time to finished project remains about 200:1. That is, for every 1 minute of finished video or audio essay, students will spend approximately 200 minutes (3 hours, 20 minutes) planning, shooting or recording, editing, and publishing their work. Thus, to produce a 5-minute video, teachers can expect students to work for at least 16 hours and 40 minutes.

In sum, teachers new to multimodal composition should bite off a reasonably sized project for their first assignment. Some teachers feel most comfortable letting a few knowledgeable students self-select the option of a multimodal composition. With this approach, teachers can identify those students who enjoy and are experienced with digital audio and video, and collect some sample projects that can be shown to other students. Other teachers will want students to experiment with one multimodal composition during the course of a term—leaving the choice of and timing of such assignments up to students. Still other teachers will want all the students in a course to be working on a multimodal assignment at once—using collaborative groups for help and support.

 What kind of computers (hardware) and software are needed to support video and audio recording?

Even short video or audio projects require a great deal of computer memory to edit, store, and publish:

> 1 minute of *raw* audio or video (before compression) can take from .5 to 1 gigabyte of memory on a computer

> 1 minute of *compressed* audio (MP3) or video takes less than 1 megabyte of memory on a computer

Although new computers feature increased amounts of memory and speed, audio and video may—nonetheless—tax those older machines to which many English composition teachers have access in institutional labs and classrooms. Next, we suggest some basic parameters for computers that teachers use for multimodal compositions. However, with rapidly changing hardware and software, such specifications will also continue to change. Hence, we recommend that teachers consult a technical support staff member—either within their department or their campus' information-technology group—about hardware and software requirements before they commit to multimodal assignments in classes.

In reference to audio and video composition, teachers can have students work alone, in pairs, or in small composing groups, depending on the amount of equipment and the numbers of computers to which the class has access. Teachers will want to look for computers that have the characteristics and software identified in Figure 12.1.

 Who has expertise in digital audio and video production to help?

This book assumes that teachers of English composition may have little or no experience with video and audio recording. If this is the case, teachers will need to learn how to

- **operate** a video camera and audio recorder

- **download** data from a video camera or an audio recorder to a computer

- **edit** video or audio in digital environments

- **compress and publish** video and audio so that a range of audiences can have access to student essays.

MINIMAL COMPUTER HARDWARE AND SOFTWARE SPECIFICATIONS FOR MULTIMODAL COMPOSING

- audio and video cards

- moderately high-speed processors (G5 processor or better for Macintosh platforms; Pentium 4/Athlon XP or better for Windows platforms)

- sufficient RAM memory (512 MB minimum, 1 GB recommended)

- CD or DVD burners, and CD or DVD burning software (such as Roxio's Toast for Macintosh or Nero's 6 Ultra for Windows machines)

- audio-editing software (either free software like Audacity or inexpensive software such as Apple's GarageBand for the Macintosh; Adobe's Audition for Windows machines)

- video-editing software (such as iMovie for Macintosh; Movie Maker for Windows machines)

- Free media playing software that can be downloaded from the Internet (e.g., RealMedia Player, Quicktime Player, Windows Media Player)

- Several portable hard drives for storing and backing-up class projects (120 GB each) or individual jump drives (which students can purchase).

FIGURE 12.1 Computer hardware and software specifications for multimodal composition

Teachers considering a multimodal assignment will want to try each of these processes themselves, taking careful notes as they do so. These same notes can be used later to help students learn the same processes.

There are multiple sources that teachers can go to for help in learning these processes:

- **students** (who may do audio or video recording and editing as a hobby)

- **technical support staff members** (working within a department or out of a campus-wide instructional-technology office)

- **colleagues** (in English, or other disciplines, who have done some audio or video recording)

- **family members or friends** (who have done some audio or video recording)

Where can I get digital video cameras and audio recorders? How many are needed?

Teachers who want to provide students the opportunity to work with digital audio and video need some basic access to digital video cameras and digital audio recorders. Check the following sources for such equipment:

- **Students**. Increasing numbers of students have access to digital video cameras and digital audio recorders that they can use for multimodal assignments. If they don't have access to their own equipment—and many students will not because this equipment remains relatively expensive—students can often borrow such equipment from friends or roommates.

- **Colleagues**. Other faculty may have access to video cameras and digital audio recorders that they are willing to loan to students in class.

- **Other units** within the university. The library or campus instructional-technology office may have digital video cameras and digital audio recorders that students can check out. Also check digital arts departments, history departments, education departments, and film studies.

The exact number of audio recorders and digital video cameras that a class will need for a multimodal assignment will depend on the approach that a teacher takes.

For teachers and students who have no access to video cameras and digital audio recorders, we suggest assignments for multimodal essays that use video and audio clips downloaded from the web, or photographs that have been scanned and made into digital images. To create audio and video essays of this kind—using images, photographs, video clips, or audio clips that someone else has made—teachers do not need access to video- or audio-recording equipment at all. They do, however, need to advise students about how to seek material with open-source licenses, how to cite all sources appropriately and—if students plan to distribute their projects outside the classroom—how to follow licensing or copyright guidelines in obtaining permissions (see Chapter 6).

Most teachers, however, will want students to shoot their own video or record their own audio. If this is the case, then the number of video cameras and audio recorders a class needs depends on whether students work alone or on teams, and whether students will all work on projects at the same time or at different times. If, for example, each of the students in a class produces a multimodal composition, the class will need access to more equipment. If teachers don't mind students working on collaborative teams for multimodal assignments, less equipment will be required. Similarly, if a teacher wants all students to work on a multimodal composition at the same time during a semester, more equipment will be needed than if students have the option of completing a multimodal essay in response to one of four essay assignments over the course of a semester.

For teachers who have access to a limited number of digital audio recorders, digital video cameras, and computers, we suggest the practical approach of collaboration. Working together on teams, students can share equipment and help each other as they learn to operate computer hardware and software (see Chapter 4). A class of 20 students, formed into five collaborative teams, for example, can share four video cameras and four digital audio cameras with relative ease if the teacher establishes a careful program of equipment scheduling and checkout (see Appendices 23 and 24) and provides plenty of advance planning time for assignments (see Chapter 3).

Teachers who have access to only one or two video cameras and audio recorders may want to offer the option of doing a multimodal essay to only one collaborative team for each major essay they assign during a term. Faculty may even want to further limit this option to individual students who have previous experience with audio and video as composing tools.

What do I need to know/learn about computer hardware/software, about audio and video recording and editing, to make this project work smoothly for students? Who can help me learn what I need to learn?

The best way for teachers to learn what they need to know about composing an audio or video composition is to create a practice composition themselves. Cindy Selfe, for example, created the practice video "The Changing Nature of Literacy" in order to learn about *iMovie*—the program she used to sequence and edit this short video. Similarly, she created the audio essay "Band Practice" by using a single microphone and a digital audio recorder in order to experiment with *Audacity,* an audio-editing program. Neither project was meant for distribution, but both provided the teacher a great deal of insight into the processes that students would have to go through when they composed their own multimodal compositions.

As Aaron Toscano and John Branscum note in Chapter 7 on staying flexible and experimental, teachers can use their procedural notes and production logs for such practice projects to write documentation for students.

 What do students need to know about audio- and video-recording equipment, about audio- and video-editing software, and about computer hardware for this assignment?

Because students may not be familiar with composing in multiple media, they often have a great many things to learn in connection with such efforts. In Figure 12.2, we list just a few of the skills and understandings students need to acquire.

 What do technical support staff need to know about multimodal composition assignments? About plans for hardware, software, equipment?

The more teachers can tell technical staff members about plans for multimodal composing, the more help staff members can provide. Staff members can be most effective when they have full information about a multimodal composition project. We have listed some questions that teachers should be able to answer—for themselves and for the technical support staff with whom they work—in Figure 12.3.

 What do program/departmental administrators need to know about multimodal composition assignments? About plans for hardware, software, equipment?

Teachers who take care to keep program and departmental administrators informed about their plans for integrating multimodal composing into their classes make life easier for everyone in the department. Administrators can help teachers avoid problems with scheduling, curriculum committees, and student complaints. Teachers can help administrators learn how much work experimentation with digital media can be and make some of their most innovative teaching visible to a person who is bound to take an important role in departmental tenure and promotion decisions. In Figure 12.4, we list some questions that teachers should be able to answer—for themselves and for the administrators with whom they work.

 How will I need to shift my teacherly expectations to sustain this type of technology-rich instruction? Can I expect students to work individually or in groups? What can I expect students to learn themselves? What will I have to teach them?

Composing with video and audio

- How to operate a digital video camera, a digital still camera, and an audio recorder (See operators' manuals for instructions on using equipment)

- How to download digitized video, still photographs, and audio to a computer (See Chapter 6)

Editing audio, video, and still images

- How to edit audio with audio-editing software

- How to edit video with video-editing software

- How to edit images with image manipulation software (See software manuals and online help files for various packages)

Publishing multimodal compositions

- How to compress files and burn compressed files onto a DVD or CD (See Chapter 7)

Planning, revising, and evaluating multimodal compositions

- How to plan effective audio and video compositions (See Chapter 4)

- How to think rhetorically about multimodal compositions (See Chapter 8)

- How long assignments are likely to take (See Chapter 3)

- How to maintain a positive attitude about experimenting with such compositions (See Chapter 7)

- How to work productively on collaborative compositions (See Chapter 4)

- How to interview people and obtain their informed consent for interviews (See Chapter 3)

- How to document sources of video clips, audio clips, and images (See Chapter 6)

- How composing efforts will be assessed (See Chapter 8)

- How to provide helpful feedback for revision (See Chapter 9)

- How to deal with the problems during a project (See Chapter 10)

FIGURE 12.2 Student skills and understandings about multimodal composition

Teachers and students who work with multimodal composition will need all the help they can get. We have found the following hints useful in reducing the demands on individual teachers and students and sustaining programs of multimodal composing.

 Invite administrators, staff members, and colleagues interested in multimodal composing to form a community of practice. Engage these folks in discussions of assignments, technical support, computer technology, studio critiques, and assessment. Invite them to showcase sessions of multimodal compositions, demonstrations, and so on.

ASSIGNMENT GOALS

- What does the teacher expect students to accomplish?
- What kinds of projects are to be produced?

PROJECT DESCRIPTION

- How long are projects?
- How many projects will a class produce?
- What are the main project due dates?
- Will students work alone or in groups?

EQUIPMENT NEEDS

- How many audio recorders, video cameras, and still digital cameras will be needed?
- Where can teachers and students go for equipment within their home department? Within the university?
- How many students have access to their own equipment?
- How compatible are various pieces of equipment with existing hardware and software?

COMPUTER HARDWARE NEEDS

- How many computers will students need?
- When will these machines be needed?
- Where will students work on projects?
- What are the memory storage and processor speed requirements for computer hardware?
- Where will students store projects and for how long? Who will have access to such files? Who will decide issues of access?
- WIll students use their own computers or university computer facilities?

COMPUTER SOFTWARE NEEDS

- What audio-editing software will be used?
- What video-editing software will be used?
- What image manipulation software will be used?
- What word processing software will be used?
- What compression software is needed?
- Are online tutorials available so that students can teach themselves how to use software packages?
- Will students download software and use it on their own computers? Will they use the software available on university computers?
- How will projects be burned to DVD or on portable hard drives?
- Will compatibility be a problem?

TEACHER'S SKILL LEVEL

- How much experience does the teacher have?
- How much help does the teacher need?
- What online resources does the teacher use?

FIGURE 12.3 Some helpful questions to discuss with technical staff members

TEACHER GOALS AND UNDERSTANDINGS

- Why does the teacher consider multimodal composition important in terms of students' education?

- What does the teacher expect students to accomplish in multimodal compositions?

- How are the teacher's efforts to integrate digital technology into classes connected to various scholarly interests?

STUDENT LEARNING

- What do students say about their experiences in this class? What are they learning? What are their concerns?

- Are students realistic about the technological resources teachers can provide in classes? Are students blaming faculty for outdated or scarce equipment?

RESOURCE NEEDS

- What are the teacher's/students' equipment needs (e.g., audio recorders, video cameras, digital still cameras)? Where is the teacher getting this equipment?

- Can departmental support staff help in any way? When? Where? How?

- Are program/department computer resources (e.g, computer hardware and software, computer-supported classrooms, labs) adequate to the teacher's needs? Students' needs?

- Will this class conflict with/contend with other classes for scarce program/department/institutional resources?

- Has the teacher identified technical support staff—within the department or the university—who can help them?

- What low-cost/no cost resources (e.g., communities of practice, student technology assistants, lunch time presentations on teaching with technology, teaching awards) can the program/department provide faculty who explore innovative options for teaching with technology?

- What sources of funding are available for teachers who want to explore multimodal composing (e.g., summer programs, professional development grants, sabbatical leaves)?

FIGURE 12.4 Some helpful questions to discuss with administrators

Create a class expertise grid so that students can help one another (see Appendix 9).

 Ask knowledgeable students to give class demonstrations of equipment use, software programs, editing techniques, problem-solving strategies.

 Have individual students use free online tutorials to teach themselves how to use video- and audio-editing software (Chapter 7).

 Have students plan their production schedules before they check out digital cameras or recorders. Create an equipment schedule and checkout sheets so that staff members and students can help keep track of equipment (see Chapter 4, Appendix 23 and 24).

 If your program, department, or school doesn't have access to audio and video equipment, encourage students to create multimodal compositions from video clips, audio clips, and still images they can find online. For such work, they do not need to shoot their own video or record their own audio. Make sure all sources are documented, cited, and used according to copyright or licensing restrictions.

 If equipment is scarce, borrow it from other units in the university or see if students can borrow some items from friends.

 Stay flexible and maintain an experimental frame of mind (see Chapter 7).

 Schedule studio reviews so that students can contribute peer responses and help each other refine projects.

 Ask knowledgeable colleagues in your department and other departments for help. Or, join online discussion groups like <techrhet@interversity.org> (Primarily, college-level participants. Send a note to <techrhet-owner@interversity.org> to join) and <wwwedu@yahoogroups.com> (Primarily, K-12 participants. Visit <http://groups.yahoo.com/group/wwwedu> to join).

 Design multimodal assignments to support the department's Writing Across the Curriculum program. Have students document important work going on in other places in the university. Such projects will help increase interest in multimodal composition, involve other teachers from other disciplines in students' composing practices, and highlight interesting work at the university (see Chapter 11).

Sustainable Relationships

What makes an effort in multimodal composition sustainable? Primarily, we suggest, it is the people involved—the communities of practice that can, under the right circumstances and with the right leadership, form around such efforts. The people who are motivated to form such communities will have an interest in multimodal composing; they will have an interest in teaching, learning, studying, and supporting new ways to make meaning and new semiotic systems. They will stay involved and remain supportive if their contributions, talents, and the constraints under which they must operate are appreciated. We consider the task of valuing these communities and their members an important part of teaching in a sustainable multimodal classroom—it helps to talk, tell stories, and laugh with each other. It might help to eat and drink together and spend some time off project. It might help to know a bit about each others' personal, professional situation, if people are willing to share. It helps to give credit and celebrate work well done.

All this is easier said than done. Communities of practice, when they work best, require teachers to think outside the academic boxes called classrooms and disciplines. But such efforts are worthwhile because they can result in a unique educational experience, and one that is sustainable over a longer period of time than most individual efforts. When students have a chance to become involved in such communities, what they can gain are not only the literacy skills and approaches that the rest of this volume is focused on, but also new strategies for learning and new appreciations of interpersonal connections with faculty and others. For teachers, communities of practice provide unusual opportunities to pay attention to people in new ways and learn more about the skills and talents they bring to the table—to learn about the many literacies that students bring into classrooms, the concerns of administrators, and the understandings of staff members.

REFERENCES

Brown, J. S., & Duguid, P. (2000). *The social life of information.* Boston: Harvard Business School Press.

Hull, G. (2003). Youth culture and digital media: New literacies for new times. *Research in the Teaching of English, 38*(2), 229-333.

Kist, W. (2003). *New literacies in action: Teaching & learning in multiple media.* New York: Teachers College Press.

Lave, J., & Wenger, E. (1991). *Situated learning: Legitimate peripheral participation.* Cambridge: Cambridge University Press.

Nardi, B., & O'Day, Vicky. (1999*). Information ecologies: Using technology with heart.* Cambridge, MA: MIT Press.

Selfe, C. (1999). *Technology and literacy in the 21st century: The importance of paying attention.* Carbondale: Southern Illinois Press.

Selfe, R. (2003). Techno-pedagogical explorations: Sustainable technology-rich instruction. In P. Takayoshi & B. Huot (Eds.), *Teaching writing with computers: An introduction* (pp. 17-32). Boston: Houghton-Mifflin.

Selfe, R. (2004). *Sustainable computer environments: Cultures of support for teachers of English and language arts.* Cresskill, NJ: Hampton Press.

Williams, S. (2002). Why are partnerships necessary for computer classroom administration? *Technical Communication Quarterly, 11*(3), 339-358.

Wills, K. (2004). A study of technological literacy in writing programs. Unpublished dissertation. AAT 3134206.

Photograph by Gail E. Hawisher

CHAPTER 13
Learning Digital Literacies

Marilyn M. Cooper

The importance of learning digital literacies—reading, writing, and exchanging multimodal information in online environments—is inescapable, but many teachers worry that they don't know how to teach these skills or that doing so will take up too much time, time that should be devoted to teaching "content" rather than skills.

To gain some perspective on this problem, I asked some students about their experiences in using and learning digital literacies. From these interviews with nine second-year college students, I learned that helping students to acquire digital literacies need not take up a lot of class time, and that the principles of teaching multimodal composition are much the same as those involved in teaching any other subject. I also learned that teaching the digital literacies associated with multimodal composing is not a matter of simple instruction in skills and that certain kinds of instruction definitely help more than others.

I interviewed six women and three men who had completed the second-year course in written, oral, and visual communication at Michigan Technological University.[1] These interviews lasted between 30 and 60 minutes, with most lasting about 40 minutes. Although this sample is small and localized, it does provide some important insights about how these nine students acquired digital literacies. In this short chapter, I share my findings from these interviews, framing them in terms of five strategies of effective instruction. I also recommend that teachers who provide instruction in multimodal composition pursue similar research with the students in their own classes. Paying close attention to students' learning strategies, literacy practices, and literacy values can improve the instructional efforts of any teacher.

---

[1]The study was approved by the IRB of Michigan Technological University, and students are quoted anonymously with their permission. The numbers following quotations are codes for the individual students.

PAYING ATTENTION TO DIGITAL LITERACIES

The nine students I interviewed were typical college age (late teens-early 20s) and this group—characteristic of Michigan Tech's larger population—was not ethnically diverse. Five were majoring in engineering, two in business, one in psychology, and one in social sciences. They had differing levels of affinity for and expertise with digital literacies, but, as Cindy Selfe and Gail Hawisher have observed of the young people they interviewed for their book *Literate Lives in the Information Age,* all of these students "have a great deal of situated practice with new media literacies" (p. 209). All nine use instant messaging prolifically, all use email, and all use the Internet as a major source of information on everything from weather to shopping, to research for their class papers, to learning about places where they are planning to work or study. Eight of the nine reported having a computer at home since they were in primary school and using email and the Internet since they were in secondary school. Five of them regularly read newspapers online, their hometown newspaper or newspapers from places they plan to visit. Four have experience constructing Web sites; three are ardent bloggers; and three others participate in the *Face Book*, an online directory that enables students to connect with classmates at their college in an unthreatening way. Although one student described himself as "computerly inept," he regularly uses the Internet to get information, uses IM and email, and is part of the *Face Book* because, he says, it sends you reminders of your friends' birthdays.

Although these nine students sometimes worry that they are less competent than they feel they should be, they are comfortable with digital literacies. One woman said, "with our generation, we grew up with them." One result of this comfort is that they learn new digital applications quickly, and they recognize that their "learning curve" when undertaking such activities is different from those of other generations. As one woman commented on her mother's attempts to learn a word program, "even though she's taken I don't know how many computer classes, she still, I think just because she never used it when she was young, but her learning curve is way different." Often, however, these young people feel that their teachers expect them to already be proficient in many digital literacies.

All nine of the young people I interviewed have had instruction in digital literacies in school. One said she received instruction on computers throughout her primary school years, starting with games in kindergarten, typing in first and second grade, making a simple brochure with *Microsoft Word* in fourth grade, and doing research online for a research paper in fifth grade. Six reported a variety of computer classes in their secondary schools, on how to use spreadsheets, word processing, *Power Point*, online research, and graphics programs. In college, all received some instruction in online research in their first year, and all received instruction on Photoshop in the second-year communications class. They also reported instruction in digital literacy applications in many other college classes, including business, engineering, and social sciences. Although they said that the instruction was helpful, they clearly considered much of it as less than ideal. All reported a lot of learning on their own, often supported by help from friends or family or online help systems.

Indeed, for many of the students I interviewed, the preferred method of learning digital literacy applications, even complicated ones like *Photoshop*, is just figuring them out for themselves. One student said, "A lot of the way I learn a lot of technologies is by opening the program and messing around and finding out what commands will get you where" (002). Others said, "the best way to learn is just playing around with it" (007), and "most of my learning has been trial and error" (008). As one observed, "You just pick them up because they're all pretty similar" (007). And one student noted, "I like to learn programs on my own because the speed I learn it is different from others" (005).

Nevertheless, these students recognize that some applications can't be learned this way, and some instruction is necessary. One woman complained about an assignment to complete a complicated Web site project for which "we had very little instruction, but [the teacher] said that was the point because he wanted us to learn to do it ourselves, but when you're using programs like making queries and *Microsoft Access* it's not something you're supposed to learn for yourself." She explained that, "there were people in the lab every night struggling and relying on older students and then when someone would figure something out—oh this is how you put a picture in, oh this is how you make your text wrap." The teacher, she said, "told us nothing" (009).

The most commonly used methods of instruction among teachers of multimodal composition—tutorials and in-class demonstrations—drew decidedly mixed reactions from the students I interviewed. One student, for instance, who learned *Pagemaker* from a tutorial in a book in a business class in secondary school was scathing:

> It went step-by-step, it was just boring, sitting there reading a book. You look at the book over here, okay, step one, you do the step, you look back over at the book. You're going back and forth, it was just boring. You couldn't really play around with what you wanted to do, you had to do exactly what the book had. You didn't really have a chance to explore the program. There was no creativity. (003)

Two students mentioned that they were "too impatient" to work through long tutorials. Others, however, found tutorials helpful. A student who learned *Photoshop* from tutorials designed by the teacher noted that in contrast to the *Pagemaker* tutorial just described, the teacher's tutorial didn't have "too many restrictions." She said,

> We had to make a calendar, we had to bring in a couple of pictures, and we could make the picture look any way we wanted it to as long as we did certain [effects], but it was kind of open to us what we wanted to do and where we wanted to put it. (006)

Another student found tutorials more helpful than learning on your own: "If you just want to find out how to do a specific thing, fooling around is good, but if you really want to use [an application], expand into other uses, the tutorial is best" (004). And another noted that tutorials were better than in-class explanations: "I liked the tutorials better, they were hands on. I work better when I can do things for myself and try it out" (008). Like figuring things out for yourself, tutorials also allow for different speeds of learning, as one student noted.

In-class demonstrations are useful in showing what applications can be used for, but as direct instruction they are not very effective. The "computerly inept" student was particularly frustrated with instruction in *Photoshop* that consisted mostly of demonstration: "We were shown a few things and then we were to play with it. . . . It was a nightmare. We weren't shown enough of the basics" (004). Another student who was in the same class said, "It was hard for me. She showed us things we could do. My housemate came in and sat with me and I told her how I wanted it to look and she showed me what effects to use" (005). Being unable to work with the application during instruction is the main problem with in-class demonstrations, as two students noted: "When you're shown it in class, you can't remember how to do it" (006); "When you're not on a computer and following along for yourself I don't think demonstrations do a lot for you" (009). Nonetheless, demonstrations can be helpful in orienting students, as one said: "I think it's nice to get an overview of how to do it. It's nice to know the basic stuff and then you can play around with it" (006).

Although many rely on friends and classmates for tips about how to use applications, none feel that this is a good way to learn digital literacies. They tend to ask for help from friends and classmates only on specific questions. One said, "sometimes you just need quick little help and friends are great with that" (007); another said, "for basics, classes work, for specific stuff your friends work better" (001). Another noted, "Friends are more likely to just do it for you, so it's better to have formal teaching," and he added, "If you have a friend and they have time to help you then it's better, but usually they have their own projects to do and don't have time" (004). Another noted the interpersonal problems of working with friends, "Sometimes you don't want to tell them you don't get it. If it's someone you're comfortable with it works better" (005).

FIVE STRATEGIES FOR INSTRUCTION

What do these students find most helpful in learning how to use digital applications for multimodal composition? No one strategy, of course, works for every student—students and their learning styles are far too different. However, a combination of five strategies stand out in these students' comments: knowing what an application is intended to do and what it can do, being allowed to be creative and actually do things with an application, having the time to learn the application to do a project well, having a teacher who is knowledgeable and available to answer questions, and working with peers on projects.

 Strategy #1: Provide an adequate context for learning. Tell students what an application is intended to do and what it can do. Tell them what the application is for—that is, why you are asking them to use it for this composing task.

One student was particularly succinct when I asked what kind of information about applications would help her most; she said, "What it does, how to open it, and what not to do." She elaborated a little with reference to one experience: "They didn't explain what it was for, to begin with. I need the program explained to me, what it's basically supposed to do" (008). Knowing what an application does and how to get started using it are what other students called learning the basics, and this is when demonstrations, particularly in a situation in which students can immediately try out the application, can be helpful, as another student explained: "a couple of demonstrations when we're all on the computer and we can do it" (009). Good demonstrations enable students to understand what can be achieved with the application and what they might want to use it for.

 Strategy #2: Provide an adequate motivation to learn. Make sure there is enough room in multimodal composition assignments for creativity and personal investment.

As other chapters in this collection suggest, the best multimodal assignments allow room for both creative approaches and personal investment. The students I interviewed indicated that they learn how to use applications better and have a more extensive understanding of applications' uses when projects allow them to be creative and achieve things they want to do. As one student said, "You have to have something specific to do and really want to learn it." One student, who hated the tutorial for *Pagemaker* that he was asked to do, found it boring because it didn't allow any exploration on his own (003); a student who liked the tutorial her teacher made for *Photoshop* enjoyed playing around with the application because the teacher didn't put too many restrictions on what she was to do (006).

Other students learned applications in order to accomplish projects of their own: one collaborates with a friend to compose music, exchanging versions and new phrases online; another learned *Photoshop* and HTML coding in order to "make stuff" for her blog. When students are motivated to learn, they have a stake in the instruction and the outcome.

 Strategy #3: Provide adequate time for both learning and doing a project well, one of which students can be proud.

Several students commented on how much time it takes to do digital literacy projects well, and one, the student who had ongoing instruction in digital literacies in primary school, was especially concerned that in college she wasn't given enough time to learn how to use applications well. She commented, "In Revisions [the second-year communications course], we had the option of using

Dreamweaver, but that's another program I don't understand and we had such a short deadline, we couldn't use it" (009). Later in the interview when I asked her what was the best way to learn digital literacies, she said, "Just give me time, time to figure out how to use it for myself . . . having time to work in the lab with a teacher there who can help you. I guess I don't see the point in assigning things if you're not going to give the students, if they've never used the program, enough time to do it" (009).

Having time to really work with an application and understand its possibilities, being able to, as one student said, "expand into other uses" (004), is essential in developing what James Paul Gee calls one's appreciative system, an individual's "set of goals, desires, feelings, and values in respect to the domain [of the application] being engaged with" (p. 97). Gee explains that an appreciative system merges affect and cognition and is what one uses to determine the significance and acceptability of the results of one's actions in a domain. Students who are not given the time and resources to engage deeply with applications to complete projects to their satisfaction have not really acquired digital literacies, as this student's comments insightfully suggest.

Strategy #4: Provide adequate assistance for learning. Make yourself available for teaching.

The availability of the teacher to answer questions and give support is also important—as several of these students noted. One woman said, "you have to make yourself available as a teacher" (009). Students also commented on their teachers' availability on email. One in particular said about his teacher, "She was the best professor I've had as far as replying, because I could write her probably two emails in a day and she'd get back to both of them and they wouldn't be one-line answers, they'd be thoughtful answers explaining to me and I think that really helped me out" (004). Others noted that working in a computer lab with the teacher available to help them was always useful.

Strategy #5: Provide students with opportunities to learn and solve problems collaboratively, with the help of peers.

Working with peers on a project or sharing with each other the work classmates are individually doing also promotes faster, more comprehensive understanding of the possibilities and uses of digital literacies. One student said,

> The best way of learning is first letting the person fool around and then gathering together and then looking at it and looking at other people's work, and realizing, you look at someone else's and that doesn't look right, that doesn't look good, and then you realize, hey, I did the same thing myself. (003)

He added, "Working with peers is the major thing . . . we almost felt we don't even really need [the teacher] in the sense that we can critique each other's work so well" (003). Another student, when I asked how he would go about learning new applications, said,

> You slowly pick things up. If you're submerged in people always using [a program] you're going to pick things up. It's just like if you're trying to learn French, if you go over to France you're going to learn it faster than if you're here trying to take a class. (004)

These comments reflect Gee's contention that learning to use applications (or in his study, learning to play video games) involves entering a semiotic domain, "a set of practices that recruits one or more modalities . . . to communicate distinctive types of meanings" (p. 18). Learning the practices of various semiotic domains, which include academic disciplines and workplace occupations, as well as particular literacy genres and digital literacy applications, is, he argues, more important than learning content, and practices are learned in interaction with others.

THE IMPORTANCE OF DIGITAL LITERACIES

These perspectives on what students are learning when they learn different digital literacy applications well suggests why teaching digital literacies is so important. It is not just that learning such applications involves acquiring essential skills for workers and citizens in our electronically connected world. Rather, digital literacies are social practices through which we define meanings and values and discover the effects of our meanings and actions on others. Recognizing the social and rhetorical effects of digital literacies is an important goal for students, one that will enable them not only to survive in this world but to create better worlds for themselves and others.

Selfe and Hawisher note that students with a great deal of situated practice still "need help in framing their understandings critically so that they can question their own judgment and look at their work from the perspectives of audiences increasingly different from themselves" (p. 209). One student I interviewed demonstrated this sensitivity to audience as he explained why he took his blog offline; he said, "Since the Revisions class I started taking audience and context into account and that kind of contradicted the point of me writing down my thoughts if I'm tailoring it to everyone who's reading it. It became writing for someone else instead of writing to learn so eventually I just made it private" (002). Later in the interview, he said that learning the rhetoric of digital literacies was the most useful thing he took from his Revisions course.

As I have pointed out, the nine students I interviewed form only a very small and local sample of convenience for the instructional conclusions I draw here. And, thus, I will not claim that my suggestions are based on generalizable data. I do claim, however, that they make sense in light of what I know about effective instruction of any kind. I also encourage readers of this book to conduct similar research with the students they teach—learning for themselves how and why students acquire digital literacies, what instructional strategies work well and fail to work for them, and what literacy means to them and for them.

Personally, I believe that students can best develop the ability to reflect critically on their uses of digital literacies when they have the time to work through meaningful projects together and with the support of teachers. In such contexts, students can come to understand digital literacies as involving much more than the exercise of simple skills and gain insight into how such literacies figure into social relationships. Perhaps most important of all, students can gain confidence in their own ability to create meaning in semiotic domains, thus exercising their social agency in increasingly effective ways.

REFERENCES

Gee, J. P. (2003). *What video games have to teach us about learning and literacy.* New York: Palgrave Macmillan.
Selfe, C. L., & Hawisher, G. A. (2004). *Literate lives in the information age: Narratives of literacy from the United States.* Mahwah, NJ: Erlbaum.

AFTERWORD

Debra Journet

As students and teachers of English, and more particularly of rhetoric and composition, our colleagues and we have begun to consider how digital media and new technologies are expanding and revising our understanding of literacy. Yet, even as many are beginning to compose in multiple modes and media and encouraging their students to do so as well, there is still sometimes a gap between theories of multimodal communication and effective classroom practices. This book is a result of efforts to address such gaps. In the spring of 2004, Cindy Selfe was the Thomas R. Watson Visiting Distinguished Professor of Rhetoric and Composition at the University of Louisville. As Watson Professor, Cindy offered a graduate seminar entitled "Literacy, Technology, and Education" and gave several presentations to students and faculty. Much of this book is the result of the fruitful conversations that were stimulated and enriched by Cindy's visit. The book's authors outline some of the achievements and complications inherent in integrating multimodal literacies into writing classes. As practitioners (and lovers) of narrative, we preface their work with a set of stories that we hope will locate the challenges that students, teachers, and writing program administrators face as they move toward multimodal literacies. This book captures the energy and creativity that inspired these innovative projects and practices so that others can both learn from them and explore new ways of writing and communication.

LEARNING BY DOING: OBSERVATIONS IN A MULTIMODAL CLASSROOM

Why should we include multimodal forms of literacy in our writing classes? This is not a question I would even have considered until recently. However, in the spring of 2004, I had the opportunity to observe what happens when students are asked to expand their sense of literacy and complete projects incorporating multiple modes and media when I "sat in" on Cindy's seminar. I was particularly intrigued with the seminar's topic because I've always thought of myself as relatively nonliterate about technology. This class offered a good chance, I thought, to begin changing that. So, eagerly and enthusiastically, I planned to tackle all of the class's assignments. However, even as the seminar began I felt daunted and a bit overwhelmed by what was going to happen. We would, Cindy explained to us, compose sound and video projects that explored the way multiple literacies functioned in our own lives and in the lives of other groups in which we were interested. We would learn to use these nifty digital video and audio recorders and edit our work using such programs as Audacity and MovieMaker. This all sounded exciting but a little scary, and very time-consuming. Soon, pleading the normal complications of classes and committees and deadlines, I began to be less and less a participant in the seminar and more and more an observer. In the end, I decided not to do the assignments myself, but to observe closely what other seminar participants did. This was, as I later realized, a *big mistake* and one that I came more and more to regret. Because a key lesson Cindy's class taught me was that one learns not just by listening and reading and talking, but also by doing. This is obviously true of many things, and it is certainly—and importantly—the case with technology. Thus, I watched the students become more and more expert as I remained a novice.

Because I did not "do" in Cindy's class, I can only still speak of multimodal literacy as a relative outsider. But I am an outsider who knows more than I used to because I was able to observe 15 students who are now definitely insiders. My story, then, recounts what I saw as I watched a talented group of graduate students gain the technical and critical skills associated with new forms of literacy and reflect on what they hoped to carry away in their own teaching and learning.

Meeting Technological and Rhetorical Challenges

The participants in the "Literacy, Technology, and Education" seminar brought with them different degrees and kinds of technological expertise. Some were extraordinarily fluent with what technology the course would involve and interested not only in "what to do," but also the more theoretical "why"; others knew and used only the minimum that they needed. At the beginning of the semester, then, some participants seemed to approach new technologies as a challenge, whereas others expressed my own kind of nervousness and trepidation. And in most cases, this trepidation seemed to me to be entirely appropriate. Putting projects together required enormous time and effort. Participants spent literally hours and hours working in the computer lab. In progress reports during class sessions, we heard maddening stories about whole days' work that produced only 2 or 3 minutes of tape, or tragic tales of lost files. As we looked at projects in progress, we saw and heard inaudible sounds or missing images. Together we experienced the wobbles of production: "I don't know where that file is," or "It didn't do that when I played it earlier."

However, in every instance, members of the seminar overcame technological challenges expertly enough to produce complex and polished sound and video projects. The audio projects mixed diverse kinds of sounds—usually incorporating music, interviews, voice-overs, and other recorded sounds. Video projects combined still and moving images, verbal texts, music, and spoken words. Although some were obviously more sophisticated than others, all the projects demonstrated a technological competence that was to me (and to some of the participants as well) astounding.

I do not want to underestimate the difficulties I witnessed as people composed for the first time in new and variably demanding media. But I do believe, at least from my own observations, that what was accomplished more than made up for the frustrations. The general level of success is likely the result a number of factors. The seminar was, in many ways, a best-case scenario. The students, as doctoral candidates in rhetoric and composition, knew they were gaining important professional skills and were thus willing and eager to commit uncommon amounts of time and energy. The topics of their assigned projects concerned literacy—a subject central to their intellectual lives. Moreover, the resources for this course were unusual: students benefited from an extraordinarily enthusiastic and experienced teacher, whose sole responsibility during the semester was to this one class, as well as from a generous (although inevitably not large enough) budget for technology. But the class also succeeded because of a kind of shared problem-solving approach that is, I suspect, common to many technological situations. Because no one in the class claimed professional expertise in technology (at least of the sort that class participants were learning to claim in rhetoric and composition) it was relatively easy and natural to ask for and offer help. This sense that "we were all in this together" was strongly complemented by the workshop environment of the class, in which we spent much of our time watching and listening to each other's projects and offering suggestions. Moreover, technological assistance flowed easily into other kinds of collaboration. Indeed, trying to figure out how to solve technological problems often went hand in hand with trying to work out more substantive rhetorical challenges.

The two multimodal assignments students produced asked them to "employ the affordances (capabilities) of the medium and modes in effective rhetorical ways." That is, technological innovation was meant to serve a larger rhetorical purpose. In particular, students were expected to create projects that used sound and visual effects to say something interesting and persuasive about a form of literacy. During the course of the semester, we saw and heard projects about the way literate agency was modeled by nuns in a Catholic school or how a Kentucky family's traditions of craftsmanship were passed from one generation to the next. We learned about literacy as it related to country music and heavy metal, bus signs in the Civil Rights period, and cross-cultural eating styles. We learned about the literate development of a young American child and a bilingual Nepalese student.

As experienced readers and writers, all these students were already highly fluent in print literacy and very familiar with the genre of the academic essay or research article. But for most, this was the first time they had worked extensively to produce work that depended primarily on audio or visual material. Accordingly, many produced drafts or early versions of projects that looked or sounded like written academic texts simply transposed to different media. Video projects, for example, often contained too much verbal text; audio projects tended to sound as though they had been written out in advance and were subsequently being read aloud. Other projects simply had too much going on to make sense: viewers and listeners were inundated with clever video or sound effects that had only a loose relation to the rhetorical point of the piece. But again, the collaborative workshop environment of the class helped students make the transition from purely verbal to sound and visual modes. As class members were shown projects in progress, they were able to suggest ways in which audio and visual elements of the projects could be highlighted or manipulated for better effect. Projects became more adventurous and began to look less like transcriptions of academic verbal texts. Visual and sound material became more than simply an adjunct to the verbal, but the way experience itself was narrated.

Extending What We Learned

The class drew (in an unusually hands-on way) on the shared expertise and experience of its members, their collective sense of "being in this together," their facility with written texts, and their general history as consumers of visual and sound rhetoric. But the seminar also encouraged us to move "doing" to "reflecting" and consider how we might frame and extend this experience, both as producers and teachers of sound and visual "texts."

Because we are all writing teachers, we tended to talk and think in terms of the writing process theories we had all been taught. As participants reflected on the process of authoring video and audio texts, we often employed a familiar vocabulary: we talked about "invention" or "revision," "collaborative learning" and "feedback," "peer response" or "editing." The process model and its language seemed useful in suggesting connections between what we did and knew as writing teachers and what we were hoping to do as multimodal teachers. But many of the participants also emphasized their sense that visual and audio modes allowed them to make new kinds of arguments or explore different kinds of experiences. Consequently, we became conscious of the differences between "composing" a written essay and "composing" an audio or sound project, and we began to speculate on how our assumptions about writing did and did not translate into other modes of representation.

The differences we have begun to recognize as we compose in verbal, visual, and sound modes raise important questions for us as teachers, students, and producers or recipients of new media.

Aside from mastering the technology, what else should we learn? What do we need to understand about visual or auditory rhetoric? What about principles of design? How do we analyze the audience for visual or sound projects? What do we need to know about how listeners and viewers understand and remember? These are not the kind of questions writing teachers have been trained to consider. And although it is tempting to think that we can negotiate some of these questions by drawing on the theoretical or empirical knowledge we already possess about writing processes and written texts, we may also need to consider gaps in our understanding of the full range of representational possibilities, and what a concomitantly wider range of disciplines can offer us as an aid to filling in some of those gaps.

Beyond such theoretical concerns, we remained conscious of the need to consider the problems and issues that will arise as we extend the experiences of this class into other situations, particularly those in which students and teachers don't have as much time or commitment or as many resources as we had in Spring 2004. Although we talked about these challenges during the seminar, most of us don't yet know how well we will be able to incorporate multiple modes of literacy into our traditionally organized classes. Moreover, we were mindful of a larger disciplinary challenge: the need to articulate to our colleagues why—given inevitable limited time and resources—it is necessary or even beneficial that we do so. In the past, English departments have been very effective in making arguments for devoting time and resources to the teaching of writing—not only in composition but also in literature and other textually oriented classes. Our arguments that writing is a tool for both learning and assessing have been effective, for example, in providing university-wide resources to keep our classes small (at least in relation to other university offerings). But if we are to move our classes toward multimodal forms of literacy, we will need to ground our arguments in similarly appropriate theoretical and empirical research.

In particular, we need to consider how we will answer a question frequently raised in our seminar and in other conversations around our department: "Why should we be doing this in English?" Inherent in that question are two assumptions that seem to me unnecessarily limiting, but that may be common to the thinking of many of our colleagues. One is that other disciplines or departments may be better suited to take on this task. The response to this suggestion is fairly clear, as no other academic unit appears (at least at my institution) eager or willing to do so. The second assumption is more complicated and has to do with the question of what the work of English departments is and should be. This question is clearly too difficult—and controversial—to answer fully here. But what I observed in Cindy's seminar helped change my own thinking—offering me an important glimpse into what I am coming to see as one of the next steps in the inevitable evolution of the academic discipline of "English."

Addressing multimodal literacy in a sustained way is clearly not part of the mission of the typical English department—especially if that mission remains defined solely in terms of print literacy, particularly the reception of literary works. But it is worth noting that English departments have a history of successfully expanding their mission in many ways—the incorporation of rhetoric and composition into the discipline being a clear case in point. We were able to bring the teaching of writing into a disciplinary domain partly because we were no longer willing to draw a categorical line between the production and reception of "texts" and partly because of theoretical and material redefinitions of "textuality" itself. Thus, we now regularly include as part of "English" all kinds of "texts"—from canonical literature to creative writing, from business and technical writing to popular culture. All these "texts" are, we understand, a way of making meaning; all are rhetorical; and all may be the proper work of an English Department.

Most of us live in a world where our students are already far more fluent in multiple modes and media than we are. The question for them is not "why" or "if' we will move to multimodal literacies, but "how" and "when." For me, much of the answer to these questions lies in what I saw in the spring of 2004. The seminar resulted in some stunning projects that show extraordinary imagination and technological fluency. Even those others that were not yet so polished or finished, however, were impressive—demonstrating an amazing leap from where students started to where they were at the end of the semester. At their best, projects didn't simply attach illustrations or sound bits to what was really a conventional essay or academic presentation (as, for example, my own Power Point presentations tend to do). Rather, new media and modes embodied new forms of representation—new ways of thinking and communicating. But I also believe that the real fruits of the seminar were not just the products that the students completed but also, and perhaps more importantly, the embodied processes of composing, learning, and teaching that they practiced: learning by doing.

Note: In the summer of 2006, Debra Journet attended a two-week institute on Digital Media and Composition (DMAC) at The Ohio State University. At DMAC, Debra experimented with digital audio recording and created her first digital video ("Rough Edges"). She is learning by doing—and setting an example for us all.

Bosco, Erin Smith

GLOSSARY
Technical
Terms

GENERAL TERMS

Affordances: The particular representational capabilities associated with a modality of composing. Video, for instance, is particularly capable of representing movement, process, and the passage of time. Audio has the capability of representing accent, tone of voice, mood, or music. An affordance of alphabetic writing is the ability to represent linear propositional logic in structures like sentences and paragraphs.

Alphabetic compositions (composing with words): Compositions that rely on words as the primary modality for making meaning—although other modalities (such as the visual) are involved.

Audio compositions (composing with sound): Compositions that rely on audio as a primary modality for making meaning—although other secondary and tertiary modalities may be involved.

Author(s): The person—or people—who compose and convey meaning in any modality or medium.

Bit rate: A measure of file quality, referring to the number of data bits per second transmitted by an audio or video file—often expressed in thousands of bits per second (kilobits or kbits) or millions of bits per second (megabits or mbits). Bit rate is used to identify acceptable quality for compressed media files. For audio files, the following bit rates are considered minimally acceptable:

- 4 kbits—recognizable speech
- 8 kbits—telephone quality speech
- 96 kbits—FM radio quality audio
- 128 kbits—CD quality audio

For video files, the following bit rates are considered minimally acceptable:

- 2 Mbit/s—VHS quality video
- 8 Mbit/s—DVD quality video
- 55 Mbit/s—HDTV quality video

(See also **Compression** and **Sampling Rate**)

Compression: The task of reducing the size—and resolution—of digital files, using a computer pro-gram—so that they can be more easily stored and accessed. Compression rates are expressed in ratios that indicate how much compression has occurred: a 20:1 compression rate is high and a 2:1 compression rate is low. With an audio file, most people can't easily detect a 10:1 compression ratio. The lower the rate of compression, the better the quality of a file—but also the more memory it requires to store on a computer. Students' video and audio projects, typically, are compressed when completed so that they can be stored on some portable medium like a CD or a DVD. (See also **Bit Rate** and **Sampling Rate**)

Copyright: Laws that govern the use of intellectual property, including creative works such as alpha-betic texts, audio and video texts, and images. Copyright law is designed to protect the rights and economic interests of authors and artists with regard to the distribution and use of their original work. (See also **Copyleft, Fair Use, Open-Source Licensing,** and **Public Domain**)

Copyleft: A movement that advocates the open sharing of intellectual property and the use of copy-right law "to ensure that every person who receives a copy or derived version of a work, can use, modify, and also redistribute . . . the work." Artists and authors attach copyleft licenses to their work in order to grant particular rights and ensure that their intellectual property circulates without typical copyright restrictions. (See also **Copyright, Fair Use, Open-Source Licensing,** and **Public Domain**)

Digital environments: Environments within which information (e.g., words, pictures, video, sound), at its most basic level, is coded/modified/conveyed in some combination of 1s and 0s: for instance, personal computers, computer networks (both local-area and wide-area networks), hard disks, the WWW.

Fair use: A doctrine that allows the use of copyright-protected works for commentary, parody, news reporting, research and education. As Copyright.com <http://www.copyright.com/ccc/do/viewPage ?pageCode=cr11-n#copyfaq7> notes,

> . . . fair use is not an exception to copyright compliance so much as it is a "legal defense." That is, if you use a copyright-protected work and the copyright owner claims copyright infringement, you may be able to assert a defense of fair use, which you would then have to prove. Whether a certain reproduction or other use of a copyright-protected work is considered fair use is not specifically set out in the Copyright Act. As such, you must determine, based upon the factors in the Copyright Act, whether that particular act may be considered fair use.
>
> Fair use considers:
>
> 1. The purpose and character of the use, including whether such use is of a commercial nature or is for nonprofit, educational purposes.
> 2. The nature of the copyrighted work.
> 3. The amount and substantiality of the portion used in relation to the copyright protect-ed work as a whole.
> 4. The effect of the use on the potential market for or value of the copyright-protected work.

Teachers can compare key definitions of Fair Use at <http://www.answers.com/Fair%20Use> (See also **Copyleft, Copyright, Open-Source Licensing,** and **Public Domain**)

Media: The technology on which—and the technological systems through which—information is delivered or stored: computers, drawing paper, photographic paper, television, CDs, DVDs.

Open-Source Licensing: The open-source movement has encouraged authors and artists to make their creative material—software, code, video, music, writing—available to the public under a licensing agreement. Open-source types of licenses, typically, allow people to use protected material as long as they adhere to a flexible set of conditions (some rights reserved—such things as attribution, commercial/noncommercial use, changes, sampling, and sharing). These rights are determined by the original authors/artists.

Originally aimed at the software coding community <http://opensource.org/>, the open-source movement has had an impact on video, audio, and image artists and authors as well, and its tenets are developed most fully, perhaps, by Creative Commons.org <http://creativecommons.org>. The Creative Commons site is useful for teachers and students in multimodal composition classes because it offers a wide range of free audio files, video files, and image files. Students can use these files without charge in their own multimodal texts as long as they adhere to the artist's/author's conditions (as expressed by the Creative Commons license attached to their work). (See also **Copyleft, Copyright, Fair Use,** and **Public Domain**)

Public Domain: A part of copyright law that allows the public use of materials not currently protected under copyright law. Teachers can compare key definitions of public domain at <http://www.answers.com/topic/public-domain>. (See also **Copyleft, Copyright, Fair Use,** and **Open-Source Licensing**)

Reader(s)/Viewer(s)/Listener(s): The person (people) who reads/views/listens to the essay or project.

Modalities: Visual, audio, gestural, spatial, or linguistic means of creating meaning.

Multimodal composing: Using multiple modalities to compose and convey meaning. The goals associated with multimodal composition assignments include the following: helping students understand the power and affordances of different modalities—and to combine modalities in effective and appropriate ways—multiplying the modalities students can use to communicate effectively with different audiences, and helping students employ modalities to make meaningful change in their own lives and the lives of others.

AUDIO

Ambient Noise: Background noise that often gives a sense of location and realism, but should not obscure or distract from the signal sound.

Cartiod (and Hypercartiod): Microphones that pick up sounds primarily in front of the microphone and limit sound pick up from the sides and rear. (Also see **Omnidirectional**)

Clipping: A special kind of audio distortion that occurs when sound is recorded at such a high level that the recording device cannot capture the entire signal. When viewed as a waveform, clipped sound is flat on the top and the bottom of the track.

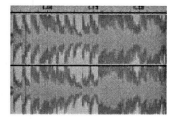

Compression: When a raw sound file is reduced by a digital formula to a smaller size. Compression results in some loss of sound quality, so the desire for high-quality audio must always be balanced against the desire for smaller files.

Fade in/Fade Out: To begin an audio segment/element by having sound build gradually, fading up from silence. Or to end an audio segment/element by having sound gradually disappear, usually fading to silence. The image below shows a segment of audio that fades in and fades out.

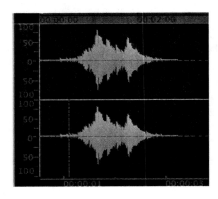

Gain: The process of digitally amplifying or lowering the volume in a piece of audio.

Keynote: A sound that serves as a fundamental tone, orienting the audience to a piece's overall meaning. A keynote may not always be heard consciously, but it adds meaning to the surrounding tones (Schafer, 1997).

Noise: Unwanted sound such as clicks, pops, the noise of air conditioners, the hum of fluorescent lights.

Levels: The level of volume as represented on an audio-recording device. The picture below shows an audio level meter on a computer.

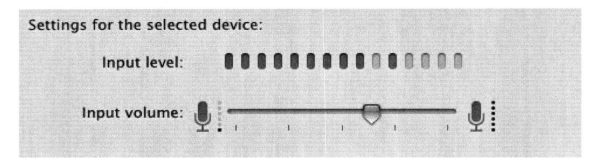

Omnidirectional: Microphones that pick up sound from all directions. These microphones cannot be aimed and, thus, are less useful for interviews in which the subject's responses are the primary focus. (Also see *Cartiod*)

Sampling: The process of recording sound and turning it into a digital file. During this process, a real-world sound is sampled at regular intervals and transformed into bits of data. The sampling process determines the resolution, or quality, of the digital file that results. The faster the *sampling rate* (how many times per second a sound wave is measured) and the larger the *sample size* (the range of numbers used to record each measurement), the more accurate the digital recording—but also the more memory it will take up on a computer. *Sampling rate* is expressed in hertz (hz) and thousands of hertz (khz). And *sample size (or bit depth)* is expressed in bits. Typical sampling sizes for audio files include 8 bit, 16 bits, 24 bits, and 32 bits.

Typical sampling rates for audio are as follows:

- 8,000 Hz—telephone quality audio
- 22,050 Hz—radio quality audio
- 44,100 Hz—compact disc quality audio
- 48,000 Hz—films and professional quality audio
- 96,000 or 192,400 Hz—DVD quality audio

Audio files on commercial CDs, for instance, are typically recorded at the rate of 44,100 samples per second, with a 16-bit sample size. (See also **Bit Rate** and **Compression**)

Signal: Foregrounded sounds that are to be given direct attention by the listener (Schafer, 1997).

Soundmark: A sound that has a unique meaning to a community (Schafer, 1997).

Soundscapes: Audio compositions that attempt to capture and represent some of the essential meaning, emotion, importance, or content associated with a particular sonic environment—often a site, place, event, or natural or artificial location (e.g., county fair, factory, ice skating rink, fox's den) (Schafer, 1997).

Sound Portraits/Biographies/Autobiographies: These compositions are biographical—focusing either on an individual human or animal subject (person living on the street, nurse, centenarian, twins, race horse) or a group of such subjects (Schafer, 1997).

Sound Documentaries: Aimed at capturing and representing the importance of a noteworthy cultural, social, or political event, trend, or pattern, sound documentaries can vary from short to feature-length compositions. They often involve some combination of interviews, shadowing, first- and second-person commentary, participant observation, and so on. They may involve individuals, groups or their representatives, or even large crowds .

Sound Performance: If soundscapes, sound portraits, and sound documentaries are akin to the "nonfiction" of the audio world, sound performances are closer to "fiction" or artistic performance. Sound performances—which include audio-based renditions of music, drama, prose, or poetry (either conventional "word" poems or audio poems made up entirely of sounds)—focus on the interpretation of works of art by individuals or groups.

Track: One layer of audio in an essay. Audio essays often layer several tracks on top of one another (background noise, voice over, music). The image below shows audio tracks. It represents an essay in Audacity with two tracks—the top track is loud and the bottom track is soft.

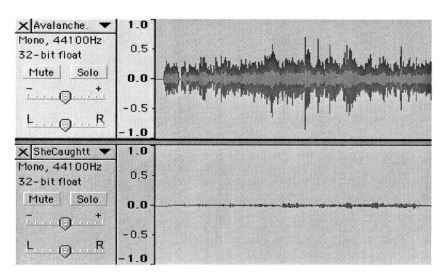

Transport Controls: The controls in an audio-editing program. The picture below shows a common transport bar with the following controls from left to right: Fast Back, Play, Record, Pause, Stop, and Fast Forward

Voice over: Commentary added to an audio essay to explain, clarify, or narrate action. The voice over is recorded separately from other audio elements.

Waveform: The sound wave pictured in an audio-editing program. The picture below shows a waveform.

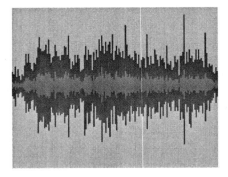

Windscreen: Foam cover that fits over the end of a microphone so that the noise of the wind blowing across it will not be heard on the recording. If you do not have a real windscreen, place a small square of foam material—about 1/4-1/2 inch thick—over the end of the mic and secure with a rubber band.

VIDEO

Camera Angle: The position from which the camera records. Videographers need to walk around their subjects to ascertain the best angle for their shots. Videographers will also want to shoot from different angles to provide viewers with the sense of a three-dimensional world.

Compression: When a raw video is reduced by a digital formula to a smaller size. Compression results in some loss of video quality, so the desire for high-quality video must always be balanced against the desire for smaller files.

Cut: The act of moving from one scene/sequence/element to another scene/sequence/element—thus suggesting a connection by placing them in the same sequence.

Cut Away: A technique used during post-production editing to combine attention to primary (A roll) and secondary (B roll) footage. For example, an editor will cut away from a primary shot of an interview subject to shots that will show examples of what the subject is talking about. The final effect is a sequence that shows a shot of the interview subject talking, then a transition to several examples (while the subject continues talking), and finally a return to the interview subject. Cut away sequences are used to avoid a static "talking head shot" that can be boring and doesn't take rhetorical advantage of video as a modality.

Dissolve (or mix): A particular kind of transition between scenes in which one scene changes gradually into another image or scene.

Duration of Shot: How long—in terms of time—a camera shot should last. This decision depends on what's going on in the shot and what the videographer is trying to accomplish with the shot, sequence, and composition.

Fade (in or out): A way of beginning a scene/element by having an image/clip appear gradually, fading up from black. Similarly, a way of ending a scene/element by having an image/clip gradually disappear, usually fading to black.

Framing: Deciding what should appear in a shot, where it should appear, and how much detail or background should be included.

Headroom: The space between the top of a person's head and the top of the frame.

Jump Cut: A technique used during editing, in which the middle section of a continuous shot is removed, and the beginning and ending are joined together. This approach creates a discontinuity in time and a noticeable jump. It calls attention to the unreality of time as represented in film or video.

Shots: What is composed for and captured by the video camera. A videographer will want to mix the kinds of shots included in an essay to provide viewers with some visual variety.

> **Close up:** A shot in which the camera is zoomed in as tightly as possible, showing a small field, but with great detail.

> **Dolly shot:** A shot in which the camera follows the action of a character, moving along with him or her. The trick with dolly shots is to keep the camera shot looking smooth instead of jumpy. In Hollywood, the professionals use a camera cart that moves along fixed rails to accomplish this feat. To simulate a dolly shot, have the cameraperson sit in a desk chair with wheels and brace his or her elbows on the arms. Then, have another person roll the chair (and the cameraperson and the camera) along a smooth floor.

> **Shot - Reverse Shot (over the shoulder):** A term used most frequently in interviews to show how a secondary subject responds to a primary subject—the camera cuts away from the interviewer (secondary subject) asking a question to the person being interviewed (primary subject). Often the shot looks over the shoulder of one person (from the back) and focuses on the other person's face.

Establishing Shot/Sequence: A shot/sequence that opens a video, providing an orientation for the viewer. Often, an establishing sequence begins with a wide or long shot that provides maximum context and, then, zooms into a more particular location that marks the beginning of the action.

Full shot: On a person, a shot that captures the whole body from head to toe.

Long shot: A camera shot from some distance away to provide context for the action.

Medium shot: A shot at the medial level that limits some background context, but provides a focus for viewer's attention. On a person, a shot from the hips up.

Two Shot/Three Shot: A two shot captures two people in the frame, and a three shot captures three. Such a shot is usually medium or wide.

Pan (left and right): The act of turning or swiveling a video camera horizontally, left or right.

Tilt: The act of tilting a camera up or down.

The rule of thirds: To compose a shot, divide the frame into thirds—both by length and width. Put the focal point for a shot in the left or right third of the frame rather than in the center third and in the upper third rather than in the lower two thirds.

Wide shot: A shot that captures the widest picture possible in the frame to show a landscape, scene, or context.

Transitions: The way in which videographers join or combine two sequences or elements within a video.

Sequence: A series of related shots that have a unifying idea or concept. The three shots above, for example, form a sequence.

Shooting into the light (backlighting): When a videographer records a subject against a window or some other light source. The camera adjusts to the brighter light, leaving the subject in darkness. Avoid this unless you wish to keep people anonymous.

Sound track: The audio portion of a video. Often a video will have several tracks (music, voice over, sound effects, background noise, etc.).

Title Screen; A screen that uses alphabetic text to convey information about the video.

Videoscapes: Compositions that use digital video, digital photography, digitally scanned images or illustrations, and so on, to capture and represent some of the essential meaning, emotion, importance, or content associated with a particular location or visual environment. Videoscapes can focus on natural or artificial environments (i.e., football stadium, the interior of a car, campaign headquarters), or large or small places (i.e., room, city, neighborhood, classroom, park).

Video Portraits/Biographies/Autobiographies: Video compositions focusing on either an individual human or animal subject (person living on the street, nurse, centenarian, twins, race horse) or a group of such subjects. Often video portraits focus on people whose lives have not been documented and whom many would consider unimportant. These segments attempt to convey some sense of the subject's life or personality through the words and sounds they use. If the video composition focuses on a human subject, an author/sound designer generally identifies a series of questions to ask. But some authors/videographers also follow their subjects around and record their interactions with others and the world.

Video Documentaries: Aimed at capturing and representing the importance of a noteworthy cultural, social, historical, or political event. Video documentaries can vary from short to feature-length compositions. They often involve some combination of interviews, shadowing, first- and second-person commentary, participant observation, and so on. They may involve individuals, groups or their representatives, or even large crowds. Because of their length and complexity, video documentaries often require a great deal of planning, recording, shaping, and editing.

Video Performances: These videos are akin to "fiction" or artistic performance. Video performances—which include visually based representations of music, drama, prose, or poetry—focus on the visual interpretation of works of art by individuals or groups.

Video Arguments: These projects are targeted at making a convincing visual case. Authors use video, still photographs, comic strips, and the like, and draw on logos, pathos, and ethos to persuade an audience.

Voice over: Commentary added to a video to explain, clarify, or narrate action. The voice over is generally recorded separately and imported into a video as an audio track.

COLLECTED RESOURCES

WORKS CITED

Abel, J., & Glass, I. (1999). *Radio: An illustrated guide.* Chicago: WBEZ Alliance Inc.

Anderson, D. (2003). Presume approaches to new media composition: Consumption and production in continuum. *Kairos, 8*(1). Accessed March 28, 2005, from <http://english.ttu.edu/kairos/>.

Ball, C. E., & Arola, K. L. (2004). *ix visual exercises* (CD-ROM). Boston: Bedford/St. Martins.

Barton, D., & Hamilton, M. (2000). Literacy practices. In D. Barton, M. Hamilton, & R. Ivanic (Eds.), *Situated literacies: Reading and writing in context* (p. 7-15). London: Routledge.

Barnhart, J. B. (2005). Sample statement page 1. Sample statement from the Web site of the U.S. Social Security Administration. Retrieved July 5, 2005, from <http://www.ssa.gov/mystatement/sample1.htm>.

Bernhardt, S. (1986). Seeing the text. *College Composition and Communication, 37,* 66-78.

Boxer, S. (2005). Digital 'antigrafitti' peels away the years. Web site review 'Graffiti Archeology,' Arts Section. *The New York Times* Web site accessed June 22, 200, from <http://www.nytimes.com/2005/06/21/arts/design/21boxe.html?ex=1120017600&en=a03801f5a29ef085&ei=5070&emc=eta1>.

Brown, J. S., & Duguid, P. (2000). *The social life of information.* Boston: Harvard Business School Press.

Brummett, B. (1991). *Rhetorical dimensions of popular culture.* Tuscaloosa: University of Alabama Press.

Bull, M., & Back, L. (Eds.). (2003). *The auditory culture reader.* Oxford: Berg.

Carbone, N. (2004). Visual rhetoric in tutor training. Online posting. July 1, 2004. Wcenter Listserv. July 2, 2004 <wcenter@lyris.ttu.edu>.

Daly, E. (March/April 2003). Expanding the concept of literacy. *EDUCAUSE,* pp. 33-40.

D.C. Comics. (2005, June). *Harper's Magazine,* p. 22.

Dewey, J. (1938). *Experience and education.* New York: Touchstone.

Educators, entertainment industry team up to fight peer-to-peer copyright piracy. (2003). *Patent Trademark & Copyright Journal, 65.* Retrieved April 25, 2005, from <http://ipcenter.bna.com/pic2/ip.nsf/id/BNAP-5KA85M?OpenDocument>.

Gantz, J., & Rochester, J. B. (2004). *Pirates of the digital millennium: How the intellectual property wars damage our personal freedoms, our jobs, and the world economy.* New York: Prentice-Hall.

Gee, J. (2004). *What video games have to teach us about learning and literacy.* New York: Palgrave Macmillan.

George, D. (2002). From analysis to design: Visual communication in the teaching of writing. *College Composition and Communication, 52*(1), 11-39.

Hacker, D. (n.d.). Humanities: Documenting sources. On Diana Hacker's *Research and Documentation Online* Web site. Retrieved July 8, from <http://www.dianahacker.com/resdoc/p04_c08_o.html>.

Harper, G. (2004). *Crash course in copyright*. Web site of the Office of the General Counsel, The University of Texas System. Retrieved March 28, from <http://www.utsystem.edu/ogc/IntellectualProperty/cprtindx.htm#top>.

Hemmens, A. (2005). *Information on obtaining copyright permissions*. Resources on the University of Washington Web site. Retrieved July 8, 2005 at <http://lib.law.washington.edu/ref/copyright.html>

Holmes, A., & Martin, F. (n.d.). Home page for audio production and contemporary culture. Retrieved June 7, 2005, from <http://www.infocom.cqu.edu.au/Courses/2002/T3/MMST12016/course_site/tut%203.ht>

Hill, C. A., & Helmers, M. (Eds.). (2004). *Defining visual rhetorics*. Mahwah, NJ: Erlbaum.

Hocks, M. (2003). Teaching and learning visual rhetoric. In P. Takayoshi & B. Huot (Eds.), *Teaching writing with computers: An introduction* (pp. 202–216). Boston: Houghton Mifflin.

Hull, G., Mikulecky, L., St. Clair, R., & Kerka, S. (2003). *Multiple literacies: A compilation for adult educators*. A report of the Center on Education and Training for Employment, The Ohio State University, Columbus. Retrieved June 26, 2005, from <http://www.cete.org/>.

Huot, B. (2002). Toward a new discourse of assessment for the college writing classroom. *College English, 65*(2), 163-180.

Kalantzis, M., Varnava-Skoura, G., & Cope, B. (Eds.). (2002). *Learning for the future: New worlds, new literacies, new learning, new people*. Altona, Victoria, Australia: Common Ground Publishers.

Keyes, E. (1993). Typography, color and information structure. *Technical Communication, 40*(4), 638-654.

Kress, G. (1999). "English" at the crossroads: Rethinking curricula of communication in the context of the turn to the visual. In G. Hawisher & C. Selfe (Eds.), *Passions, pedagogies, and 21st century technologies* (pp. 66-88). Logan: Utah State University Press.

Kress, G. (2003). *Literacy in the new media age*. London: Routledge.

Kress, G., & van Leeuwen, T. (1996). *Reading images: The grammar of visual design*. London: Routledge.

Lankshear, C., & Knobel, M. (2003). *New literacies: Changing knowledge and classroom learning*. London: Open University Press.

Lave, J., & Wenger, E. (1991). *Situated learning: Legitimate peripheral participation*. Cambridge: Cambridge University Press.

Lea, H. C. (1902). The eve of the Reformation. As reproduced in *The Cambridge Modern History* (A.W. Ward, G.W. Prothero, & S. Leathes, eds.). New York and London: The Macmillan Company.

Lindemann, E. (1987). Making and evaluating writing assignments. In *A Rhetoric for writing teachers* (pp. 91-224). New York: Oxford University Press.

Marc, D. (1995). *Bonfire of the humanities: Television, subliteracy, and long-term memory loss*. Syracuse, NY: Syracuse University Press.

McCloud, S. (1993). *Understanding comics: The invisible art*. New York: Harper Perennial.

McFedries, P. The word spy. <http://www.wordspy.com/words/drivewayeffect.asp>.

Moran, C., & Herrington, A. (2003). Evaluating academic hypertexts. In P. Takayoshi & B. Huot (Eds.), *Teaching writing with computers: An introduction* (pp. 247-257). Boston: Houghton Mifflin.

Nardi, B., & O'Day, V. (1999*). Information ecologies: Using technology with heart*. Cambridge, MA: MIT Press.

Pemberton, M. (2003). Planning for hypertexts in the writing center . . . or not. *Writing Center Journal, 24*, 9-24.

Plato. (1956). *Phaedrus* (W. C. Helmbold & W. G. Rabinowitz, Trans.). Indianapolis, IN: Liberal Arts Press.

Ross, H. (2003). Digital video and composition: Gauging the promise of a low-maintenance high-reward relationship. *Kairos, 8*(1). Retrieved March 28, 2005, from <http://english.ttu.edu/kairos/>.

Schafer, R. M. (1997). *Our sonic environment and the soundscape: The tuning of the world*. Rochester, VT: Destiny Books.

Selfe, C. (1999). *Technology and literacy in the twenty-first century: The importance of paying attention*. Carbondale: Southern Illinois University Press.

Selfe, C. (2004). Toward new media texts: Taking up the challenges of visual literacy. In A. F. Wysocki, J. Johnson-Eilola, C. Selfe, & G. Sirc (Eds.), *Writing new media: Theory and applications for expanding the teaching of composition*. Logan: Utah State University Press.

Selfe, R. (2003). Techno-pedagogical explorations: Sustainable technology-rich instruction. In P. Takayoshi & B. Huot (Eds.), *Teaching writing with computers: An introduction* (pp. 17-32). Boston: Houghton-Mifflin.

Selfe, R. (2004). *Sustainable computer environments: Cultures of support for teachers of English and language arts*. Cresskill, NJ: Hampton Press.

Sheridan, D. (2002). Visual rhetoric in tutor training. Online posting. July 2, 2004. Wcenter Listserv. <wcenter@lyris.ttu.edu>.

Sirc, G. (2002). *English composition as a happening*. Logan: Utah State University Press.

Snyder, I., & Beavis, C. (Eds.). (2004). *Doing literacy online: Teaching, learning and playing in an electronic world*. Cresskill, NJ: Hampton Press.

Sparks, J. R., Areni, J. R., & Cox, K. C. (1998). An investigation of the effects of language style and communication modality on persuasion. *Communication Monographs, 65,* 108-125.

Stephens, M. (1998). *The rise of the image the fall of the word.* Oxford: Oxford University Press.

Sullivan, P. (2001). Practicing safe visual rhetoric on the world wide web. *Computers and Composition, 18*(2), 103-122.

Tagg, P. (1986). *Reading sounds: An essay on sounds, music, knowledge, rock, and society.* <http://www.theblackbook.net/acad/tagg/articles/readsound.html>.

Takayoshi, P. (1996). The shape of electronic writing: Evaluating and assessing computer-assisted writing processes and products. *Computers and Composition, 13,* 245-258.

The New London Group. (1996). A pedagogy of multiliteracies: Designing social futures. *Harvard Education Review, 66*(1), 60-92.

Thompson, H. S. (1973). The Kentucky Derby is decadent and depraved. In T. Wolfe (Ed.), *The new journalism.* New York: Harper and Row.

Trimbur, J. (Dec 2000). Composition and the circulation of writing. *CCC, 52(*2), 188-219.

Tufte, E. R. (1990). *Envisioning information.* Cheshire, CT: Graphics Press.

Tufte, E. R. (1997). *The visual display of quantitative information.* Cheshire, CT: Graphics Press.

Tufte, E. R. (2001). *The visual display of quantitative information* (2nd ed.). Cheshire, CT: Graphics Press.

Tufte, E. R. (2003). *The cognitive style of PowerPoint.* Cheshire, CT: Graphics Press

Wolfe, T. (1973). Introduction. In *The new journalism.* New York: Harper and Row.

Wysocki, A. F. (2001). Impossibly distinct: On form/content and word/image in two pieces of computer-based interactive multimedia. *Computers and Composition, 18*(3), 207-234.

Wysocki, A. F. (2003). With eyes that think, and compose, and think: On visual rhetoric. In P. Takayoshi & B. Huot (Eds.), *Teaching writing with computers: An introduction* (pp. 182–201). Boston: Houghton Mifflin.

Wysocki, A. F., & Johnson-Eilola, J. (1999). Blinded by the letter: Why are we using literacy as a metaphor for everything else? In G. E. Hawisher & C. L. Selfe (Eds.), *Passions, pedagogies, and 21st century technologies* (pp. 349-368). Urbana: University of Illinois Press.

Wysocki, A. F., Johnson-Eilola, J., Selfe, C. L., & Sirc, G. (Eds.). (2004). *Writing new media: Theory and applications for expanding the teaching of composition.* Logan: Utah State University Press.

Zebroski, J. (1994). *Thinking through theory: Vygotskian perspectives on the teaching of writing.* Portsmouth, NH: Boynton/Cook.

ONLINE RESOURCES

Citation and Documentation

"Citing Sources: Online Style Sheets," Evaluating and Citing Web Sources
<http://www.library.vanderbilt.edu/romans/polsci/evalweb.html#style>.

"Electronic References" (2003). APA Style
<http://www.apastyle.org/elecref.html>.

Style Guides and Resources
<http://www.ifla.org/I/training/citation/citing.htm>

"Using Modern Language Association (MLA) Format"
<http://owl.english.purdue.edu/handouts/research/r_mla.html#Electronic>

Landmark's Citation Machine
<http://citationmachine.net/>

Copyright and Copyleft

§ 107. Limitations on exclusive rights: Fair use. Copyright Act of 1976. Title 17
<http://www.copyright.gov/title17/>

Copyright Act of 1976. Title 17.
<http://www.copyright.gov/title17/>

Copyright.com.
<http://www.copyright.com/>

Crash Course in Copyright, Georgia Harper
<http://www.utsystem.edu/ogc/IntellectualProperty/cprtindx.htm#top>

Creative Commons
<http://creativecommons.org>

Electronic Frontier Foundation
<http://www.eff.org/>

"How to Cite Film, Video, and Online Media"
<http://www.lib.berkeley.edu/MRC/mla.html>

"Humanities: Documenting Sources"
<http://www.dianahacker.com/resdoc/p04_c08_o.html>.

Information on Obtaining Copyright Permissions
<http://lib.law.washington.edu/ref/copyright.html>

"Public Domain"
<http://www.answers.com/topic/public-domain>

Stanford Law School's Center for Internet and Society
<http://cyberlaw.stanford.edu/>

Journals

Computers and Composition Online
<http://www.bgsu.edu/cconline/>

Enculturation: A Journal for Rhetoric, Writing, and Culture
<http://enculturation.gmu.edu/>

KAIROS
<http://english.ttu.edu/kairos/>

Multimodal Examples and Resources

BBC News
<http://news.bbc.co.uk>

Current_TV: VC^2 Survival Guide
<http://www.current.tv/make/training>

Digital Documentaries
<http://www.atschool.org/digidocs/index.htm>

Digital Story Telling Education
<http://story.e2bn.net/index.php>

Electronic Literature Project Directory
<http://directory.eliterature.org>

Heightened Student Voice through Digital Storytelling
<http://www.kenton.k12.ky.us/DigitalStory/dstindex.htm>

Home Page for Audio Production and Contemporary Culture
<http://www.webfuse.cqu.edu.au/Courses/2002/T3/MMST12016/course_site/index.htm>

Internet Archive
<http://www.archive.org>

Listening Booth
<http://www.poets.org/booth/booth.cfm>

Lost and Found Sound: From NPR's All Things Considered
<http://www.npr.org/programs/lnfsound/>

The Movie Sounds Page
<http://www.moviesounds.com/>

Multimedia Seeds: A Starting Point for Audio, Video, and Visual Resources
<http://eduscapes.com/seeds/>

National Public Radio Website
<http://www.npr.org>

New York Times Multimedia Page
<http://www.nytimes.com/pages/multimedia/index.html>

Online Multimedia Gallery, Duke Center for Documentary Studies
<http://cds.aas.duke.edu/exhibits/multimedia.html>

Online Speech Bank
<http://www.americanrhetoric.com/speechbank.htm>

"On Viewing and Visually Representing As Forms of Literacy"
<http://www.ncte.org/about/over/positions/category/literacy/107573.htm>

Open Video Project
<http://www.open-video.org>

Our Media
<http://ourmedia.org>

Poems that Go
<http://www.poemsthatgo.com>

Project-Based Learning with Multimedia
<http://pblmm.k12.ca.us/>

Public Broadcasting Station
<http://www.pbs.org>

Public Radio Exchange
<http://www.prx.org/home.do>

Radio College: A Project of the Association of Independents in Radio
<http://www.radiocollege.org/>

RadioDiaries on NPR
<http://www.radiodiaries.org/>

<remix culture>, Lawrence Lessig.
<https://netfiles.uiuc.edu/jlsolber/www/lessig/>

Rhetorical Figures in Sound: Revised and Improved
Web site retrieved July 13, 2005, from <http://www.americanrhetoric.com/figures/antithesis.htm>

Sound Portraits.org
<http://www.soundportraits.org/>

StoryCorps
<http://storycorps.net/about/>

Stories1st.org
<http://www.stories1st.org/>

"Reading Sounds: An Essay on Sounds, Music, Knowledge, Rock, and Society," Phillip Tagg
<http://www.tagg.org/articles/readsound.html>

Talking History: Aural History Productions
<http://www.talkinghistory.org/>

Technology Showcase: Videography for Educators
<http://ali.apple.com/ali_sites/ali/exhibits/1000019/>

The Language of Film and Video
<http://english.unitecnology.ac.nz/resources/resources/film.html>

The Veterans History Project, Library of Congress
<www.loc.gov/vets/>

Third Coast International Audio Festival
<http://www.thirdcoastfestival.org/pages/archive848.html>

This American Life: From WBEZ Chicago
<http://www.thislife.org/>

Transom.org
<http://www.transom.org/>

WAV Central
<http://WavCentral.com/movies/>

Youth Media Distribution
 <http://www.ymdi.org/index.php>

Software/Hardware Documentation

Apple iMovie Support
<http://www.apple.com/support/imovie/>

Atomic Learning
<http://www.atomiclearning.com/moviemaker2>

Audacity
<http://audacity.sourceforge.net/>

Digidesign
<http://www.digidesign.com/>

MightyCoach.com
<http://www.mightycoach.com/articles/mm2/>

Sony Product Support
<http://www.ita.sel.sony.com/support/>

Windows MovieMaker
<http://www.windowsmoviemakers.net/Tutorials/Index.aspx>

APPENDICES

APPENDIX 1
Sample Assignment #1

DIRECTIONS

Compose an audio essay that explores the role of sound in your own personal literacy history and that will help class members gain a broader understanding of your literacy practices and values.

This project should *not simply record and reproduce sounds*. Rather, it should use sound to *tell a story, make meaning about, create some commentary on, offer some insight into your literacy practices and values*. Most importantly, it should help listeners *reflect* on what they are hearing. Your essay can take the form of a sound portrait, soundscape, audio documentary, or sound reflection.

Other than these requirements, the assignment is wide open—and purposefully so! I want you to exercise your own creativity in the service of teaching us all something about literacy.

In class, we will listen to the audio essays below to explore sound. Listen to them yourself as well.

* **sound portrait:** an audio essay that focuses on some aspect of a person's life. It is often biographical.

    "Willie Young Rabbit Hunter" (sound portrait, 1:37)
    <http://www.soundportraits.org/on-air/rabbit_hunter/>

    "Reggie Jones, Lifeguard" (sound portrait, 3:45)
    <http://www.soundportraits.org/on-air/lifeguard/>

* **audio documentary:** an audio essay that records the sounds of an important event or time in history when something momentous is happening, some change is taking place, or some trend/pattern is observed in society.

    "Woolworth's Lunch-Counter Waitress" (audio documentary about the original civil rights sit-in at a Woolworth's lunch counter, 4:58)
    <http://www.soundportraits.org/on-air/lunch-counter_waitress/>

    "Street Dogs" (audio documentary about dogs who live with street people, 12:06)
    <http://www.transom.org/shows/2001/200108.shows.streetdogs.perrywarga.html>

HINTS FOR SUCCESS

* Make sure to plan for your sound project. Writing will help you here and you should hand in all the written materials that support your project. For example, be sure to keep a written production log of the time you spend on your project. Here is a sample entry for that log:

27 November 2006
9:40-11:00   In class, spent 40 minutes uploading audio and 40 minutes editing audio
                    according to plan. PLAN FOR NEXT SESSION: Continue to edit audio.

—record citations for the audio clips you download from the web
—write a reflection on a draft

- Make sure you know how to use your recording equipment! Read the documentation that comes along with the digital sound recorders!

  —always wear isolating headphones so that you can hear what you are recording
  —whenever possible, connect the audio recorder to a power source with an adapter;
    batteries fail at the worst possible times.

  Other written documentation will also come in handy. Careful written documentation will help your teacher understand how much work you have put into your project. Here are some suggestions for the documentation you should be keeping:

  —storyboard your audio essay or write a scene-by-scene outline
  —write out interview questions beforehand and share them with the person(s) you are
    interviewing.
  —make a list of sounds/people/activities you need to record
  —make sure you are not recording sounds (e.g., air conditioning hum, a lawn mower going by, a
    nearby source of electrical power, ambient noise in a room) that will obscure or contaminate the
    sounds you want to capture

- Schedule more time than you think you need for editing with Audacity—it always takes *much much* longer than the original recording!! Before you begin editing, be sure to go through the Audacity tutorial on the SourceForge web site <http://audacity.sourceforge.net/help/> or the Audacity overview at the Transom Web site <http://www.transom.org/tools/editing_mix ing/200404.audacity.html>.

- Before you edit—draw a visual plan of how you want the essay to be structured—what anecdotes go where, where you are going to include soundmarks, signal sounds, keynote sounds, silence, music, narration, and so on. Identify when and where you are going to *layer* these sounds to create a rich texture for your project.

- Make sure to provide some kind of focused reflective frame for your audio project—some way of helping listeners understand what they are hearing, why it is significant, and what you are trying to convey about your subject. (Read the excerpt from Abel and Glass [1999] *An Illustrated Guide for Radio*.)

- Select/edit/winnow! Make sure your sound composition is tightly and effectively composed. Cut everything that doesn't directly contribute to your intended message. (Read *An Illustrated Guide to Radio*.)

- Make sure your sound project effectively takes advantage of the specific affordances (capabilities) of the medium. What can sound capture best (e.g., tone, emotion, accent)? What escapes the affordances of sound (e.g., a wink, a hand gesture, a facial expression)?

- **SAVE OFTEN, SAVE OFTEN, SAVE OFTEN!!!**

- **BACK UP YOUR WORK, BACK UP YOUR WORK, BACK UP YOUR WORK!!!**

- See the attached evaluation sheet for the criteria on which this assignment will be graded.

EVALUATION SHEET
Audio Autobiography: Sound and Literacy

| | 1 | 2 | 3 | 4 | 5 |

Little evidence of careful <————————————————————————————> Lots of careful planning/
planning/composing/producing   composing/producing
Comment:

| | 1 | 2 | 3 | 4 | 5 |

Reveals very little <————————————————————————————> Reveals a great deal
about role of sound in life   about role of sound in life
Comment:

| | 1 | 2 | 3 | 4 | 5 |

Lack of reflective focus <————————————————————————> Great reflective focus
on personal literacy practices   on personal literacy practices
Comment:

| | 1 | 2 | 3 | 4 | 5 |

Ineffective use of affordances of audio<————————————> Effective use of affordances of audio
Comment:

| | 1 | 2 | 3 | 4 | 5 |

Ineffective attention to audience/purpose <—————————> Effective attention to audience/purpose
Comment:

| | 1 | 2 | 3 | 4 | 5 |

Less than careful <————————————————————————————————> Very careful
approach to citation,   approach to citation, documentation,
documentation, copyright, licensing   copyright, licensing
Comment:

| | 1 | 2 | 3 | 4 | 5 |

Less than careful approach <————————————————————————> Very careful approach
to permissions/releases   to permissions/releases
Comment:

| | 1 | 2 | 3 | 4 | 5 |

Poorly written documents/ <—————————————————————————> Excellent written
supporting materials   documents/supporting materials
Comment:

| | 1 | 2 | 3 | 4 | 5 |

Less creative/insightful <———————————————————————————> Very creative/insightful
Comment:

GRADE:

APPENDIX 2
Sample Assignment #2

VIDEO BIOGRAPHY: LITERACY VALUES AND PRACTICES

DIRECTIONS

Compose a video text about literacy (using Video Studio, I-Movie, or some similar software that you have access to) that provides an insightful representation of the literacy issues/themes we have identified thus far in this course.

In your video, combine still images, video, music, written words, narration, and/or sound to compose **a narrative documentary. You can use one or more of the following focus ideas:**

- an individual's or group's interesting or unusual literacy practices/values
- an interesting or unusual place in which this individual's literacy is practiced or valued
- an individual who practices an interesting or unusual literacy that represents a larger trend
- a person who practices an interesting or unusual kind/type/genre of literacy

Your literacy video text should have the following characteristics:

- Some video or still images, some narration or voice over, and some music that adds significant information about the topic
- Information that is valuable to our class discussion of literacy issues/themes
- **a title screen** for your video
- **a credit screen** that include full citations for video clips, images, music that you download and use

The project should employ the affordances (capabilities) of the media you are using in effective rhetorical ways. It should be characterized by careful design that helps to convey meaning. The project should be both instructive and creative.

The project should do more than simply *depict* a literacy practice/value/issue/place/event/genre—it should help readers/viewers *reflect on/gain insight into the subject of the video.*

For this assignment, you will probably need to do several of the following tasks:

- **record some video** (use a digital video camera)
- **use some digitized images** (shoot your own video or download video clips from a collection on the web)

- **use some music and sound/narration/voice over** (use a digital sound recorder to capture sound and or download music/sound from the Internet). This will involve cutting out the parts that you don't need, re-arranging the parts that you do need, and layering these semiotic elements in Video Studio. You may also need to edit your sound using Audacity
- **write** supporting materials and documents

If you don't have access to your own digital camera, see me to check out a digital video camera or a digital still camera. I can also help you check out a digital audio recorder and microphone. You will need time to learn how to work these pieces of equipment, so plan ahead to read the documentation.

You will also need to buy a set of inexpensive headphones.

I will demonstrate in class how to use digital cameras and edit video at various times, but you can also follow the directions for using VideoStudio at <http://www.ulead.com/learning/vs.htm> and those I have written in the Downloading Sound and Images handout.

Want to see some sample student-made videos? Look at some of the examples on the DVD at the back of this book.

EVALUATION SHEET
Video Biography: Literacy Values and Practices

```
                    1              2              3              4              5
Little evidence of careful <————————————————————————————————————> Lots of careful planning/
planning/composing/producing                                      composing/producing
Comment:


                    1              2              3              4              5
Teaches viewers very little about literacy <—————————————————> Teaches viewers a great deal about literacy
Comment:


          1      2      3      4      5
Ineffective attention to audience/purpose<————————————————————> Effective attention to audience/purpose
Comment:


                    1              2              3              4              5
Lack of reflective focus on literacy practices <————————————> Great reflective focus on literacy practices
Comment:


                    1              2              3              4              5
Ineffective use of affordances of video and audio<———————————> Effective use of affordances of video and audio
Comment:


                    1              2              3              4              5
Less than careful <—————————————————————————————————————————————> Very careful approach
approach to citation, documentation,                              to citation, documentation,
copyright, licensing                                              copyright,licensing
Comment:


                    1              2              3              4              5
Less than careful approach <————————————————————————————————————> Very careful approach
to permissions/releases                                              to  permissions/releases
Comment:


                    1              2              3              4              5
Few written <———————————————————————————————————————————————————> Extensive written
documents/supporting materials                                    documents/supporting materials
Comment:


                    1              2              3              4              5
Less Creative/insightful/ <—————————————————————————————————————>Very Creative/insightful
Comment:


Grade:
```

APPENDIX 3
Sample Assignment #3

DOCUMENTARY AS CREATIVE NONFICTION

GEARING UP: We've read and discussed Hunter S. Thompson's article "The Kentucky Derby is Decadent and Depraved," and analyzed his gonzo journalism approach in the context of other forms of creative nonfiction writing such as reportage and memoir. We've considered how Thompson's style connects to Tom Wolfe's definition of new journalism, Lee Gutkind's discussion of techniques for creative nonfiction, and Jessica Abell and Ira Glass' theories of drawing out stories in audio interviews. Now you'll form your own approach, in response to, or in extension or rejection of, the styles we've talked about.

In this assignment, your job is to document an event/trend/situation/experience that interests you.

YOUR ASSIGNMENT: Compose a piece of creative nonfiction, You can select any medium or combination of media (print, computer, radio, etc.), any modality or combination of modalities (still or moving images, words, sound, etc.), and any genre you choose (conventional essay, audio memoir, comic book, web site, 'zine, newspaper, video documentary, or some combination thereof) to document an event, trend, situation, or experience interesting to you. Capture what the event/trend/situation/experience means, why it exists, why people attend or do it, what you're doing there. Develop a theme, make a point. Your goal is to both entertain and inform viewers/readers/listeners, to give them a sense of how you see or understand the event/trend/situation/experience and its import.

YOUR APPROACH: Your approach is your choice. Will you follow Thompson's lead and focus on the seedy underbelly of the event/trend/situation/experience you have chosen? Will you seek out important or interesting interview subjects? Will you portray people who embody the event/trend/situation/experience?

Whatever the approach, your project should represent the event/trend/situation/experience from your perspective, from the angle you want to present it. At all stages, reflect on your role as the author/composer. Can you be an impartial observer behind the scenes, or should your role be explored in the text itself? What can you do to assure you're not taking over the stories of other people, but instead working to represent them as fairly as possible? Will you limit yourself to "detached" observation, will you participate in the festival and interact with people, or will you combine the two approaches? What choices will you make in the stages from your initial observation/participation in the festival (in the form of written notes, raw camera footage, raw audio recording, etc.) to showcasing your project in a more final form?

MEDIUM, MODALITY, AND GENRE: You can choose any medium, modality, or genre for your final documentary. We'll talk in class about how and why you make the choices you do, and why you believe them best for your approach and your project, so keep these questions in mind as you work: What can words do that video or audio cannot do as well, and vice versa? What are the advantages and weaknesses of the genre you have chosen for your project? How will your audience engage with your medium? What expectations for themselves as readers (or viewers or listeners) will they bring with them? I'm thinking here of the Abel and Glass book, *The Illustrated Guide to Radio*, which explains radio as a very didactic medium in which the points of stories often need to be stated very specifically. How would you describe the way your documentary needs to be told in the medium, the modality, and the genre you choose?

OPTIONS: Work with a group or go solo. Visit the festival for a one-night stint; or contrast morning observation with late night; or force yourself to stay awake to attend three days in a row, start to finish, in true gonzo journalism fashion!

APPENDIX 4
Sample Timeline

Timeline for Audio/Video Assignment in a Documentary Course

Weeks 1-2: Have students read about video and audio documentaries and their historical importance. Have students come up with a definition of documentary as a genre. Focus on audio documentary and video documentary as communicative forms. Have students complete a series of reflective writing assignments about these readings. Consider some of the following readings and resources:

Documentary Films and Documentary
<http:/www.trinity.wa.edu.au/plduffyrc/subjects/english/media/docfilms.htm>

Theory into Practice: Stanley Hawes and the Commonwealth Film Unit
<http://www.latrobe.edu.au/screeningthepast/firstrelease/fr0799/ibfr7d.htm>

Defining Documentary Film: The Question of Roger and Me
<http://doc.weinberger.us/>

Week 3: Conduct two discovery workshops: one on using a digital audio recorder, and one on using a video cameras. Practice interviewing skills with other students in class. Have students write a list of questions (see Appendix 5).

Week 4: View or listen to sample documentaries from the following sites. Have student groups showcase their favorite examples. Have them write short responses that analyze samples for structure, content, organization, audience, purpose.

Teaching Matters: Digital Documentaries
<http://www.atschool.org/digidocs/index.htm>

PBS Youth Media Network
<nethttp://www.pbs.org/merrow/listenup/index.html>

Apple Learning Interchange

Documenting Child Labor in Nepal
<http://ali.apple.com/ali_sites/ali/exhibits/1001479/>

The Life of a Veteran
<http://ali.apple.com/ali_sites/ali/exhibits/1000925/>

Australian Film Commission/Australian Broadcasting Corporation: Documentary Online
<http://abc.net.au/documentaryonline/default.htm>

Center for Documentary Studies: Online Multimedia Gallery
<http://www-cds.aas.duke.edu/exhibits/multimedia.html>

Week 5: Brainstorm about possible student-made documentary projects. Form student collaborative groups. Have groups submit a short proposal for the project to the instructor and to another peer-review group. Students reserve equipment for recording in weeks 8-9 (see Appendix 23-24).

Week 6: Have students plan audio or video projects using sample diagrams in Appendix 12-13, or storyboarding techniques from the following web sites:

Memory's Voices
<http://www.storycenter.org/memvoice/pages/cookbook.html>

Teaching Matters: Digital Documentaries
<http://www.atschool.org/digidocs/info4.htm>

Weeks 7: Students record and document their experiences—recording audio and video, taking notes on observations, interviewing subjects.

Week 8: Hold two workshop sessions on audio-editing and video-editing software. Students download and begin work on projects.

Week 9: Conduct studio critiques of works-in-progress. Students show works, reflect in writing on works, and provide revision suggestions.

Week 10: Revision of projects.

Week 11: Showcase documentary projects. Have students write curatorial or authorial statements about their projects.

APPENDIX 5
Interviewing

- Plan ahead and present your project to possible interview subjects as early as possible. Agree to a specific interview date and stick to it. Alternatively, you can plan to interview on site at an event/situation/experience (attendees, operators, spectators, speakers, etc.). Your questions may be carefully planned ahead and go in-depth for more formal interviews, or be more spontaneous for interviews on site, when you might speak to several people rather than going in-depth with one.

- Be clear about what your project entails, what kinds of questions you'll be asking, and what audiences will see the finished product (e.g., "I'll be asking you questions about your role as a festival organizer as part of a project for my W311, Writing Creative Nonfiction course at Indiana University Southeast. My work will initially be seen by my instructor and classmates, but I would also like to ask your permission to post the final version online.") **Make sure to have all subjects sign a release consent form (Appendix 6) prior to their interview.** Remember interview subjects are putting their stories in your hands, so you want to establish a level of trust and let them know of your intentions to represent them fairly and accurately.

- Invite interview subjects to become active participants in the project. Offer to show them your project in process, rather than asking them to wait for the final version. You may find their feedback on your project very valuable.

- Ask your subjects to tell stories.

- Consult the following sites for hints on interviewing:

  Ivideotape: Camera Techniques for Interviewing
  <http://www.nextexit.com/production/ivideo.html>

  General Guidelines for Conducting Interviews
  <http://www.mapnp.org/library/evaluatn/intrview.htm>

  Interview as a Method for Qualitative Research
  <www.public.asu.edu/~kroel/www500/Interview%20Fri.pdf>

  Oral History: Conducting Interviews with Survivors of the Holocaust
  <http://www.history.ucsb.edu/projects/holocaust/Oralhistory/>

  Folklife and Fieldwork: A Layman's Introduction to Field Techniques
  <http://www.loc.gov/folklife/fieldwork/howto.html#preparation>

  Advice on Videotaping Interviews
  <http://pblmm.k12.ca.us/TechHelp/VideoHelp/bProduction/AdviceOnInterviews.html>

  The Heart of Oral history: How to Interview
  <http://www.baylor.edu/Oral_History/index.php?id=23611>

INTERVIEW RELEASE/INFORMED CONSENT FORM

I hereby give _____ (insert student interviewer's name) the right to record this interview, to edit the material that I provide in this interview, and to create a composition (audio, video, alphabetic) that uses this material for educational purposes.

I understand that this composition will not be sold. I understand it may be distributed for educational purposes within classes and among teachers who could use this material for their classes.

I also give/do not give permission to use my first and last name in connection with the publication of the composition.

I give/do not give permission for my interview material to be posted on the www as part of this composition.

Note: Individuals under 18 years of age must have the permission of a parent.

Signature: _____

Date: _____

Parent's signature (if applicable): _____

Date: _____

Print name: _____

_____
Note: Teachers should check with the institutional review board (IRB) at their college or university before conducting any research involving human subjects.

What you will need:

To download photographs from a digital camera to a PC, you will need the following equipment.

- a digital camera like this Sony Cybershot

- a USB cable (USB A –USB B)

- a PC with a USB port

What to do:

1. Carefully attach the small end of the USB cable to the camera using the appropriate port.

2. Carefully attach the large end of the cable to the USB port on the computer.

3. Boot up the computer, Then turn on the digital camera.

4. Open My Computer and wait until the camera appears, and click twice on it.

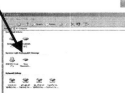

5. Wait until the Camera
   Wizard screen pops up.
   Click on the Next button.

6. Select the photograph
   you want to download.

   When there is a blue box
   around it, put a check
   in the small box in the
   upper right-hand corner.

   Click Next.

7. Give your picture a
   descriptive title.

   Click Browse and make
   sure you save it
   in your own project
   file.

   Click Next.

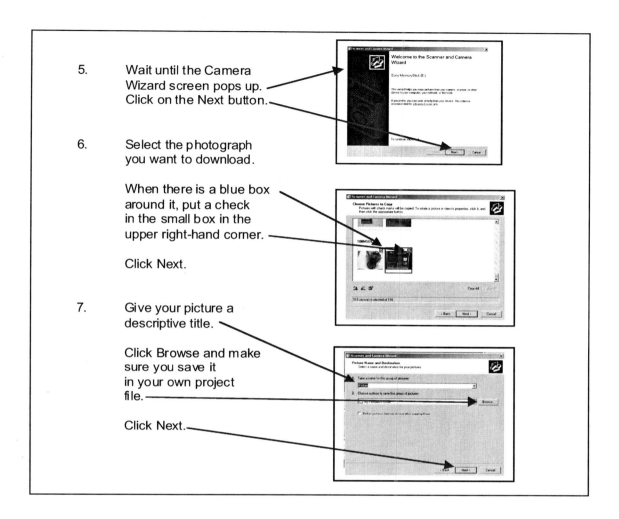

APPENDIX 8
Technology Survey

1. How often do you use a computer? Email? The Internet?

2. How would you describe your level of fluency with computer-based technologies?

3. How comfortable are you working with new technologies and new computer programs?

4. Have you ever worked with audio-editing software? If so, what program(s) have you used?

5. Have you ever worked with video-editing software? If so, what program(s) have you used?

6. What experiences have you had composing, arranging, or performing audio compositions (e.g., compiling mix tapes, monitoring volume levels on microphones in plays and musicals, playing musical instruments, or writing music)?

7. What experiences have you had composing, arranging, or performing video compositions (e.g., recording and editing home movies, taking and editing digital photographs, or composing visual artwork)?

8. How do you best learn about technology? Choose all that apply.

   a. Demonstration

   b. One-on-one

   c. By yourself through trial and error

   d. Other—please explain

9. What technologies could you teach other students about (e.g., audio recording, audio editing, audio mixing, video recording, video editing)?

Name:_____ Email Address:_____

APPENDIX 9
Student
Expertise Grid

	CAROL S.	SAM C.	BETH R.	JON M.	MARC D.	JEFF W.	JACI E.
E-mail	E	E	M	E	E	M	E
Internet	E	E	M	E	E	M	E
Audacity (audio software)	B	B	E	D	D	B	D
GarageBand (audio software)	M	B	D	D	E	D	B
IPod/iTalk Recorder	B	E	D	D	E	B	D
iMovie (video software)	M	D	E	D	E	D	B
Video Studio (video software)	B	D	D	D	D	D	E
Digital Video Camera	B	D	E	D	E	D	B
Digital Camera	B	D	E	D	E	D	E

D = Don't know it at all, but I want to learn
B = I am a beginner and need help
M = I have some experience and am willing to help
E = I am fairly expert and can teach, but I want to learn more

APPENDIX 10
Collaborative
Project Log

Name:_____   Date:_____

Here's what I accomplished today:

Make sure you look at or listen to this:

Here's what I suggest working on next:

Here's my list of what we still need to do:

Other thoughts and questions:

Directions: In your groups, discuss the following list of key elements in composition and come to a consensus on how they will function in your project. You're probably familiar with these key elements from your work with alphabetic texts; however, you will need to work with them in new ways because you're composing in a new mode—sound.

Consider how you can use both composing strategies that apply across modes (such as repetition and emphasis) and composing strategies unique to sound:

Keynote Sounds: Sounds that set the tone of an audio essay or sonic landscape and orient the audience to the piece's overall meaning. They help situate the piece. They may be subtle and go unnoticed by the audience.

Signal Sounds: Sounds to which the audience pays immediate attention. They are in the foreground, rather than the background, and provide a focus on the key theme of the audio essay.

Soundmarks: Audio's version of visual landmarks. These are important, explicit reference points to a sonic landscape (Schafer, 1997, pp. 9-10).

KEY ELEMENTS IN COMPOSITION

1. **Thesis Statement:** Will your project have a thesis statement? Will it be implicit or explicit? Which type of thesis (explicit or implicit) would make your project more or less effective?

2. **Structure:** How will you structure your audio composition? Consider how and why you might apply these typical organizational models to audio compositions:

    Chronological Order
    General to Specific/Specific to General
    Question/Answer
    Problem/Solution

3. **Introduction:** How will you introduce your project, and how will that introduction add to the project's effectiveness as a whole? Will you use conventional introduction strategies? Will you "hook" the audience with something immediately compelling? Why or why not?

4. **Conclusion:** How will you conclude the project, and how will it add to the project's effectiveness as a whole? Will you use conventional conclusion strategies? Will you summarize the main point or points of your composition, while at the same time offering something new to your audience? Why or why not?

5. **Transitions:** How will you transition from one idea to the next?

6. **Coherence:** How will your composition work as a unified whole? What will you do to make sure that the project hangs together?

APPENDIX 12
Planning
Audio Essays

SEQUENCING: SINGLE AUDIO TRACK

(fade in) music file A ···· (fade in) Children reading aloud ···· silence ···· (fade in) Narration (How do children learn to read?) ···· (fade out) ···· (fade in) breakfast table chatter ···· (fade out) ···· (fade in) music file
(fade out) ···· in classroo (fade out) ···· B (fade out)

LAYERING: MULTIPLE AUDIO TRACKS

Audio track #1
(background) ···· (fade in) Children reading aloud in classroom (fade out) ···· (fade in) Teacher instructing in reading ···· (fade out) ···· (fade in) breakfast
···· table chatter (fade out)

Audio Track #2
(music) ···· music file A—(fade out) ···· (fade in) music file B (fade out)
Note: find a Sesame St. song ···· Note: use ABC song

Audio Track #3
(narration/ ···· voice over (How do children learn to read?) ···· (fade out) ···· Mother's narrative
voice over) ···· comments about Johnny

AUDIO

■ sound file (music)

▨ silence

▤ sound file (background sound)

■ sound file (narration/voice over)

228

Video & stills
- title screen
- (cross fade)
- video segment A (reading groups) (jump out)
- Still shot — (cross fade) (Johnny reading & teacher sitting in class)
- Still shot — (cross fade) (Johnny reading a computer screen)
- Still shot — (cross fade) (Johnny reading - talking to him)
- video segment B (Johnny at breakfast table playing video game and chatting while mom is talking to him)

Audio track #1 (background)
- (fade in) kids reading aloud (fade out)
- (fade in) Teacher talking to reading groups (fade out)
- aloud in classroom
- (fade in) breakfast table chatter (fade out)

Audio Track #2 (music)
- music file A—(fade out)
- Note: find a Sesame St. song
- (fade in) music file B (fade out)
- Note: use ABC song

Audio Track #3 (narration/voice over)
- voice over
- narration (How do children learn to read?) (fade out)
- (fade in) voice over (Mother's comments about Johnny's video gaming)

AUDIO
- sound file (music)
- silence
- sound file (background sound)
- sound file (narration/voice-over)

VIDEO
- title screens
- video segment
- still shot
- cross fade (still to still)

Name:_____   Date:_____

Describe your knowledge/comfort level before beginning the audio project and your current knowledge/comfort level. Rate your knowledge/comfort level in the following areas as high, good, average, poor, or absent. Explain or add comments if necessary.

<u>BEFORE</u>   <u>NOW</u>

Working with recording devices:

Working with sound-editing software:

Transferring audio data (from recorder
to hard drive, from program to program,
within the editing program, from hard
drive to CD):

Arranging and composing audio
in meaningful ways:

APPENDIX 15
Group Evaluation—
Video Essays

Name:_____ Date:_____

Describe your group members' participation in each of the following aspects of your video project as high, good, average, poor, or absent. Explain or add comments if necessary.

Group Member Names: _____

_____

_____

Working with recording devices:

Working with video-editing software:

Transferring video data
(from camera/disc to hard
drive, from program to program,
within the editing program,
from hard drive to CD):

Arranging and composing images
and sound in meaningful ways:

Willingness to share what he
or she knows or has learned:

APPENDIX 16
Collaboration
Checklist

_____ I experimented with aspects of the project that were unfamiliar to me. (List these aspects below.)

_____ I experimented with recording equipment.

_____ I experimented with transferring files or clips.

_____ I experimented with editing and arranging recorded data in meaningful ways.

_____ I experimented with adjusting pieces of the project for overall coherence and consistency by adjusting volume, selecting transitions, and inserting signposts for viewers or listeners to follow.

_____ I taught something I learned to someone else. (List what you taught and to whom below.)

_____ When teaching, I made sure to let the learner practice instead of showing him or her what to do.

_____ I regularly provided encouragement to other students.

APPENDIX 17
Bridging Alphabetic and Multimodal Composition

DIRECTIONS:

In the space below, or on separate sheet, brainstorm lists for the aural and visual affordances offered by alphabetic texts:

AURAL AFFORDANCES   VISUAL AFFORDANCES

Next, select a particular alphabetic essay that you have written. Examine your text and choose a small portion of it that could be represented in some visual or aural form. (For instance, you could transform the portion into an oral reading, a recorded conversation, a comic strip, or a video clip—less than one minute is recommended for this brief exercise.)

Now, show how this segment would work in the new modality you have chosen: create a storyboard (for a video), a script (for an audio essay), a draft strip (for a comic strip), and so on. Don't worry about the final quality—the goal is to produce a draft.

As you work, think about the following questions and respond to them in writing once you're done:

- What is gained and/or lost, emphasized and/or underplayed with each modality? Why?

- How does the author's relationship to the audience (ethos) change?

- If appeals to logic (logos) and emotion (pathos) are made in print texts, how does the change of modality alter the effectiveness of the appeal? Why?

Purpose: Through watching portions of a video essay and discussing the essay's visual effectiveness, you can start thinking about how and why images can be rhetorically powerful.

Directions: As a class, first discuss ideas about what makes a video image or frame powerful. Come up with specific examples and theorize as to why they might be powerful. Then, in small groups, watch the following sections of Kara Alexander's video essay "Literacy Practices and Literacy Events of a 21st Century American Child" several times, pausing on certain images and rewatching the section several times to write about and discuss the following questions:

Introduction: (0:00-0:57)
Choose three specific video images or frames that stand out to you as a viewer in terms of their power, pausing the video at these points. What does the content of each specific image or frame make you feel or think? How is the author's use of each image or frame related to her rhetorical purpose? Audience? Why? The content? Why? If text accompanies the image or frame, how is it related to her rhetorical purpose? Audience? Why?

1.

2.

3.

Choose one sequence of images/frames in the video that you consider especially effective. Watch the entire section several times. Identify at least one sequence of images or frames that you feel is particularly powerful. Why are these images or frames powerful when put together this way? How is this sequence related to the author's rhetorical purpose? Audience? The content? Why? Consider multiple influences in terms of logos, ethos, pathos.

Watch the entire section one more time, without pausing. What does the accumulation of images or frames make you feel or think? How is this accumulated imagery related to the author's rhetorical purpose? Audience? The content? Why?

APPENDIX 19
Rhetorically Powerful Sounds

Purpose: Through listening to portions of an audio essay and discussing its effectiveness, you can start thinking about how and why sounds can be rhetorically powerful.

Directions: As a class, first discuss ideas about what makes an audio element powerful. Come up with specific examples and theorize as to why they might be powerful. Then, in small groups, listen to the following sections of Sonya Borton's audio essay several times, pausing on certain audio elements and listening to the section several times to write about and discuss the following questions.

Sonya's Grandfather: (1:53-3:01)
Choose three separate audio elements that stand out, pausing the clip after playing each. What does the content of a specific element—whether narration or music—make you feel or think? How is the author's use of each audio element related to her rhetorical purpose? Her audience? The content? Why? If a sound is accompanied by narration in one of the elements you have chosen, how might there be something powerful about that combination—especially in terms of its rhetorical appeal?

1.

2.

3.

Listen to the entire section several times. Identify at least one juxtaposition or layering of sounds that seems particularly powerful to you as a listener. Why are these sounds powerful when put together this way? How is the author's use of sound related to her rhetorical purpose? Her audience? The content? Why? Consider multiple influences in terms of logos, ethos, pathos.

Listen to the entire section one more time, without pausing. What does the accumulation of sounds make you feel or think as a listener? How is the accumulation of sounds related to the author's rhetorical purpose? Her audience? The content? Why?

1.

2.

3.

Conclusion: (4:19–5:30)
Play this section at least four times and listen closely to it. Choose three audio elements within this section that stand out—that seem particularly powerful—to you as a listener. What does the content of each specific element—whether narration or music—make you feel or think? How is the author's use of each audio element related to her rhetorical purpose? Her audience? If a sound is accompanied by narration, how does that combination relate to the author's rhetorical purpose? Her audience? The content? Why?

1.

2.

3.

Listen to the entire section several times. Identify a specific sequence or layering of sounds that seems particularly powerful to you as a listener. Why are these sounds powerful when put together this way? How is the sound related to the authors' rhetorical purpose? Her audience? The content? Why? Consider multiple influences in terms of logos, ethos, pathos.

Listen to the entire section one more time, without pausing. What does the accumulation of sounds make you feel? Think? How is this accumulation of sounds related to the authors' rhetorical purpose? Her audience? The content? The appeals of logos, ethos, pathos? Why?

APPENDIX 20
Rhetorically Powerful Camera Work

Purpose: Through watching portions of a video essay and discussing it in terms of camera shots, angles, and sequences, you can rehearse ways to talk and write about the structural elements of your own projects.

Directions: Read over the following terms* to become familiar with them for your analysis.

Wide Shot (a.k.a. Establishing Shot or Long Shot): A shot that sets the scene, orienting viewers to the main subject or important people involved. Such a scene might include a small group of people.

Medium Shot: This shot is closer to the subject and shows less of the scene than the wide shot. This shot is also useful as a transition between a wide shot and a close-up shot. In the scene with the small group, this shot might focus more closely on one person in that small group.

Two Shot/Three Shot: A two shot captures two people in the frame, and a three shot captures three. Such a shot is usually medium or wide.

Close-Up Shot: A shot that gets even closer to the subject, ideal for showing detail. In the scene with the small group of people, this would focus on one person's face.

Extreme Close Up Shot: This shot is even closer, possibly focusing on a person's eyes or mouth.

Over the Shoulder or Cutaway Shot: A cutaway moves away from the main action. In an interview, a cutaway might transition from the interviewee to the interviewer. Such shots can be helpful for transitions when editing.

Sequence: A series of related shots. A sequence of classroom shots, for instance, might start with a wide shot of a classroom, followed by medium shots of a few students, and then a close-up of one student.

Length of Shot: Determining how long to hold a shot depends on what's going on in the shot and what you're trying to accomplish.

---

*Adapted from the Web site of Project-Based Learning with Multimedia: <http://pblmm.k12.ca.us/PBLGuide/Activities/Powerful Images.html>.

Lydia's Religious Literacy: (8:25-8:57)
Choose a sequence from this section and analyze its rhetorical effectiveness:
Describe the rhetorical purpose for the entire video and then identify the more specific rhetorical purpose for this particular sequence. Finally, describe the even more specific purpose of each shot *within* the sequence. Are there any shots that work particularly well? Why? Are there any shots that should be eliminated? Why?

Choose a sequence with at least two shots and describe how logos, ethos, and pathos might be bound up in each constituent shot.
What is the purpose and message of each shot within this sequence? How does each shot connect to the rhetorical appeals?

Choose a sequence from this section and analyze camera logistics:
Identify the use of two specific transition shots and/or effects within a sequence. How are transitions constructed? Which transitions work well? Which don't work as well? Why? How do the transitions relate to the rhetorical purpose of the video? The audience? The content? Why?

Locate the movement from wide to close-up shots. What does this movement do to viewers' focus? Attention? Why? How do the shots/the movement relate to the rhetorical purpose of the video? The audience? The content? Why?

Identify at least one specific example of a shot held too long and one of a shot not held long enough. How does the length of shots relate to the rhetorical purpose of the video? The audience? The content? Why?

APPENDIX 21
Discovering about Audio

TRYING OUT THE MINIDISC AUDIO RECORDER....

1. As a group of four—take a digital audio recorder, a pair of headphones, and a microphone. Sit near a plug so that you can plug in the audio recorder.

2. As a group, read the documentation (the User's Manual); figure out how to use the equipment.

3. In *What Can Video Games Teach Us About Learning and Literacy*, James Gee says "Literacy . . . is not a unitary thing, but a multiple matter" (p. 14). He explains that literacies are ways of making meaning within certain semiotic domains (e.g., biology, mathematics, video games, music, painting, fashion design, movies, journalism, dance) that "recruit" certain communication modes (e.g., sound, equations, writing, gestures, still images, moving images, movement).

   In a digital audio interview (no longer than 5 minutes), answer the following questions:

   - What literacies do you practice and value? In your life? At home? In the classroom?

   - What literacies are most important to you? Why?

   - In what areas are you illiterate? Talk about an area of illiteracy that matters to you. Tell why.

4. Make sure that each member of your group takes one turn at the following roles:

   - the interview subject (the person responding to questions and prompts)

   - the interviewer (the person reading the questions, and following up if necessary)

   - the audio engineer (the person responsible for making sure the recorder is recording when the interview subject is talking and stopped when the subject is finished

TRYING OUT THE DIGITAL VIDEO CAMERA....

 1. As a group of four—take a digital video camera and a tripod. Sit near a plug so that you can plug in the video recorder.

 2. As a group, use your collective expertise (and the user documentation) to figure out how to use the equipment

 3. In a videotaped interview, answer the following questions:

- What is literacy to you?

- What are some of your earliest literacy memories? How was literacy practiced or valued in the house where you grew up? Consider telling a story about the first book you remember reading or telling a story about a book that was important to you.

- What literacy stories did your family tell you as a child? Or sayings that your mother and father/grandmother and grandfather repeated about literacy? Education?

 4. Make sure that each member of your group takes one turn at being the interview subject (the person in front of the camera) and videographer (the person in back of the camera).

 5. If you are the interview subject—no notes! Speak from the heart and from memory. Speak no more than 5 minutes.

 6. When you are the videographer, make sure the red "Record" light is on when you are recording. Make sure to turn off the camera when you are done. DO NOT REWIND—each videographer will start where the last left off on the tape. If you rewind, you will tape over someone else's effort!

TRYING OUT THE DIGITAL VIDEO CAMERA.... *(continued)*

As videographer, make sure you experiment with the following techniques:

- Framing—try for shots other than those with the interview subject's head in the middle of the frame. Seek unusual framings. For instance, zoom in on only half of the subject's face, or one eye, or only one part of his/her body.

- Movement—try moving around with the camera. Take it off the tripod and try some hand-held shots. Try zooming in and zooming out. Think Blair Witch . . .

- Low light—see what difference the low-light setting makes. This might be a good artistic effect.

 7. If you are neither videographer nor interview subject:

- Read the manual and see what you can learn.

- Play crew to the videographer.

- Keep time—no longer than 5 minutes per interview subject.

- Stand behind the camera and give the interview subject someone to whom they can talk and make eye contact.

- Figure out what you are going to say as interview subject.

SONY HANDYCAM TRV38 (CS)

Name_____ E-mail_____ Telephone_____

Out _____ In _____
(Date/Time/Your initials)   (Date/Time/My initials)

Out   In (Initials)

CAMERA

_____ _____   Sony HandyCam (TRV33)

BATTERY

_____ _____   Medium Battery

PERIPHERALS

_____ _____   64 MG Memory Stick

_____ _____   Tripod

EXTRA CABLES

_____ _____   USB-camera cable

SONY MINIDISC RECORDER AND MIC

Name_____ **E-mail**_____ **Telephone**_____

Out _____ **In** _____
  (Date/Time/Your initials)   (Date/Time/My initials)

Out   **In (Initials)**

SONY MINIDISC RECORDER

_____ _____   Sony Minidisc recorder
              (MZ-NHF800)

CABLES

_____ _____   1/8" to 1/8"
              mini-to-mini plug,
              MD recorder to computer

_____ _____   XLR to mini plug
              mic to MD recorder

MIC

_____ _____   Shure SM86 mic

HEADPHONES

_____ _____   Sony Studio Headphones

CANNON DIGITAL STILL CAMERA

Name_____   E-mail_____   Telephone_____

Out _____   In _____
      (Date/Time/Your initials)   (Date/Time/My initials)

Out   **In (Initials)**

CAMERA

_____ _____   Canon PowerShot S1 IS

CABLES

_____ _____   AV DC300
                            Camera to computer

PERIPHERALS

_____ _____   Camera Flash Card
                            512 MB

_____ _____   Compact Flash Reader
                            USB connection

IF SOMETHING IS MISSING—ANYTHING—CALL MY ATTENTION TO IT IMMEDIATELY.

APPENDIX 24
Class Equipment Reservations

Mon. 11 Oct.	Tues.12 Oct.	Wed. 13 Oct.	Thurs. 14 Oct.	Fri. 15 Oct.
(9:00-am-2:45)	(9:00-am-2:45)	(9:00-am-1:45)	(9:00-am-2:45)	(9:00-am-2:45)
VIDEO CAMERAS:	**VIDEO CAMERAS:**	**VIDEO CAMERAS:**	**VIDEO CAMERAS:**	**VIDEO CAMERA:**
Sony TRV38 (#1)	Sony TRV38 (#1)	Sony TRV38 (#1)	Sony TRV38 (#1)	Sony TRV38 (#1)
Time out: _____ or Time in: _____	Time out: _____ or Time in: _____	Time out: _____ or Time in: _____	Time out: _____ or Time in: _____	Time out: _____ or Time in: _____
Sony TRV38 (#2)	Sony TRV38 (#2)	Sony TRV38 (#2)	Sony TRV38 (#2)	Sony TRV38 (#2)
Time out: _____ or Time in: _____	Time out: _____ or Time in: _____	Time out: _____ or Time in: _____	Time out: _____ or Time in: _____	Time out: _____ or Time in: _____
STILL CAMERA	**STILL CAMERA**	**STILL CAMERA**	**STILL CAMERA**	**STILL CAMERA**
Canon PowerShot	Canon PowerShot	Canon PowerShot	Canon PowerShot	Canon PowerShot
Time out: _____ or Time in: _____	Time out: _____ or Time in: _____	Time out: _____ or Time in: _____	Time out: _____ or Time in: _____	Time out: _____ or Time in: _____
MD RECORDERS	**MD RECORDERS**	**MD RECORDERS**	**MD RECORDERS**	**MD RECORDERS**
Sony MDRecorder (#1)	Sony MDRecorder (#1)	Sony MDRecorder (#1)	Sony MDRecorder (#1)	Sony MDRecorder (#1)
Time out: _____ or Time in: _____	Time out: _____ or Time in: _____	Time out: _____ or Time in: _____	Time out: _____ or Time in: _____	Time out: _____ or Time in: _____
Sony MDRecorder (#2)	Sony MDRecorder (#2)	Sony MDRecorder (#2)	Sony MDRecorder (#2)	Sony MDRecorder (#2)
Time out: _____ or Time in: _____	Time out: _____ or Time in: _____	Time out: _____ or Time in: _____	Time out: _____ or Time in: _____	Time out: _____ or Time in: _____

APPENDIX 25
Check-In and Check-Out Procedures

Equipment Check-Out Procedure

Step #1:   Reserve the equipment you need on the **Class Equipment Reservation sheet** outside my office. Indicate the time and date you plan to check equipment out and the time and date you will check it back in.

(This will let other members of the class know when equipment will be available.)

Step #2:   On the designated date, come in and get the camera, audio recorder, or mic from the equipment shelf in my office (Walker 310).

Step #3:   Fill out the appropriate Equipment Check-Out Sheet.

Step #4:   File this sheet in the **Equipment Check-In Files** under the day you will bring the equipment back.

Call my attention to any missing parts immediately—anything at all— or be prepared to pay replacement costs on check-in.

Equipment Check-In Procedure

Step #1:   Bring in your equipment at or before the designated time and date to my office (Walker 310).

Step #2:   Find your Equipment Check-Out Sheet under the day you filed it in the **Equipment Check-In Files.**

Step #3:   Show me each piece in the equipment bag so that I can initial your **Equipment Check-Out Sheet**

Class members need to depend on a timely and reliable check-in and out. Don't be late.

VIDEO AND AUDIO PRODUCTION

Technology Showcase: Videography for Educators
<http://ali.apple.com/ali_sites/ali/exhibits/1000019/>

Heightened Student Voice through Digital Storytelling
<http://www.kenton.k12.ky.us/DigitalStory/dstindex.htm>

Digital Documentaries
<http://www.atschool.org/digidocs/index.htm>

Transom
<http://www.transom.org>

Radio College
<http://www.airmedia.org/PageInfo.php?PageID=3>

AUDIO EQUIPMENT

Sony Product Support
<http://www.ita.sel.sony.com/support/>

AUDIO SOFTWARE TUTORIALS AND SUPPORT

Audacity

Transom.org
<http://www.transom.org/tools/editing_mixing/200404.audacity.html>

Audacity.SourceForge
<http://audacity.sourceforge.net/>

ProTools Free

Digidesign
<http://www.digidesign.com/>

Transom.org
<http://www.transom.org/tools/index.html>

VIDEO EQUIPMENT

Video Cameras

Sony Product Support
<http://www.ita.sel.sony.com/support/>

VIDEO SOFTWARE TUTORIALS AND SUPPORT

Mighty Coach
<http://www.mightycoach.com/articles/mm2/>

Windows MovieMaker
<http://www.windowsmoviemakers.net/Tutorials/Index.aspx>

VIDEO SOFTWARE

Movie Maker

Atomic Learning
<http://www.atomiclearning.com/moviemaker2>

MightyCoach.com
<http://www.mightycoach.com/articles/mm2/>

Windows MovieMaker
<http://www.windowsmoviemakers.net/Tutorials/Index.aspx>

Atomic Learning
<http://www.atomiclearning.com/imovie2x.shtml>

iMovie

Apple iMovie Support
<http://www.apple.com/support/imovie/>

APPENDIX 27
Web Sites for Audio and Video Genre Examples

Web sites with Audio and Video Projects

Video/Multimedia/Animation

- Apple Learning Exchange:
  <http://ali.apple.com/ali_sites/ali/index.html>
  Video essays, music videos, documentaries, public service announcements created by students
- BBC News:
  <http://news.bbc.co.uk>
  Video and audio news essays on various subjects
- Electronic Literature Project Directory:
  <http://directory.eliterature.org>
  Multimodal poetry, fiction, drama, and nonfiction
- *New York Times* Multimedia Page:
  <http://www.nytimes.com/pages/multimedia/index.html>
  Audio essays, audio interviews, audio and video slideshows, and video essays focused on news
- Poems that Go:
  <http://www.poemsthatgo.com>
  Multimodal poetry incorporating or relying on visual, video, and audio
- Public Broadcasting Station Web site:
  <http://www.pbs.org>
  Multimodal essays and projects
- Digital Documentaries
  <http://www.atschool.org/digidocs/index.htm>
  Student videos, personal narratives, and informational documentaries
- ListenUP!:
  <http://www.listenup.org/>

Open-Source Video Archives

- Open Video Project
  <http://www.open-video.org>
  open-source video examples
- Internet Archive
  <http://www.archive.org>
  open-source audio and video examples
- Creative Commons
  <http://creativecommons.org/>
  open-source audio and video examples

- Our Media
  <http://ourmedia.org>
  open-source audio and video examples

Audio

- Online Speech Bank
  <http://www.americanrhetoric.com/speechbank.htm>
  Collection of major speeches in U.S. political history, including those of John F. Kennedy and Martin Luther King, Jr.

- National Public Radio Web site:
  <http://www.npr.org>
  Audio compositions on varying subjects and in varying styles

- Lost & Found Sound:
  <http://www.npr.org/programs/lnfsound/>
  Audio essays and artifacts

- Acoustic Ecology Institute:
  <http://www.acousticecology.org/soundscapes.html>
  Soundscapes, essays, articles, links for audio representations of the natural world

- Talking History: Aural History Productions
  <http://www.talkinghistory.org/>
  Collection of audio documentaries, speeches, debates, oral histories, conference sessions, commentaries, archival audio, and aural history resources

- Online Multimedia Gallary, Duke Center for Documentary Studies
  <http://cds.aas.duke.edu/exhibits/multimedia.html>
  Video, audio, and photographic documentaries

- WAV Central
  < http://WavCentral.com/movies/>
  .WAV files and sound-effect files

- The Movie Sounds Page
  <http://www.moviesounds.com/>
  Audio clips from movies

- Sound portraits.org
  <http://www.soundportraits.org/>
  Audio documentaries, personal narratives, sound portraits

- StoryCorps
  <http://storycorps.net/about/>
  Recorded personal stories of, and about, U.S. citizens

- RadioDiaries on NPR
  <http://www.radiodiaries.org/>
  Oral history and documentaries, recorded audio of peoples' lives

- This I Believe
  <http://www.npr.org/templates/story/story.php?storyId=4538138>
  Short recorded audio about peoples' personal beliefs, famous and not-so-famous citizens

- Public Radio Exchange
  <http://www.prx.org/home.do>
  Exchange for radio and recorded audio essays

- Transom
  <http://www.transom.org>
  Recorded audio documentaries and essays, great technical advice about audio recording

- Stories1st.org
  <http://www.airmedia.org/PageInfo.php?PageID=3>
  Personal narratives in video, word, and audio art forms

- Radio College
  <http://www.radiocollege.org/>
  Recorded audio documentaries and essays, great technical advice about radio recording, sponsored by National Public Radio

- Third Coast International Audio Festival
  <http://www.thirdcoastfestival.org/pages/archive848.html>
  Archives of recorded audio essays, documentaries, audio art

- Listening Booth
  <http://www.poets.org/booth/booth.cfm>
  Recorded audio of poets past and present

Open-Source Audio

- Internet Archive
  <http://www.archive.org>

- Creative Commons
  <http://creativecommons.org/>

- Our Media
  <http://ourmedia.org>App 30

APPENDIX 28
Teacher's Progress–Assessment Journal

TEACHER'S PROGRESS-ASSESSMENT JOURNAL

STUDENT: _____

Project Description:

Purpose:

Audience:

PROGRESS-ASSESSMENT NOTES:

Date: _____ Time on project: _____

Date: _____ Time on project: _____

Date: _____ Time on project: _____

APPENDIX 29
Student's Progress Journal

STUDENT'S PROGRESS JOURNAL

NAME: _____

Project Description:

Purpose:

Audience:

Media/Modalities:

PROGRESS NOTES: (Focus on rhetorical rational for changes. Include date, hours logged on project.)

- ❖ Poster with pictures and words
- ❖ Video—video tape yourself and talk
- ❖ Audio—record yourself or the interview
- ❖ Pamphlet
- ❖ Music Video
- ❖ Video game
- ❖ Chat Log (AIM)
- ❖ Collage
- ❖ PowerPoint presentation
- ❖ HyperStudio
- ❖ Sculpture with text on it
- ❖ Banner/Flag
- ❖ Text on object related to your major
- ❖ Webpage
- ❖ Message Boards
- ❖ Screen Shots
- ❖ Interactive website
- ❖ Interactive website
- ❖ Oral speech with visual aids
- ❖ Written text with visuals
- ❖ Taped speech
- ❖ Newspaper article
- ❖ Letter to the class with pictures
- ❖ Interview on camera
- ❖ Photo album
- ❖ Oral demonstration or presentation
- ❖ Skit, drama
- ❖ Song
- ❖ Short film
- ❖ Commercial
- ❖ Magazine article
- ❖ Newsletter
- ❖ Advertisement
- ❖ Animation
- ❖ Diagram of all the characteristics and functions of the job
- ❖ Visual display of job
- ❖ Question and answer session with charts, graphs, etc.
- ❖ Handouts on job
- ❖ Handouts with pictures
- ❖ Movie
- ❖ Written paper and a commercial
- ❖ Written paper and a movie clip
- ❖ A model
- ❖ Brochure
- ❖ Board game
- ❖ Design a cereal box
- ❖ Include actual movie, television show, or commercial clips
- ❖ Talk show
- ❖ Speech and handout
- ❖ Essay with pictures
- ❖ Slide show
- ❖ Scrapbook
- ❖ Computer game
- ❖ Journal/diary
- ❖ Comic strip

This list was generated by students in Kara Poe Alexander's Spring English 102 class.

APPENDIX 31
Affordances of Modalities

SOUND (AUDIO)	MOVING IMAGES (VIDEO)	ALPHABETIC LANGUAGE (WORDS)
Representation through sound waves that can be captured, edited, and reproduced in digital contexts.	Representation through light waves that can be captured, edited, and reproduced in digital contexts.	Representation through alphabetic symbols that can be typed or scanned into digital contexts, edited, and reproduced.
ability to represent accent	ability to capture movement and action	ability to represent linear propositional logic
ability to distort sound, create special audio effects	ability to capture facial expressions	portability, cost effectiveness, spatial fixedness
ability to represent musical sounds	ability to represent color	ability to combine color, font, layout, language
ability to represent vocal tones, sounds, animal noises	ability to change view (e.g., zoom in and out, to pan, tilt, focus and unfocus)	
ability to represent silence	ability to convey body language	
ability to represent rhythm, interruption, tempo	ability to combine sound, still images, words, font, color, and moving images	
ability to represent sound effects, ambient sound, layered sound, words	ability to create special visual effects	
ability to represent changes in volume		
ability to represent through vibration		

Excerpted from Kara Poe Alexander's Spring English 102 class.

APPENDIX 32
Audio Checklist

	CHECKLIST FOR WORKING WITH AUDIO
	Blank storage media is **available**.
	Blank storage media have been labeled with topic, date, and time.
	The audio recorder is plugged in or operating on new (or fully charged) batteries.
	Background noise is controlled or eliminated.
	"Do not disturb—audio taping session" sign has been hung up (if applicable).
	Microphone is turned on (if applicable).
	Microphone is securely plugged into audio recorder.
	An empty disk is inserted in the recorder.
	Isolating headphones are securely plugged into the audio recorder.
	Volume on the audio recorder is turned up to an appropriate level.
	Volume bars appear in the audio recorder window.
	Sound test has been conducted—sound can be heard clearly on the headphones and is registering on the audio recorder.
	4-5 seconds of silence (in this location) has been recorded for later use in editing.
	People have been informed about the project and have signed release consent forms.
	People have been given copies of interview questions (if applicable).
	Audio recorder is recording.

CHECKLIST FOR WORKING WITH VIDEO

	Several empty video tapes or CDs are available.
	Video tapes or CDs have been labeled with topic, date, and time.
	The video camera is plugged in or operating on new (or fully charged) batteries.
	Background noise is controlled or eliminated.
	Lighting contributes to the tone/content of the video. Viewers can see clearly what needs to be seen.
	"Do not disturb—video taping session" sign has been hung up (if applicable).
	Outboard microphone is turned on (if applicable).
	Volume in internal microphone is turned up on video camera.
	An empty video tape or CD is inserted in the recorder.
	Video test has been conducted—sound can be heard clearly, subject is visible and framed appropriately, focus is sharp, strong light sources are behind the camera person.
	Camera is fixed on tripod (if appropriate) or focused for the first shot.
	People have been informed about the project and have signed consent release forms.
	People have been given copies of interview questions (if applicable).
	Video camera is recording.
	Lens cap is off.

TRACKS	ACTION [what you do]	TIMELINE [note minutes, seconds, duration]
TRACK ONE		
TRACK TWO		
TRACK THREE		

APPENDIX 35
Video-Editing Log

SEGMENTS	ACTION [what you do]	TIMELINE [note minutes, seconds, duration]
SEGMENT ONE		
SEGMENT TWO		
SEGMENT THREE		

APPENDIX 36
Connecting
Sound and Writing

BUILDING BRIDGES TO AUDIO COMPOSITION

✓ **Select an audio essay from one of these sources.**

- *This American Life* archive: <http://www.thislife.org/>
- *Lost and Found Sound* archive: <http://www.npr.org/programs/lnfsound/stories/031003.green-street.html>
- *Kentucky Works* (Listen to the sound without the images): <http://www.wfpl.org/KY_works/default.htm>
- NPR's *Radio Expeditions* archive: <http://www.npr.org/templates/topics/topic.php?topicId=1023> (Select a story that is not identified as an "interview.")
- NPR's *Present at the Creation* archive: <http://www.npr.org/programs/morning/features/patc/>

✓ **Listen to the essay once to get a sense of the whole: purpose, audience, dominant rhetorical strategies.**

PART I

✓ **Listen again to a segment of no more than 2–3 minutes. Using only alphabetic text, reproduce that short segment. Allow yourself to listen as many times as you'd like. The goal is to experiment with the affordances of different modalities and to make an effective audio essay into an effective alphabetic essay. You will, of course, have to make many changes to accomplish this task.**

✓ **Review your translation. Compare it with a colleague's.**

- Does your written text capture the spirit, nuances, purpose of the audio text?
- What is missing? What is gained?
- What did you add in order to replace the missing sounds?
- What work could you accomplish in writing that you couldn't make happen with sound? Why?
- How are the effects similar? How are they different?

PART II

✓ **For several short segments, identify all the sounds that are not spoken words.**

✓ **Identify any significant voice inflections or changes in tone or volume.**

✓ **How is each identified sound or voice change connected to the author's purpose or audience?**

✓ **What rhetorical strategy is facilitated by each sound?**

✓ **Compare your list with that of another class member.**

Index

A

Actions
    studio sessions, 121*t*
Activism, 79–80
Administrators
    multimodal composition efforts, 169
Affordances (capabilities), 52*f*, 60–61, 193
    audio and video
      composing multimodal assignments, 33*t*
    audio project, 20
    video documentary, 55
aiff. *See* Audio interchange file format (.aiff)
Alphabetic compositions, 193
Alphabetic essays, 155*t*–157*t*
Alphabetic texts
    visual issues crossing, 158*t*
Alphabetic writing
    importance, 9
Ambient noise, 195
American Psychological Association (APA)
    Publication Manual of the APA, 158
Animation
    importance, 9
APA. *See* American Psychological Association
    (APA)
Archiving and showcasing
    composing multimodal assignments, 35
Arrangement, 5
Assessment, 99–11, 100–102
    coherence, 108*f*, 109*f*
    criteria sheets, 118
    documentation style, 108*f*, 109*f*
    example, 107–109
    formative, 100
      criteria, 101*f*
      progress journals, 104–105
      studio assessments, 103–104
    instructive, 100
      shaping assignments, 102*f*
    multimodal texts, 102–106
    sample group-presentation rubric
      rhetorically-based criteria, 108*f*
    student journal, 106*f*
Audacity, 69, 135
Audience
    awareness, 5
    crossing forms, 155*t*
Audio, 195
    publishing in digital formats, 137–138
    recording, 134, 135
    special challenges of teaching with, 17, 18*t*
Audio and video affordances
    composing multimodal assignments, 33*t*
Audio and video analysis
    specialized terms, 52*f*
Audio and video compositions
    communication rhetorical principles, 5
Audio and video essays
    places to submit, 80*f*
Audio and video projects
    collaborating
      benefits, 39–43, 43*t*
      challenges, 44–46, 46*t*
      composition principles, 42
      encouragement, 41
      fragmentation, 44–45
      groups, 44
      indications, 40*t*
      resource utilization, 41–42
      shared knowledge, 40–41
      shared visions, 45–46
      technological limitations, 44
Audio autobiography
    sound and literacy
      evaluation sheet, 22
      sample assignments, 19–22
Audio clip
    audio essay, 58, 59
Audio composition, 193
    listening and speaking advice, 160*t*
    rhetorical power, 159

Audio documentary, 20
Audio editing log, 137*f*
Audio editing program
    digital
        corrupted files, 141*t*
Audio essays, 155*t*–157*t*
    audio clip, 58, 59
    human-computer interaction, 58–60
    layered, 59*f*
    logos, 59
    sample assignment, 211–213
Audio failure
    troubleshooting, 134*t*–141*t*
Audio files
    downloading from Internet, 140*t*
        finding files, 140*t*
    downloading onto computer, 135–136
    editing, 136–137
    problems, 138*t*–141*t*
    publishing, 134
Audio images
    sample citations, 76*f*
Audio interchange file format (.aiff), 70*f*
Audio texts, 14
Audio/video assignments
    sample timeline, 218–219
Authoring composition
    engaging, 4–5
Authors, 193
Autobiography
    audio sound and literacy, 22

B

Backlight, 201
Behavior
    studio sessions, 121*t*
Bitmap (bmp), 71*f*
Bit rate, 193–194
bmp. *See* Bitmap (bmp)
Buses
    place for community, 58*f*

C

CAC. *See* Communication-across-the-curriculum
    (CAC)
Camera angle, 52*f*, 198
    video documentary, 53, 56
Capabilities. *See* Affordances (capabilities)
Cartiod, 195
Circulation
    composing multimodal assignments, 30*f*, 34–35
Citation and documentation
    online resources, 205
Civil rights era
    historical images, 54*f*
Clipping, 195
    digital, 145*f*
Cloning, 96–97
Close up, 199
Coaching
    digital, 95–96

Coherence
    assessment, 108*f*, 109*f*
Collaborating on multimodal projects, 39–47. *See
    also* Audio and video projects
Collaborative learning
    digital literacies, 184
Collaborative partners, 93–94
Collages
    feedback and revision, 123
Collected resources, 203–208
Color
    importance, 9
Comic strips
    feedback and revision, 123
Communication
    cross-cultural, 2
    digital, 2
Communication-across-the-curriculum (CAC), 157
    web site, 157
Communication rhetorical principles
    audio and video compositions, 5
Communities of practitioners. *See* Sustainable com-
    munities of practitioners
Community
    buses, 58*f*
Compatibility, 89–90
    flexibility and experimental, 85*t*, 86, 91*t*
Composing multimodal assignments, 29–38
    archiving and showcasing, 35
    audio and video affordances, 33*t*
    circulation, 30*f*, 34–35
    consultants, 36
    designing assignments, 35–37
    elements, 30*f*
    exploration and questions, 32
    group work, 32
    modalities, 32
    peer response, 36
    research, 37
    revising and testing composing theory, 30–31
    structure and choice, 30*f*, 32–34
    structure and strategies, 33
    student reflection prompts, 34*f*
    technical production, 36
    theory, 30*f*
    timelines, 35–36
    writing, 37
    written reflection, 33
Composing theory
    revising and testing, 30–31
Composing with sound, 14, 15*f*
Composing with video, 15–16, 16*f*
Composing with words, 13, 14*f*
Composition authoring
    engaging, 4–5
Composition class
    multimodality detractions, 9
Composition instruction
    change, 2–3
Composition online
    computers and, 80*f*

Composition principles
    audio and video project collaboration, 42
Compressed video files
    formats, 71*f*
Compression, 194, 196, 198
    formats
        rhetorical considerations, 72*f*
Computer
    and composition online, 80*f*
    downloading audio files onto, 135–136
    effects, 7
Computer hardware
    defined, 27
Computer software
    defined, 27
Conferencing
    listening and speaking advice, 160*t*
Confidence
    flexibility and experimental, 85–86, 85*t*, 91*t*
Constructive responses
    studio sessions, 121*t*
Consultants
    composing multimodal assignments, 36
Content
    assessment, 109*f*
Context
    crossing forms, 155*t*
Convergence
    digital production technologies, 7
Cool
    flexibility and experimental, 85*t*, 88
Copyleft, 194
    online resources, 205–206
Copyright, 194
    online resources, 205–206
Copyright holders
    obtaining permission, 75–77
Copyright law, 73
Correctness, 5
    crossing forms, 156*t*
Corrupted files
    digital audio editing program, 141*t*
Creative commons, 74–75
Creative nonfiction
    documentary
        sample assignment, 217
Creativity, 90
    flexibility and experimental, 85*t*, 87–88, 91*t*
Criteria sheets
    assessment, 118
Critical thinking skills
    assessment, 108*f*, 109*f*
Cross-cultural communication, 2
Cut, 198
Cut away, 198

D

Detail
    crossing forms, 156*t*
Difficulty
    assessment, 108*f*

Digital audio editing program
    corrupted files, 141*t*
    losing files, 141*t*
    varying sound quality among segments, 141*t*
Digital clipping, 145*f*
Digital coaching, 95–96
Digital communication, 2
Digital environments, 194
    effects, 7
Digital equipment
    multimodal composing teaching, 10
Digital files
    downloading from digital recorder
        transferring problems, 139*t*
Digital formats
    putting video in, 144
        problems and troubleshooting, 146*t*
Digital literacies, 181–187
    collaborative learning, 184
    comfort with, 182
    importance, 186–187
    instruction, 182–183
    instructional strategies, 184–186
    learning curve, 182
Digital materials
    web resources for citing, 78*f*
Digital production technologies
    convergence, 7
Digital recorder
    downloading digital files from
        transferring problems, 139*t*
Digital sound recorder
    recording sound with
        background noise, 139*t*
Digital technologies
    compatibility, 86
Digital video. *See also* Recording digital video with
        video camera
    downloading from web
        video clip downloads, 147*t*–148*t*
    editing
        audience can't follow story line, 150*t*
Digitized still images
    formats, 71*f*
Dissolve, 199
Documentary
    audio, 20
    as creative nonfiction
        sample assignment, 217
Documentation
    online resources, 205
    style, assessment, 108*f*, 109*f*
Dolly shot, 199
Downloading
    audio files from Internet
        finding files, 140*t*
        respecting intellectual property, 140*t*
    audio files onto computer, 135–136
    digital files from digital recorder
        transferring problems, 139*t*

digital video from web
    video clip downloads, 147*t*–148*t*
    sound, 134
    still images from web for video
      incompatible formate, 148*t*
      poor quality, 148*t*
      public domain images, 148*t*
    video, 142–143
Driveway effect, 5
Duration of shot, 199
DVDs, rewritable, 68

E
Editing
    audio files, 136–137
    digital video
      audience can't follow story line, 150*t*
      audio and video don't match, 149*t*
      audio doesn't enhance video, 150*t*
      boring video, 150*t*
      choosing video to include, 149*t*
      learning software, 149*t*
      loosing data, 149*t*
    video, 143–144
Education
    progressive, 5
Encouragement
    audio and video project collaboration, 41
Enculturation, 80*f*
Equipment
    keeping track, 94–95
    sample assignments, 25–26
Essays
    alphabetic, 155*t*–157*t*
    audio, 155*t*–157*t*
      audio clip, 58, 59
      human-computer interaction, 58–60
      layered, 59*f*
      logos, 59
      places to submit, 80*f*
      sample assignment, 211–213
    video, 155*t*–157*t*
      places to submit, 80*f*
Establishing shots, 200
    video documentary, 55
Ethos
    vs. pathos
      video documentary, 53
      print and multimodal text, 50*t*
Evaluation
    instructive, 100
Exigence, 5
Experiments
    benefits, 84–89
Exploration and questions
    composing multimodal assignments, 32

F
Fade in, 52*f*, 196, 199
    video documentary, 55
Fade out, 52*f*, 196, 199
Failure, 133–152

troubleshooting, 134
    audio, 134*t*–141*t*
    video, 142–151
Fair use doctrine, 74, 194–195
Feedback
    collages, 123
    comic strips, 123
    sheets
      sample, 119*f*–120*f*
      studio sessions, 122
File management, 68
Flexibility
    benefits, 84–89, 91*t*
    challenges, 89–91
    four Cs, 85*t*
Focus
    crossing forms, 156*t*
Form
    crossing forms, 155*t*
Formative assessment, 100
    criteria, 101*f*
    progress journals, 104–105
    studio assessments, 103–104
Fragmentation
    audio and video project collaboration, 44–45
Framing, 199
Friends
    digital literacies, 183
Full shot, 200
Future literacy, 114*f*
Future technology, 114*f*

G
Gain, 196
GIF. *See* Graphics interchange format (GIF)
Graphics interchange format (GIF), 71*f*
Group-presentation rubric
    assessment, 108*f*
Group work
    composing multimodal assignments, 32

H
Hardware
    computer
      defined, 27
    documentation
      online resources, 208
    sample assignments, 25–26
    specifications
      multimodal composing, 172*f*
Headroom, 199
Historical images
    civil rights era, 54*f*
Homegrown multimodal specialists
    creating, 95–96
Human-computer interaction audio essay,
    58–60
Hypercartiod, 195

I
Image files
    sample citations, 78*f*

Images
  audio
    sample citations, 76*f*
  importance, 9
  public domain
    downloading still images from web for video, 148*t*
  still
    digitized, 71*f*
    downloading from web for video, 148*t*
  video
    sample citations, 76*f*
  visual
    video documentary, 54
iMovie, 69
In-class demonstrations
  digital literacies, 183
Informed consent, 78–79
Instruction
  digital literacies, 182–183
Instructive assessment, 100
  shaping assignments, 102*f*
Instructive evaluation, 100
Intellectual property
  multimodal composing, 73–75
Internet
  downloading audio files from
    finding files, 140*t*
    respecting intellectual property, 140*t*
  intellectual property resources, 74*f*
Interviewing, 220

J

Joint photographic experts group (JPEG), 71*f*
Journals
  online resources, 206
  scholarly
    publishing multimodal essays, 80*f*
JPEG. *See* Joint photographic experts group (JPEG)
Jump cut, 199

K

KAIROS, 80*f*
Keynote, 52*f*, 196
  audio essay, 58
Knowledge, shared
  audio and video project collaboration, 40–41

L

Law
  copyright, 73
Learning, 92
  collaborative
    digital literacies, 184
  context
    digital literacies, 184
  curve
    digital literacies, 182
  by doing
    multimodal classroom observations, 187–191
    extending, 189–191

log
  technology, 93*f*
software
  editing digital video, 149*t*
Levels, 196
Licensing
  open-source, 74–75, 195
Light
  shooting into the, 201
Listeners, 195
Listening
  writing centers, 159–160
Listening and speaking advice
  audio composition, 160*t*
  conferencing, 160*t*
Literacies. *See also* Digital literacies
  future, 114*f*
  NCTE, 7–8
  pedagogy, digital technology, 2
  and public transportation video documentary
    rhetorical thinking, 53–58
Logos
  audio essay, 59
  print and multimodal text, 50*t*
  video documentary, 56

M

Media, 195
Medium shot, 200
Memory space, 68
Microphone
  recording sound with background noise, 139*t*
Mini-essay
  sample construction, 163*t*
Mix, 199
Modality, 195
  selecting effective, 9
Motivation
  digital literacies, 184
Mov. *See* Quick time movie (.mov)
MPEG-1 (.mpg), 71*f*
MPEG-2 (.mpg), 71*f*
MPEG Audio (.mpg), 70*f*
Multimodal assignments. *See also* Composing multimodal assignments
  reflecting, 130*f*
  rhetorical criteria, peer feedback, 119*f*
  sample not requiring digital tools, 114*f*–116*f*
Multimodal composing, 195
  administrators, 169
  challenges, 84*f*
  as a class, 92–93
  completeness, 110
  defined, 1–2
  examples, 97
  hardware and software specifications, 172*f*
  importance, 3
  intellectual property, 73–75
  sample assignments, 19–25
  saving, organizing and managing, 67–72

teaching
  composition, 6–7
  digital equipment, 10
  English composition faculty, 8–9
  technology expert, 9–10
  technical vocabulary, 26–27
Multimodal composition
  sustaining, 167–179
Multimodal examples and resources
  online resources, 206–208
Multimodal experimenting, 83–96
Multimodality, 1–11
  collaborating on, 39–47
  detractions
    composition class, 9
Multimodal specialists
  homegrown
    creating, 95–96
Multimodal texts, 1–2, 65–81
  ethos, 50*t*
  learning to respond to and assess, 102–106
  production and reception, 7
  saving, 65–67
    sounds and images, 66, 66*f*–67*f*
  saving and sharing, 65–67
    sounds and images, 66, 66*f*–67*f*
  saving words, 65–66, 66*f*–67*f*
Multimodal video project
  assembling files from multiple sources, 69*f*
Music
  video documentary, 54

N

Narration
  video documentary, 55
National Council of Teachers of English (NCTE)
  literacy, 7–8
Noise, 196
  ambient, 195

O

Omnidirectional, 196
Online resources, 205–208
  CAC, 157
  citation and documentation, 205
  copyright and copyleft, 205–206
  documentary films, 218
  documentation, 205
  interviewing, 220
  journals, 206
  multimodal examples and resources, 206–208
Open-ended peer-review form, 123*f*
Open-source licensing, 74–75, 195
Organization, 5
  assessment, 108*f*, 109*f*
  crossing forms, 156*t*
Over the shoulder shot, 199

P

Pan, 201
Partners
  collaborative, 93–94

Pathos
  vs. ethos
    video documentary, 53
    print and multimodal text, 50*t*
Pedagogy
  student-centered, 5–6
Peer response
  composing multimodal assignments, 36
  forms
    studio sessions, 122
Peer review
  expectations
    explaining, 118
  open-ended forms, 123*f*
  studio sessions, 113
    considerations, 125*t*
    encouraging, 116–131
    follow-up, 130
    formal and informal for formative feedback,
      117
    groups size, 127*t*
    media and modalities, 124–125
    model elements, 117
    presentations, 122
    purpose, 125*t*
    reflections, 130
    reminders, 146
    scheduling, 124
    small groups, 125*t*, 126, 127*t*
    structure, 125*t*
    teacher feedback on rhetorical considerations,
      128
    time for revisions, 130
    whole class, 127*t*
    written and verbal feedback, 128–130
Peripheral equipment
  defined, 27
Permission
  copyright holders, 75–77
PICT/PICT2, 71*f*
Point of view, 52*f*
  video documentary, 58
Portable recording equipment
  defined, 27
Preparedness
  studio sessions, 121*t*
Presentation content
  assessment, 108*f*
Presentation mode
  assessment, 109*f*
Preventative measures, 96–97
Print and multimodal text
  logos, 50*t*
  rhetorical principles, 50*t*
Print documentation
  technical concepts, 70
Print text
  ethos, 50*t*
Problem solving
  flexibility and experimental, 87–88

Professionalism
   studio sessions, 121*t*
Progress assessment
   notes, 105*f*
   teachers journal, 105*f*
Progressive education, 5
Projectors
   class troubleshooting protocol, 88*f*
Prompt
   reflection
      example, 130*f*
PSA. *See* Public service announcement (PSA)
Publication Manual of the APA, 158
Public domain, 74, 195
   downloading still images from web for video, 148*t*
Public service announcement (PSA)
   radio, 9
Public transportation video documentary
   literacies
      rhetorical thinking, 53–58
Publishing audio files, 134
Publishing audio in digital formats, 137–138
Publishing video in digital formats, 144
   audience can't open video, 151*t*
   finished video too large, 150*t*–151*t*
   low quality, 151*t*
Purpose
   crossing forms, 155*t*
Putting video in digital formats, 144
   problems and troubleshooting, 146*t*

Q

Questions
   composing multimodal assignments, 32
Quick time movie (.mov), 70*f*, 71*f*

R

ra. *See* RealAudio (.ra, .ram, .rp)
Radio
   PSA, 9
Readers, 195
Reading, responding, and revising, 113–131
RealAudio (.ra, .ram, .rp), 70*f*
RealSystem (.rm), 71*f*
Recording audio, 134, 135
Recording digital video with video camera
   dark video, 146*t*
   excessively shaky, 146*t*
   jumpy, 146*t*
   no camera screen image, 147*t*
   poor quality, 147*t*
   unclear image, 147*t*
Recording sound directly into computer
   mediocre sound quality, 138
Recording sound with microphone and digital sound
   recorder
      background noise, 139*t*
      mechanical or human failure, 139*t*
Recording video, 142
Reflection prompt
   example, 130*f*
Release forms, 78–79

Resources
   collected, 203–208
Responding and assessing, 99–11
Reverse shot, 199
Revised group-presentation rubric
   assessment, 109*f*
Revision
   collages, 123
   comic strips, 123
   encouraging, 116–131
Rewritable DVDs, 68
Rhetorical challenges
   crossing forms, 155*t*–157*t*
   learning by doing, 188–189
Rhetorical coherence and consistency, 90
   questions for, 129*t*
   video documentary, 56*f*
Rhetorical power
   audio composition, 159
Rhetorical understanding of composition, 99
rm. *See* RealSystem (.rm)
Rule of thirds, 201

S

Sample feedback sheet, 119*f*–120*f*
Sample mini-essay
   construction, 163*t*
Sample module
   components, 163*t*
Sample multimodal assignment
   not requiring digital tools, 114*f*–116*f*
Sampling, 196–197
Saving, 96–97
   multimodal texts, 65–67
   sounds and images, 66, 66*f*–67*f*
   words, 65–66, 66*f*–67*f*
Scholarly journals
   publishing multimodal essays, 80*f*
Scrapbooks
   feedback and revision, 123
Sequence, 201
Shared knowledge
   audio and video project collaboration, 40–41
Shared visions
   audio and video project collaboration, 45–46
Sharing
   multimodal texts, 65–67
Shooting into the light, 201
Shots, 199
   duration of, 199
   establishing, 200
   full, 200
   medium, 200
   over the shoulder, 199
   reverse, 199
Showcasing
   composing multimodal assignments, 35
Signal, 52*f*, 197
Software
   computer
      defined, 27

documentation
  online resources, 208
learning
  editing digital video, 149*t*
sample assignments, 25–26
specifications
  multimodal composing, 172*f*
Sound
  audio autobiography
    evaluation sheet, 22
    sample assignments, 19–22
  audio essay, 58
  autobiographies, 197
  biographies, 197
  composing with, 14, 15*f*
  documentaries, 197
  downloading, 134
  files
    formats, 70*f*
    sample citations, 78*f*
  importance, 9
  performance, 197
  portrait, 20, 197
  recording directly into computer, 138
  recording with microphone and digital sound
  recorder
    background noise, 139*t*
Soundmark, 52*f*, 197
  audio essay, 59
  video documentary, 55, 57
Soundscape, 20, 52*f*, 197
Sound track, 201
Sources
  assessment, 108*f*, 109*f*
  citing and documenting, 75–77
Southern Illinois University-Carbondale
  web site, 157
Speaking advice
  audio composition, 160*t*
  conferencing, 160*t*
Still images
  digitized
    formats, 71*f*
  downloading from web for video
    incompatible formate, 148*t*
StoryCorps, 80*f*
Student assistants, 89
Student-centered pedagogy, 5–6
Student journal
  assessment, 106*f*
Student reflection prompts
  composing multimodal assignments, 34*f*
Students
  compatibility, 86
  reading and interpreting multimodal texts, 51–52
  rhetorical coherence and consistency
    questions for, 129*t*
Student specialists, 96*f*
Studio assessments
  formative assessment, 103–104
Studio sessions. *See also* Peer review

  actions, 121*t*
  behavior, 121*t*
  conduct guidelines, 121*t*
  constructive responses, 121*t*
  responding to drafts, 121
Style
  crossing forms, 156*t*
Summative evaluations, 100
Summative function, 100
Support
  crossing forms, 156*t*
Sustainable communities of practitioners
  administrator's questions, 177*f*
  big picture, 168
  computers and software for audio recordings, 171
  digital production expertise, 171–172
  digital video cameras and studio recorders, 173
  forming, 168–169
  hardware/software knowledge, 174
  microcommunities, 168–170
  reasonable projects, 170–171
  student skills and understandings, 175*f*
  sustainable relationships, 179
  teacher expectations, 174–175
  technical staff questions, 176*f*
  technologically based efforts, 170–179
Sustaining multimodal composition, 167–179

T

Tagged image file format (TIFF), 71*f*
Teachers
  progress-assessment journal, 105*f*
  rhetorical coherence and consistency
    questions for, 129*t*
  with rhetorical experience, 50–51
Teaching, 92, 100–102. *See also* Multimodal composing, teaching
  audio special challenges, 17, 18*t*
Technical challenges
  flexibility and experimental, 91*t*
  learning by doing, 188–189
Technical concepts
  online help files, 70
Technical staff
  multimodal composition efforts, 169
Technical terms
  glossary, 193–202
Technical vocabulary
  multimodal composing, 26–27
Technological determinism, 3
Technology
  effect on conventional forms of literacy, 7
Technology learning log, 93*f*
Texts
  alphabetic
    visual issues crossing, 158*t*
  audio, 14
  create meaning in, 8
  interpret meaning from, 8
  print
    ethos, 50*t*

print and multimodal
  logos, 50*t*
  rhetorical principles, 50*t*
social nature of, 79–80
video, 15–16
Thinking rhetorically, 49–62
Thinking skills
  critical
    assessment, 108*f*, 109*f*
Three shot, 201
TIFF. *See* Tagged image file format (TIFF)
Tilt, 201
Time
  digital literacies, 184
Timelines
  audio/video assignments, 218–219
  composing multimodal assignments, 35–36
Title screen, 52*f*, 202
Track, 197
Traditional assignments
  converted into multimodal assignments, 162*t*
Transitions, 201
Transom, 80*f*
Transport controls, 198
Troubleshooting
  audio failure, 134*t*–141*t*
  putting video in digital formats, 146*t*
Tutorials
  digital literacies, 183
Two shot, 201

U

Unity
  crossing forms, 156*t*

V

Veterans History Project at Library of Congress, 80*f*
Video, 198. *See also* Digital video
  analysis, 52*f*
  arguments, 202
  autobiography, 202
  biography, 202
    literacy values and practices, 23–25, 24–25
    sample assignment, 214–216
  clips, 55–56
  composing with, 15–16, 16*f*
  compositions
    problems and troubleshooting, 146*t*–151*t*
  compressed files
    formats, 71*f*
  documentaries, 202
    affordances, 55
    camera angle, 53, 56
    establishing shots, 55
    fade in, 55
    logos, 56
    music, 54
    narration, 55
    public transportation
      literacies, 53–58
  downloading, 142–143
  editing log, 145*f*

essays, 155*t*–157*t*
  places to submit, 80*f*
failure, 142–151
files
  formats, 71*f*
  sample citations, 78*f*
images
  sample citations, 76*f*
performance, 202
portraits, 202
publishing in digital formats, 144
recording, 142
special challenges of teaching with, 17, 18*t*
texts, 15–16
  visual issues crossing, 158*t*
Video affordances
  composing multimodal assignments, 33*t*
Video analysis
  specialized terms, 52*f*
Video assignments
  sample timeline, 218–219
Video camera. *See* Recording digital video with
  video camera
Video compositions
  communication rhetorical principles, 5
Video essays
  places to submit, 80*f*
Video projects
  collaborating
    benefits, 39–43, 43*t*
    challenges, 44–46, 46*t*
    composition principles, 42
    encouragement, 41
    fragmentation, 44–45
    groups, 44
    indications, 40*t*
    resource utilization, 41–42
    shared knowledge, 40–41
    shared visions, 45–46
    technological limitations, 44
Videoscapes, 202
Viewers, 195
Visual evidence
  literacy, 57*f*
Visual images
  video documentary, 54
Visual issues
  alphabetic compositions, 158*t*
  crossing, 158*t*
  video compositions, 158*t*
Voice over, 52*f*, 198, 202
  audio essay, 59

W

WAC. *See* Writing-across-the-curriculum (WAC)
wav. *See* Windows WAVE (.wav)
Waveform, 198
Web. *See also* Online resources
  CAC, 157
  downloading audio files from
    finding files, 140*t*

respecting intellectual property, 140*t*
downloading digital video from
  video clip downloads, 147*t*–148*t*
downloading still images for video
  incompatible formate, 148*t*
intellectual property resources, 74*f*
resources for citing digital materials, 78*f*
technical concepts, 70
WID. *See* Writing-in-the-disciplines (WID)
Wide shot, 201
Windows media audio (.wma), 70*f*, 71*f*
Windows WAVE (.wav), 70*f*
Windscreen, 198
wma. *See* Windows media audio (.wma)
Words
  composing with, 13, 14*f*
  saving, 65–66, 66*f*–67*f*
Writers
  page control, 2
Writing
  alphabetic
    importance, 9
  composing multimodal assignments, 37

Writing-across-the-curriculum (WAC), 157
  crossing composing forms, 157*t*
  web site, 157
Writing centers, 153–164
  building bridges, 153–154
    resource list, 164*f*
    tools, 164*f*
  discovering rhetorical correspondences, 154–155
  listening, 159–160
  visual issues, 158–159
  workshops and collaborative learning, 160–164
Writing-in-the-disciplines (WID), 157
Writing meaning
  cultural shifts, 2
Written language
  digital enhancing understanding of, 9

Y

Youth Media Distribution, 80*f*

Z

Zooms out
  video documentary, 57